CONSCIOUSNESS
SPEAKS

Other books by Ramesh S. Balsekar

CONSCIOUSNESS SPEAKS

SPEAKS

CONVERSATIONS
WITH
RAMESH S. BALSEKAR

Edited by

Wayne Liquorman

Advaita Press

Copyright © 1992 by

Ramesh S. Balsekar

First Published in United States Of America by

ADVAITA PRESS

P.O. Box 3479

Redondo Beach, California 90277

Designed by: Wayne Liquorman

Cover Photograph: George Takamori

Printed by: McNaughton & Gunn

Library of Congress Catalog Card Number: 92-74534

ISBN 0-929448-14-6   0 9 8 7 6 5 4

Dedicated in Reverence

To the original miracle;

Consciousness,

Not aware of Itself,

Suddenly,

Inexplicably,

Causelessly,

Becoming

Aware

of

Itself.

The I Am that I Am

Table of Contents

CONTENTS

Chapter 3
THE ILLUSION OF BONDAGE....99

Chapter 4
THE MIND....117

CONTENTS

CONTENTS

CHAPTER 7 (continued)

Chapter 8

CHOICE AND VOLITION....321

Chapter 9

WHAT IS TO BE DONE....338

Chapter 10

THE GURU/DISCIPLE RELATIONSHIP....353

Chapter 11
METAPHYSICAL QUESTIONS....367

Chapter 12
REGARDING EMOTIONS....386

Glossary....391

Acknowledgments

The editor wishes to acknowledge the efforts of the following body-mind mechanisms who did all this work for Nothing: Chuck Surface, who created the skeleton on which all these words hang, *maha*transcriber Margie Harris and her beloved Mac, Norton and Albie Smith - the raiders of the lost file, Kamala Poopal, Baja Henry Swift, Roy Gibbon, Ananda Grimm, Jim Schoonover, Gail Ramey, Ardeliza Lansang, Velia Anderson, Peter Cripps, Carol Zahn, Connie Magwood, Stephanie Potter, Lisa Webber, as well as all of the others whose paths are well paved.

Blame for any and all errors should be addressed to proofreaders Lee Scantlin, Garry Dufresne, Dorothy Doyle and especially to Dr. Gary Starbuck (if you can find him) who, a split infinitive he couldn't heal, he never met.

The editor, for his part, maintains a comfortable refuge in his claim of ignorance of all things grammatical and punctuative. While in school, he was undoubtedly not paying attention when such matters were discussed—the only practice he maintains religiously to this day.

Editor's Notes

All there is, is Consciousness. If that is understood completely, deeply, intuitively then you need read no further. Put the book down and go on joyously with the rest of your life.

If, however, you belong to that massively larger group of people who consider themselves people, then perhaps there may be something here for you. As the editor, I can assure you that it is really a very good book. I've read it. Some might find it a bit short on explicit sex, violence and like entertainments, but it is a good book nonetheless. In fact, if you are one of those poor creatures who have been stripped of your certainty about who or what you truly are, then what follows might be of help.

❏❏❏

Caveat Emptor, let the buyer beware.

Embodied herein is not the Truth. The Truth cannot be held between the covers of a book. What we have here are pointers, sign posts, guides; each in a slightly different language describing, perhaps, slightly different routes, but all meant to indicate the same destination...Right Here, Right Now.

❏❏❏

Ramesh, in what I heretofore had considered to be his infinite wisdom, has asked me to tell you my story in this introduction. Those of you who have attended Ramesh's talks might already have heard parts of it. He is fond of telling it, though sometimes with questionable command of the details. Parts of it will also be found scattered about this book wherein he mentions me as something of a poster boy for Grace. I am the hang glider pilot he mentions whose life was actually *saved* by crashing through some power lines. I am also the "gentleman habituated to alcohol" (his kind way of saying, "a hopeless alcoholic") who one day wakes up after nineteen drunken and drug-addicted years to find that the obsession to drink and use drugs has been miraculously removed.

There is a *sanskrit* word, *sadhana*, which refers to the practices one does to advance along the path to enlightenment. It is generally thought of in conjunction with such practices as meditation, chanting, prayer, fasting, ritual observances, charity work etc. Its aim is to free one from total identification as the ego. At the time I was "struck sober" I had never done any of these things. I had no interest in enlightenment or anything else beyond the immediate satisfaction of my desires. I believed myself to be the center of the universe and was convinced that I could do anything I set my mind to. Spirituality, religion and "the rest of that crap" was for weaklings and cowards, people too afraid to take responsibility for their own lives. Ramesh helped me to understand that my nineteen year long *sadhana* had been to drink and drug my "self" into submission. He told me, "Nothing is wasted, everything is preparation for the next scene."

The experience of feeling such a long-standing obsession disappear in a heartbeat finally got my attention. There was no denying that *I* hadn't done it. Something had done this to me. I knew deep in my guts that some power greater than my egoic self *must* be at work and I set about finding out what that force might be. I was fortunate to then meet another recovered alcoholic who had had a similar experience and he introduced me to *The Tao Te Ching*. Despite the fact that I didn't understand them, I intuitively felt that those simple verses pointed directly to the truth.

Convinced that I needed to do something to speed the process along, I took up *Tai Chi Chuan*, dabbled in a variety of meditative practices and for the next two and a half years just generally wandered around in the spiritual marketplace.

Then, a flier arrived in the mail advertising a talk by some *guru* from India that I'd never heard of, but since admission was only a buck I thought, "What have I got to lose?" On September 16, 1987 I went with some friends to hear Ramesh at his first public talk in the U.S. (or anywhere, for that matter). I was thirty-six years old and couldn't have dreamed what was in store for me, that I was about to lose everything. I had no idea that it was a moment of *consummate* Grace. I didn't know what a *jnani* was, or that one had just bitten me. I was, at that point, a complete stranger to Advaita. I had never heard of the big Advaitic names, Nisargadatta Maharaj or Ramana Maharshi and knew the word "consciousness" only as that condition extant prior to being hit on the head with a baseball bat. This put me at a profound advantage. I had far fewer spiritual concepts to transcend than did most of the other, far more experienced, seekers in the room, though at the time I felt I had blundered into something that was way over my head. Ramesh himself, appeared in every way ordinary; a fairly intellectual, retired bank president, unpretentious and mild mannered. I left that meeting with a slight interest in seeing Ramesh again.

After returning from a two week business trip during which my *jnani* bite had incubated, I went to hear Ramesh again. This time, in the intimate confines of the magnificent hilltop home of Ramesh's host Henry Denison, I found myself transformed by Ramesh's presence and teaching. I was captivated. I was enchanted. I found myself drawn back to listen to him and be with him every day. The teaching began to sink down from my mind and go deeper. Each morning, as my car would reach the turn-off leading to Henry's house, my heart would literally begin to dance in anticipation. My mind filled with images of being with him. I was bitterly jealous of the man who was taking him for drives and out for dinners. I realized I was in love!

After a few weeks of this, I was amazed to find myself writing him this poem:

> *Who would have thought*
> *That I'd fall in love*
> *With a bespectacled banker*
> *From Bombay?*
>
> *Ridiculous*
> *Ludicrous*
> *I must be out of my mind*
> *I'm married - A father -*
> *An international businessman - A cynic*
> *Yet here I find myself*
> *Flitting about You*
> *With all the volition*
> *Of a moth at a flame*
>
> *Wondering...*
> *Afraid...*
> *Secretly hoping....*
> *That this "me" will get too close*
> *And immolate.*

During the three months that Ramesh remained in the U.S., I made a shameless nuisance of myself. I spent every possible moment in his presence and then schemed as to how I might spend more. He was characteristically patient with me.

When it came time for him to return to India, several of us gathered at the airport to see him off. We sat in the coffee shop, killing time, and the conversation turned to publishing the content of the last three months of Ramesh's talks. As the plans and schemes became more and more grandiose, the businessman in me felt compelled to point out, "You realize you're talking about starting a business, don't you? Making a book is great but what about inventory and billing and cash flow and order processing..." Henry interrupted my diatribe to inquire, "Oh, have you been in the publishing business?"

I said, "No," and then immediately Ramesh, who was sitting next to me said, "Not yet."

I felt as if I had been hit with a fist. I laughed feebly and asked, "Do you know something I don't know?" (Could there have been a stupider question?) Ramesh just smiled enigmatically and looked away but in that instant I knew I was in the publishing business; it was Advaita Press' moment of conception.

Amazingly, it was exactly the excuse I needed to go to India. After all, I wasn't going there to do something frivolous like sitting at the feet of a *guru*, I was going there to work with an author on a manuscript. It was business. Anyone could understand that. So, off I went to Bombay "to work on the manuscript." Ramesh talked and I listened. His wife, Sharda (a warm, charming lady and extraordinarily talented in the kitchen) cooked and I ate. It was heaven.

A book, *Experiencing The Teaching*[1], did come out of it, but far more important for me was the opportunity to totally immerse myself in Ramesh and the teaching. Within a year, the process was complete. As a result, I find I walk around with Ramesh as much a part of me as "me." When I mentioned to Ramesh that this was the case and that therefore I found it quite simple to edit his books, he said he had experienced the same thing while translating for his *guru*, Nisargadatta Maharaj. He said, "Sometimes someone would ask me what Maharaj had said and I would have to tell them, 'I can't always tell you exactly what he said, but I can tell you exactly what he meant'."

This book, *Consciousness Speaks*, is the fruit of the seed planted that fateful day in the airport. It doesn't always contain exactly what Ramesh said, but it does contain exactly what he meant. It has taken nearly five years to complete, though four other Ramesh books and a Ram Tzu book have come in the interim.

◨◨◨

If you are new to this subject and are confused by the terminology, be easy on yourself. Much of the material in this

---

[1]   Ramesh S. Balsekar, *Experiencing The Teaching* (Los Angeles: Advaita Press, 1988)

book is from talks I attended prior to the understanding deepening. I can remember having heard these words and the concepts they represent, but at that time much of it was meaningless. They were then describing a truth I couldn't yet comprehend; that is in fact incomprehensible. When the understanding comes, it is always intuitive and instantaneous. In fact, this whole process of seeking is just designed to keep us busy while we're waiting for *something* to happen.

Ramesh uses the analogy of trying to describe color to someone blind from birth. The description can be vivid, imaginative, accurate and truthful but it will be effective only to the extent that your listener can associate what he already knows with what you are saying. As you describe color to this blind man in more and more detail he will develop a richer and richer mental image of what he thinks color is. However, the instant he is given the gift of sight, he realizes that though the description you gave him fits, the reality of color bears no resemblance to his mental image of color because the mental image he created is of a completely different dimension.

The actual sight of the color is a transcendent experience, transcending the limitations of the mental image. So it is with Ramesh's teaching.

❏❏❏

The mere incident of enlightenment does not necessarily confer an ability to communicate the concomitant understanding. However, in Ramesh's case that ability has assumed remarkable depth. This organism known as Ramesh is amply endowed with compassion, patience, humor and eloquence. Though the dialogues in this book can convey but a fraction of the impact that his presence can have, as you read you may get a sense of the energy that fills the room as Ramesh warms to his subject.

Still, what is most remarkable about Ramesh is his very ordinariness and the very ordinariness of his teaching. Though elaborate theoretical structures may be erected around it — his concept of the working mind and the thinking mind would be a good example of this — the essence of the teaching is simplicity itself. He offers no miracles, no cures, no special powers; in fact, all he really offers is Nothing, that Nothing that we all truly Are.

And while it is often said that Ramesh appears ordinary, no one could ever say he is mediocre. It is his complete lack of pretense that moderates the light of his accomplishments from a blinding brilliance to a warm glow. In his education, both in India and at the London School of Economics, he was always *near* the top of his class but never *at* the top of his class. In his leisure pursuits, as a body builder, competitive badminton player and golfer his standings were always superior though rarely superlative.

Ramesh married Sharda in 1940 and they raised three children. The eldest was Ajit, brilliant but with a life-long history of health problems. He died in 1990 at the age of forty-nine. Next came his daughter, Jaya, who married and then moved to Bangalore where she runs a successful dairy business. His youngest son, Shivdas, is also married and is the senior executive in the Indian branch of a multi-national pharmaceutical company.

It was in his career, which began in 1940 as a clerk in the Bank of India, that Ramesh's brilliance truly shone through. Despite lacking a burning ambition, he steadily rose through the ranks until his retirement in 1977 as that bank's General Manager (what is known in the U.S. as company president or C.E.O.). During his ten years of service as its head, he guided the bank through its most rapid and successful growth period, overseeing the hiring of thousands of people and the opening of hundreds of new branches in India and around the globe.

Shortly after his mandatory retirement at age sixty, Ramesh read a magazine article about a *guru* named Nisargadatta Maharaj who was teaching about Advaita (non-duality) in a poor area of Bombay. It was a subject in which he had always had a keen interest. He went to hear him, knew at once that this was his ultimate *guru* and within three or four months began translating for Maharaj at his daily morning talks. It was not long before Ramesh too experienced the ultimate intuitive understanding. More detailed accounts of these events appear on the following pages.

Retired bank president, golfer, husband and father doesn't fit the stereotype of an Indian *guru*...and perhaps that accounts, at least in part, for the fact that 90% of the people who come to him are Westerners. His background and education combine with his Understanding to make him a master who is an ideal bridge between East and West, the spiritual and the material.

◻◻◻

All there is, is Consciousness. Those words and that message are repeated over and over on the following pages. The repetition is not gratuitous. Ramesh tells the story of being taken to a restaurant where a specialty of the house was a potato baked inside a shell of clay. The waiter came to the table and tap, tap, tapped on the clay shells with a mallet until they cracked open. Ramesh says his teaching is like that; he keeps tap, tap, tapping with the same mallet until the shell breaks, and there is no way to tell in advance how many taps it is going to take.

Wayne Liquorman
Hermosa Beach
Oct. 17, 1992

1

A BEGINNING

If there's one thing which I've always been anxious for participants in the seminars or the retreats to be sure of it's that I'm not selling anybody, anything. Then it suddenly dawned on me that that is not true. I am selling something which is nothing on behalf of the Divine Entity which is really no entity and therefore nothing either. And the biggest joke is, I'm selling this nothing to you who are all nothing! This is really the joke. But until the joke is realized as a joke, it can be a terribly tragic joke.

As was asked yesterday, "Who is seeking what?" Science tells us the "who" just doesn't exist except as a pattern of vivid energy vibrating at incredible speeds in a particular pattern. The "who" then collapses. The "what" is not something which can be perceived with any of our senses, so this too, collapses. Without any support from the "who" and "what," the seeking must collapse too! And the seeking collapses into that nothing, into that pure noumenal silence, in which there is neither a seeker nor anything to be sought nor any seeking.

What we've understood now is at an intellectual level, but it is really easy to experience this, here and now. Let's try. I suggest we keep our eyes closed and relax.

I said, "Relax," I didn't say, "Straighten your backs." Sit whichever way you are comfortable, just relax. But this is what happens. The moment we are told, "Do something," even, "Relax," the first thing we do is not to relax. You were relaxing and you suddenly straightened up. This is precisely what happens when you are seeking. The seeking is going on all the time, there is no seeker. Seeking is going on all the time. So, just close your eyes and relax, and understand that there really is no "who." The "who" is merely an imagined concept. There is no "who" and there is no "what" to be sought. When this is really understood, not intellectually, but when you *feel* this, that there is no "who"and there is no "what," then you experience that tremendous sense of nothingness, that tremendous sense of total freedom, and experience the present moment, the eternal moment. In fact, the eternal moment, the present moment, *is* the experience.

In the moment, there is no experiencer experiencing anything. All there is, is the experience which is the present moment, here and now. And in that eternal moment, the present moment, there is no "me" and there is no duration; no past, present and future. And when there is no "me" and no sense of duration, all there is, is that silence in which conceptualization cannot take place. The conceptualizing depends entirely on the "me" and the duration. If there is no "me" and no duration, there cannot be conceptualizing. That is the present moment, the eternal moment. Any experience that we "have" is only when we talk of that experience. When we talk of the experience, it is in duration. It is always in the past. The experience comes up as an event in the past when we think about it and only when we think about it. Whenever there is an actual experience, there is no experiencer. Any experience is necessarily an impersonal experience. It is an impersonal event which assumes personality, which assumes the individuality, only when the "me" thinks of the experience. But that experience is already in the past. So, in the experience itself, whether it is pain or ecstasy, in that experience there never is a "me," because the experience is always, necessarily, in the present moment—in that moment which is outside the duration. It is in a totally different dimension. It is not the present. The present moment is not the present because "the present" is related to the past and future. This experience, any experience, pain or pleasure, is the present moment. If this is understood, a lot of confusion, a lot of questions would automatically cease. Any experience that we can think of, you say, "Yes! But, in this present moment, I can think of the experience." Yes, you can, but that experience that you're thinking of is a memory. You can never have that experience again. You can have a similar experience but it will never be the same experience. The experience in the present moment is gone the moment you have thought about the experience. Also, you can imagine an experience in the future. Whether the experience is brought up from the memory of the past or is projected into the future, it is not the present moment. And this is a typical trick of the mind, to go over a past experience and either want it repeated or never to be repeated, depending on whether it was acceptable or not acceptable.

When this is understood, it creates a remarkable transformation, maybe at an intellectual level but nonetheless, it is a transformation. Even with the intellectual understanding, the result of this intellectual understanding is that gradually the involvement gives place to witnessing. This is not enlightenment. This is not true awakening.

(Ed. Note: Henceforth, questioner's questions will be displayed in *italics*.)

If there is a process of understanding, beginning at an intellectual level and going deeper into something that is referred to as

Sudden Awakening, how can this be interpreted in terms of a process?

It's a valid question. And the question can be answered this way: you are climbing—as a concept again—a staircase and you have no idea how many steps there are. All you can do is to keep climbing. The process is the climbing. And you never know how many more steps to the top. The final step is always sudden! The hindrance is, if you keep thinking about your progress, you want to hasten it. It is the nature of the mind. One of the leading psychologists in San Francisco has been attending these talks for three or four years and he still persists with this. He says, "Ramesh, I understand, but so long as it is a process, surely I must be able to hasten it." So I go back to my answer, "Who" is there to hasten this process? This progress can be felt and the process hastens itself if no effort be made to hasten it. Because, the effort is always by the "me."

So this progress can be felt, but as the progress arises, the question still remains so long as there's the "me," asking, "What do I do?" The answer is, the only thing you should do is not get involved in it, not think about the progress. The idea suddenly arises, "I've had more and more of these moments!" Fine! That is a thought that arises spontaneously over which you have no control. Or the thought may be, "I'm not making any progress." Whether it is the thought that you are making progress or the thought that you are not making progress, it is still a thought which arises in Consciousness over which you have no control. Whatever the thought, positive or negative, if it is merely witnessed then it disappears and you're no longer involved.

◘◘◘

– SCIENCE MEETS METAPHYSICS –

The basic problem of the human being is that he wants to see the whole picture, both the phenomenal picture and the non-phenomenal picture, with his limited intellect. It's like a little screw wanting to know the whole machine.

Heisenberg, who originally stated the principle of indeterminacy, says "The very attempt to conjure up a picture of elementary particles and think of them in visual terms is wholly to misinterpret them." But that is precisely what the human intellect wants to do. The human intellect wants to find out. And in trying to find out, it creates problems. So, until the human intellect accepts that all it can do is to go along with nature, the human intellect will never be able to understand nature. And that is at the level of phenomenality. So how can the human intellect hope to see the source from which this phenomenal world has arisen?

Heisenberg further says, "Atoms are not things." The electrons which form an atom's shell are no longer things in the sense of classical physics, things which could be unambiguously described by concepts like location, velocity, energy and size. These concepts the human intellect can understand, but when we get down to the atomic level, the objective world in space and time just no longer exists.

The oneness of physics is still conceptualization, isn't it? It's based on conceptualizations of sub-atomic invisible particles, totally conceptual. Isn't the conceptualization of Advaita also just conceptual, just a point of view?

Indeed, it is a point of view, it is a concept. Everything is a concept. Everything any sage, any saint, anybody has said is a concept.

So, what is not a concept?

At the phenomenal level, the only thing that is not a concept is this knowledge which every single human being, every single sentient being at every time in history has known: I exist, I Am in this moment, here and now.

And even that is a conceptualization.

Even that, ultimately, *becomes* a conceptualization.

◼◻◻

When you say we are all instruments of God, is that where the saying came from, "You are one with everything?"

You, as Consciousness, yes. Consciousness is immanent. It is the ground of all being, of everything.

That table is Consciousness? The window and everything else in the world is Consciousness, and I am one with all of that?

Yes, the mystic has been saying that for thousands of years. Now, the scientist is saying, all there is, is this wholeness and that wholeness is really and truly *indivisible*. In other words, the human mind of subject-object divides what is naturally indivisible and therefore gets into trouble.

◼◻◻

What do you mean when you say that everything is now?

That's why I give this metaphor of a painting, a mile long and ten stories high. With the limited physical sight that you have, however far back you go, you will still only be able to see a certain portion at one time. So you view it section by section and it will take you time to get to the end. But the picture has been there all the time.

What was, is. What is, is. And what is going to be, also is, now. But the human mind is incapable of knowing this except as an intuitive insight, not by reasoning. In fact, it is only when reasoning gives up that this intuitive insight erupts.

◼◻◻

2

THE NATURE OF CONSCIOUSNESS

– AN OVERVIEW –

You've said that the entire manifestation is basically impersonal. So how then does the individual fit into the picture?

What is the manifestation? It is just a sudden spontaneous concurrent appearance in Consciousness, within Consciousness, brought about *by* Consciousness. In that manifestation, the human being is just one object. Basically, as far as the manifestation is concerned, there is no difference between the human being and the inanimate object. As far as the manifestation is concerned, the human being is as much of an object as a piece of rock. So where does the question of individuality arise at all? That arises because in the inanimate object, consciousness is not there in the form of sentience. The human being is endowed with sentience, like any animal. Sentience enables the senses to work. The human being is essentially an inanimate object plus sentience, precisely like any other animal or insect which has the feeling of being present, the sense of presence. That is the sentience.

In addition to that sentience, which the insect or animal has, the human being is endowed with intellect. Intellect is what enables the human being to discriminate and interpret what is cognized, which the animal need not do. So it is this power of the intellect to discriminate and interpret what is cognized that gives the individual being a sense of individuality and makes him consider himself something special in this manifestation. What is more, he goes to the extent of believing that the entire manifestation has been created for his benefit! So, all the time he is thinking, "In what way can I benefit by exploiting nature?" And the extent to which the human being has "benefited" himself, we can all see.

So, we come back to the principle that the human being is like any other object in manifestation, and that he is merely a dreamed character with senses which enable him to perceive things and cognize and interpret and discriminate between what he sees. If he sees impersonality in all this, that he is just another object in the manifestation, with certain additional endowments, like the sentience of animals plus intellect, *that* is the first step in perceiving the impersonality of the whole manifestation. In the impersonality of this manifestation there is an inherent understanding that whatever has appeared cannot possibly have any existence of its own.

Therefore, what has appeared is merely a kind of reflection of that basic ground, call it Consciousness-at-rest, God, or whatever. Seeing the oneness, not only in the manifestation but the oneness between the manifest and the unmanifest, is all that is really meant by enlightenment. Once the individual thinks in terms of his individuality, forgetting this oneness, not only between the manifest and the unmanifest, but the manifestation as a whole, then he begins to think in terms of personal security. Once he begins to think in terms of personal security, he creates any number of problems for himself. So, at that level, the first step in the understanding of the individual is the fact that there can be no such thing as security for the individual, that movement and change are the very basis of life and living. Therefore, in seeking security, he is seeking something which just doesn't exist. That understanding is the beginning of understanding life, and through the understanding of life, to go back into impersonality. The child, in his earliest stages, has an inherent awareness of things. It is his experienced actuality. So no questions arise. But when the intellect gradually expands, the child begins to ask questions. When the child has its first confrontation with the phenomenon of death, death brings the idea of life to the child. Death and disintegration bring the idea of life and security to the child. As the intellect proceeds, the intuitive natural awareness with the Oneness gradually gets dimmed, clouded.

◻◻◻

What is a human being, really?

Zen master Tung Shan has expressed this basic fact clearly when he said, "I show the truth to living beings, and then they are no longer living beings." The end question then is, "What really am I now?" Basically all any one is, is an object. And what is this object, as seen through an electron-scanning microscope with its tremendous magnification? Even as it exists at present and based on an intelligent projection, on what the microscope has already revealed, the body appears as really nothing but emptiness and certainly not a solid object. Furthermore, deep within this emptiness, the subatomic physicist tells us, is a nucleus which, being an oscillating field begins to dissolve, showing further organized fields—protons, neutrons, and even smaller particles, each of which also dissolves into nothing but the rhythm of the universal pulse. In other words, there is no solidity at all, either at the most sublime level of the body or at the heart of the universe. The compact nucleus at the very heart of the atom, then, is nothing solid at all but rather a dynamic individual pattern of concentrated energy throbbing and vibrating at an incredible speed.

This object, the human body, can be seen from another totally different perspective, equally spectacular. The view of this object, as observed from a distance further and further back, is replaced first by a house, then in turn by a town, a country, a continent, then by the earth as a planet, followed by the solar system, the sun, a galaxy, the Milky Way, and finally by clusters of galaxies rapidly dwindling into points of light in a great vastness and about to vanish altogether.

So, the story of the outward and the inward perspectives both come to much the same thing: the human being is virtually empty space and utter illusion. The question then is, "What is our true nature? Who, really, am I or what am I?" The noumenon has become the phenomenal manifestation, the Absolute has become the relative, the potential has become the actual, and the potential energy has become the activated energy. On that empty stage comes this play, and on the empty canvas has come this painting. The source of everything is the potential nothingness. But, because of our limited perception, we think that is real which is perceptible to one of our senses, whereas the real is that which is not perceptible to the senses.

Metaphysically, we are back to the question, "*Who* is seeking *what*?" The "who," as we have seen, is nothing but emptiness, so there cannot be a real "who." There cannot be a solid "who." There cannot be a solid, individual entity which is the seeker. We have also seen that what is being sought is also nothing. The "what" that is being sought is not something which can be seen by the eye, which can be heard by the ear, which can be smelled by the nose, which can be tasted by the tongue, or touched by the fingers. So, that something which is being sought is not some thing at all.

◘◘◘

– NIRVANA AND SAMSARA ARE ONE –

This source that you speak of, is this source separate in each individual or is it like something that covers over everyone?

It's something which "covers over" everyone. It's inside everyone, every object.

Is a little piece torn off and given to me and another little piece to...

No. No. It's all one. That is the wholeness which the mystic has been talking about for hundreds of years, and which the scientist has been saying since quantum mechanics was developed. All there is, is this wholeness and oneness which cannot be separated.

The impersonal Consciousness is the *Shiva* or *Atman,* or the Self, as Ramana Maharshi used to say. And the *jiva* or the self which is the "selfish self," is the identified consciousness. What Ramana Maharshi used to say is that the Consciousness is the entire ocean. The universal Consciousness or the Self, is the ocean and the *jiva* or the identified consciousness, is a bubble. But the bubble itself, so long as it remains a bubble, is apparently separate. Nonetheless, what is the bubble other than water? And when the bubble collapses, where does it go to? It becomes the ocean.

When the understanding happens, it makes no difference which words are used or which master has used them. Each master has used different words for only one reason: his audience has been different, the circumstances different, the people different and the times different.

Maharaj once told me—I was surprised when he said it—"Many of my colleagues don't like what I say, because I am not parroting what my *guru* used to say. What comes out of my lips is what you need, not what my colleagues and I need." What surprised me was when he added, "When *you* talk, what you say will not be parroting what I have been saying." So, many people who used to go to Maharaj don't like what I say. They say, "That's not what Maharaj said!"

Of course it's not what Maharaj said!

ᗒᗒᗒ

– ETERNAL –

Consciousness, according to the very first thing you said, is everything.

Yes.

Did Consciousness create the "me"?

Yes. The "me" is nothing but Consciousness. The form is another matter. But "me" is still Consciousness which has done the identifying within the body as a "me."

There is no responsibility then for a "me."

Absolutely correct. The "me" is insubstantial. Therefore, which "me" is to be held responsible?

But if the "me" comes from Consciousness, Consciousness is going to be there, isn't it?

It is there. It is here, and it will be here even when this body-mind organism is not here. That is the point. That is why the basic Zen question is, "What was your original face? What was your true nature before your parents were born?" Your true nature did not commence with your being born and will not perish with the death of the body.

ᗒᗒᗒ

– AT REST AND IN MANIFESTATION –

In Prior To Consciousness[2], *Nisargadatta says "Consciousness is all there is." He says that a lot of the time, but sometimes he talks about Consciousness in a negative way, that you have to go prior to Consciousness. He talks about it in two different ways, as*

---

(2) *Prior To Consciousness*, ed. Jean Dunn (Durham, NC: Acorn Press, 1985)

the Absolute, and as a thing that is holding you back. He suggests we have to get beyond that. I don't understand.

Consciousness, when he talks of it as a hindrance, is the identified consciousness. Prior to Consciousness is Consciousness-at-rest, which is our real nature. So he talks about the noumenal and the phenomenal. In phenomenality, this sense of presence is the waking state, and that is when your mind is active. So the sense of presence, which he considers an obstruction, is the sense of presence in the waking state, which means the conceptualizing of the mind going on. The mind does not conceptualize, cannot conceptualize in deep sleep because the sense of presence is absent. In *Prior to Consciousness*[3], what he talks of, is the absence of *both* the presence of the sense of presence and of the absence of the sense of presence in which the question of Consciousness doesn't arise at all. Because in that state of rest, Consciousness is not even aware of itself.

Why is it not aware of itself?

Because there is no "other" to be aware of.

So, prior to Consciousness is Consciousness-at-rest? But it isn't even the absence of it. It's not just pure Consciousness is it?

It *is* pure Consciousness. It's not negating Consciousness.
It is negating this flip-flop of the presence and absence of Consciousness which is only in phenomenality, so it is negating phenomenality itself.

This negating of phenomenality, who does it?

It is the mind. So, the ultimate Reality can only be when there is negation of the negator, himself. When the mind itself is negated, there is no "one" to negate. There is no "one" to think up a concept of reality. That is the state in which no concept is possible.

---

3) ibid.

That is pure Consciousness?

Yes, you can call it pure Consciousness, Consciousness-at-rest.

Prior to identified consciousness?

So long as you understand it, there is no need of any word.

It's also impure?

The moment you call it (laughing) pure Consciousness, it is impure.

You say that this is "All a dream world, an illusion," and that we create all manifestation. At the same time you say that in order for the mind and Consciousness to appear, there has to be a body. Which came first, the body or Consciousness?

All there is, is Consciousness. In that original state, call it Reality, call it Absolute, call it Nothingness, in that state there was no reason to be aware of anything. So Consciousness-at-rest was not aware of itself. It became aware of itself only when this sudden feeling, I Am, arose. I Am, is the impersonal sense of being aware. And that was when Consciousness-at-rest became Consciousness-in-movement, when potential energy became actual energy. They are not two. Nothing separate comes out of the potential energy.

Consciousness-in-movement is not seperate from Consciousness-at-rest. Consciousness-at-rest has become the Consciousness-in-movement, and that moment that science calls the Big Bang the mystic calls the sudden arising of awareness.

You are saying that the mind and the body came about at the same time?

Simultaneously. All objects came at the same time, as parts of the manifestation. Then in certain objects, the sentience came about, sentience which enables the senses to see its objects.

So it's not sentience that creates all of this?

No.

That which is prior to sentience creates it?

Yes. First is the manifestation. Then in that manifestation, certain objects are implanted with sentience and certain others, who already have sentience, have intellect. But all of it is simultaneous, concurrent.

So it's not the chicken or the egg that is the question?

No. The chicken and the egg, both are in this manifestation.

Is the natural state Consciousness-at-rest?

It is the natural state, outside of phenomenality. In phenomenality the natural state is the non-witnessing state.

But that non-witnessing state is not Consciousness-at-rest?

Oh, no! Everything in this phenomenality is a concept, an illusion, and for practical purposes we can forget the Consciousness-at-rest because we can only talk of phenomenality. A friend of mine has been coming to me for eight years. I told him he talked of reality, but in reality, reality is a concept. He literally started tearing his hair! He said, "What do you mean, reality is a concept? Reality is reality!" So I said, "Yes, reality is reality, but not when you talk of it."

When you talk of reality, you have converted reality into a concept. Reality, as a word, is a concept. Reality, as reality, is not something that you can think of. When you *are* the reality, you cannot talk of reality. So the moment you talk or think of something, it is in phenomenality and therefore conceptual.

Can you comment on the relationship between the non-volitional aspect of what enlightenment is and the double negation that you talk about? I know the understanding of either one or both leads to enlightenment. I always thought if you understood one, the other would necessarily follow. But I can't, at least intellectually, make the connection between the two. How do they relate? I know they must in some way.

No. They are not related at all.

Aha! No wonder I couldn't understand it!

But it's a very good question. In enlightenment basically, whether it happens through devotion or whether it happens through good deeds being done in such a way that there is no "me" doing them, there is just one common thing. The common factor is that there is no sense of personal doership. There is no "me." There is no conceptualization. All that has happened is that all doubts have suddenly ceased. All concepts cease, all doubts cease. When enlightenment has happened, a doubt like that cannot remain. The double negative I mentioned is a concept which you need only so long as the doubts arise. The doubt for this double negative is, in deep sleep I have no sense of presence. The sense of presence is absent. "Is that not the noumenal state?" asks the mind.

No, it is not.

And why is it not? Because of the double negative.

Because you wake up again.

In the waking state, there is presence of presence. In deep sleep there's absence of it. When both these states are absent, conceptually, that conceptual condition is the noumenal state.

And that condition doesn't exist really... its only a concept.

Absolutely correct!

So, you cannot approach it at all.

That "you" cannot approach it, at all, is correct. But, conceptually, when this doubt arises, you have this conception, therefore that state becomes a reality.

You're not in that state all the time? No one can be in that state all the time?

No "one."

But does that state exist? Does Consciousness exist in that state?

Consciousness exists, but it doesn't know it exists. Consciousness-at-rest, without awareness, is potential energy. So that state is purely a concept. The "one" comes in when Consciousness, Subjectivity, objectivizes itself in this objective expression. That's why I say, for practical purposes, forget the noumenal state. But it's still a very good question.

Can the noumenal state express itself through the body-instrument consistently?

That is what it is doing. The noumenal state becomes the phenomenal state. Consciousness-at-rest and Consciousness-in-movement are *not* two different states. All there is, is Consciousness in one state or another.

Then you Ramesh...no, not "you," but that which is communicating to us, is Consciousness-at-rest?

No, Consciousness-in-movement.

Your words are Consciousness-in-movement?

Yes, Consciousness is in movement as soon as this I Am arises. Consciousness-at-rest doesn't even know it is at rest.

It's still pure Consciousness, only in movement?

Oh indeed! All the body-mind organisms are part of the manifestation which appears spontaneously when Consciousness begins its movement.

Does it mean that you appear within my consciousness just to awaken me? To give me that "good news" and nothing more than that?

Yes, "good news" or "bad news."

Not any more than that?

Your body-mind organism which is listening and this body-mind organism which does most of the talking, both these organisms have to be here at this place and at this time so that the one event of talking and listening can take place.

❏❏❏

– THE IMPERSONAL FUNCTIONING OF TOTALITY –

Ramesh, the Totality functions by itself. Wasn't that Maharaj's basic point?

Quite so. The same thing as your respiratory process, your digestive process, your most complicated nervous system. It works all by itself. It doesn't need any "me" to control it.

Sri Aurobindo says something like, "The hearing hears, the seeing sees, the senses are basically there themselves." There is no real subject behind the senses then? Everything is awareness?

That is correct. Therefore, it is the same thing as what I'm saying which is, there is no individual perceiver through any of the senses. The perceiving of any of the senses is taking place through the body-mind mechanism. That is all that is happening. And the reaction to that perceiving is by you.

So in the receiving of the sense impressions, whatever they may be, seeing, hearing, or touching, there is nothing that has to be there for that to occur. There is no entity, no subject. It's after the reaction occurs that I get the feeling of the "me," and the preferences and all that.

That's right. And there is one step more which is that this reactionary process is not the fault of anyone. No one need be guilty about it.

The instantaneous arising of comparing and judgment are coming up because the mind can't do anything else?

Correct. That is the nature of the mind. Therefore, in trying to suppress it, you may suppress it for a while, then suddenly it comes up with a tremendous gush.

How do you explain that one child is born in a wealthy family, another one in a poor family, another one suffers all his life, someone else comes from a middle class family, and then he becomes a beggar or is oppressed and goes to jail? All these crazy things are happening without their volition? It just happens?

Yes.

So what is the cause of all this?

The cause of this is very simple. If you accept that all there is, is Consciousness, then who is suffering this? Who is experiencing other than Consciousness? So it is Consciousness which experiences all the experiences from zero to ten through various body-mind mechanisms. But because there is identification, the split-mind says "I" am suffering or "I" am enjoying.

That's all that is happening.

You're denying any idea of a future event or a past event. What you're saying is, just consider the present. Whatever happens in the present, that's what happens.

Yes, indeed. In other words, what we think horizontally as something happening in the course of time is precisely something happening in each present moment. Not just what you are doing, but all over the world at any present moment. Whatever is happening through the billions of body-mind mechanisms is precisely what the functioning of Totality *is* at that time, including all the good deeds, including all the evil deeds, including the earthquakes and the floods, the wars, the battles, everything.

So, that way you can do away with the whole concept of time.

Which I believe is precisely what science is coming to. At one of the talks there was a mathematician, and he said that ultimately Einstein came to the conclusion that space and time do not exist. Don't take my word for it, or any other mystic. This mathematician has gone into that matter about Einstein very deeply and he said ultimately Einstein had to come to the conclusion that this space-time is not real, that space-time is only a concept, a conceptual mechanism necessary for this manifestation to take place, for three dimensional objects to be projected in space and perceived in time.

If space-time is conceptual, and space-time is a necessary mechanism, what does it make of manifestation, but also a concept? And therefore the human being as part of that manifestation is also a conceptual emptiness.

Are you saying that in the case of the lawn being watered that the thought to water the lawn rather than to take a walk or drink a cup of coffee comes from somewhere? Isn't it simply a manifestation of Totality at that time. Are you saying that there is direction in all this, intention from somewhere or somebody else?

No, except that as you said, the thought comes. You see, the basic point I'm making is, no brain can create a thought with the material of which it is. A thought can only come from outside. Then there can be a reaction at any moment, but the thought comes from outside. You see?

The concept of "outside," I find difficult. Outside what?

That is the point. Really, there is no outside or inside. All there is, is Consciousness.

So, in fact, there is no outside called "outside."

Correct. There is neither up nor down nor inside nor outside, nor without nor within. All there is, is Consciousness. And this manifestation is an appearance within that Consciousness. And even that appearance is only an objective expression of the same Consciousness. All there is, is Consciousness.

And the resistance that we have to this idea of fatalism, or non-volition, or whatever you want to call it, that, in fact, is the ego, the "me," screaming against its own annihilation.

Precisely. And a deeper point is, that there is no "me" to be blamed. There is no "me" to blame for this conditioning.

Pity. (laughter)

You can't pass the blame on to anybody. All there is, is Consciousness. Therefore, all these "me"s, the billions of "me"s, the billions of egos, who's created them? Who but Consciousness, by merely identifying itself with each individual body-mind mechanism! So there are billions of "me"s quarreling and loving and hating each other, which is what this *lila* is all about.

We had no choice in regard to our parents, our surroundings. We are just born in a particular place, with particular parents, with very definite inherent characteristics. We don't act. The body-mind mechanism merely reacts to an outside event or a thought. Each body-mind organism can react only according to its own inherent characteristics. That is why the same event produces different types of reactions in different organisms. It is not a matter of choice. Each organism reacts according to the inherent characteristics with which it has been created. Each individual organism is conceived and created with certain characteristics, so that certain actions will take place through that organism. These actions are part of the impersonal functioning of Totality. That is why you cannot be really responsible. You are only an instrument through which action is produced, impersonally. You are merely an instrument through which Consciousness is functioning.

So, I have to look at ego as also a function of Totality. Then hopefully, if I have that view, I'm in business. Is that right?

Yes, then you're in business. But if you keep fighting your ego, you are not in business. Accepting the ego and not fighting it all the time is a big step. A big step. One of the astonishing laws of the universe is that where there is no resistance, there is no conflict. If you don't put up the fight, the ego can't either. The ego must be terribly frustrated if it doesn't find resistance.

␥␥␥

The other day I stopped to feed the llamas that live in the field down the road. Watching them I remembered what you said, "When I'm hungry I eat, when I'm tired I sleep." The llama does all that, the llama has no doubts.

The llama has no intellect. In his case there is no concept of bondage. Therefore...

He doesn't know he's liberated.

No, no. There is no concept of bondage, therefore there is no need to be liberated from that concept. Since there is no concept of bondage, the question of liberation or enlightenment is irrelevant. All that happens is, a body has been "born" and will "die" in due course. That's all. Millions of bodies are created and destroyed, and that will be one of them.

How does that differ from someone who is enlightened and doesn't know he is enlightened?

No difference at all. That is precisely what I am saying. Enlightenment is merely an impersonal happening. We give it the taint of a personal achievement. Therefore the question arises, "What is an enlightened being like?" There is no such thing as an enlightened person. Enlightenment is merely another event. There is a flood, a fire, an earthquake; there is enlightenment, just one happening in the whole process, all part of the phenomenal process.

Enlightenment has significance only in phenomenality. Therefore, it is still a concept. And in phenomenality the mind wants to know what the original state of void is like. It is precisely like wanting to know what the state of deep sleep is like. Nobody asks that, because everybody has the experience of deep sleep. So the question, "What is it like?" can only happen to a person who has never slept in his life. Only he can ask, "What is that state of deep sleep like?"

It would be impossible to describe it to him.

Exactly. A more mundane example would be: how will you describe color to a man blind from birth? He can only know by touching or hearing or tasting or smelling.

◘◘◘

I find you a very interesting character. In fact, there are lots of interesting characters in this room. Why do I find some characters more interesting than others?

Basically, every individual is really an individual pattern of vibrating energy. When you find two organisms where the patterns are harmonious, you say, "I like that person."

So, the individual pattern of vibrating energy responds. It is possible then, that when I'm talking, the energy that exudes attracts certain individual patterns. To go a step further, that is why these individual patterns have been brought here together, for that purpose. It's all part of the functioning of manifestation. When you go to the potential of the Void, all this is meaningless: bondage, enlightenment, knowledge, all of it is bullshit! You don't need it. You just see the impersonal functioning of the manifestation which has simultaneously, spontaneously come about from the Unmanifest. From the Nothing, all this everything has come. Okay, that's understood. That's all that need be understood, even phenomenally. The rest of it is totally unnecessary. But as you go further down, the individual thinks he is an individual and then more words are needed.

Isn't everything you're talking about a concept?

Of course! The only truth which is not a concept is the sense of presence, here and now. In the impersonal sense of presence, "I Am," not "I am Joe or Jane." This impersonal sense of presence in the present moment is the only truth.

Whether it is Maharshi's approach, or Maharaj's or yours, it is a concept.

Oh yes, but both of them made it perfectly clear: nothing has been created, nothing has been destroyed. It's all a dream, and there is no individual, other than an appearance in Consciousness.

Does awakening lead to awareness which persists twenty-four hours a day?

Yes, but there is no one to be conscious of that awareness. That is the key to the whole thing. There is no individual, no ego to be conscious of that awareness. Awareness is just there!

But, Ramesh, if everything is dissolved, how can we surrender!

That is the point; everything dissolves. There is no "one" to surrender, no "one" to comprehend. Surrender happens. Understanding happens without any individual comprehending or surrendering. And that is the transformation; the disappearance of the "me," the "one," the "who."

So, there's no fear of surrendering, no sacrifice.

Exactly! As long as there is someone to sacrifice, it is not sacrifice. Take humility. You say, "I am humble. I'm not proud." The proudest people perform acts of humility. Real humility means the absence of that which can feel humble or proud. That is true humility. That is true compassion, when there is no one who feels, "I am being compassionate." There is love when there is no one to say, "I love." Compassion, love, humility, these are various names for that state of here and now, without the "me."

If this whole world of people and everything dissolved, what would Consciousness be?

All that remains is Consciousness. The manifestation will not be there. The appearance would not be there.

What would be there?

That which has *always* been: the Divine Ground, Consciousness, Totality, the True One Subject, the Potential Nothingness, God, whatever you call it.

I know, but what does it look like?

It doesn't look like any thing, because it is not a thing.

Is accepting life as the impersonal functioning of Totality a return to devotion?

Yes, from the devotional point of view, it is pure devotion. From the point of view of knowledge, it is the return to impersonality.

It always seems to me that if I'm to function, there has to be a desire or an expectation to produce the motivation for the function. Otherwise the functioning stops.

Every body-mind organism has been conceived and constructed with certain characteristics and those characteristics will never cease to function.

Even without desire?

Yes, even without desire, without this motivation, which brings along with it, inherently, the sense of anxiety. Without this motivation which brings with it anxiety, the work will proceed much more smoothly. The body, the mind will continue functioning. It cannot stop functioning simply because the non-existent "me" says, "I have no more motivation, therefore why should I work?" You cannot not work. The body-mind organism will continue to function according to its natural physical, temperamental, and mental characteristics to perform duties which have been programmed into it.

Seems like the desires have also been programmed in.

Yes indeed! That's why listening to what I've said could reduce the desire or suddenly bring about the flash of understanding, "That is so!" Or it may have no effect at all. The effect of what you have heard, also is not in your hands, is not a matter of volition. You can only wait and see what happens.

When you say that the environmental destruction that Consciousness is doing to our environment is supposed to happen and therefore we as...

Whose environment?! Are we different from that environment? Consciousness has created this environment of which we are a small, essential, but negligible part.

Well, on an abstract conceptual level I can follow that, but when I step into an oil slick and get crap all over my foot, it's more concrete and so that's why I talk about responsibility. We're drinking fouled water and breathing fouled air. Shouldn't I, as an individual, worry about that?

Yes. You see, *you* may worry about it. Someone else may not. They'll say, "Alright, it has to be." I'm very serious; I couldn't be more serious. If worrying and getting angry is part of the functioning of the organism, you will worry. You cannot help worrying; you cannot not get angry.

But in the same organism, if the understanding dawns, even at an intellectual level, and that understanding percolates down to the heart, and there's a conviction, that organism which used to worry may not worry all that much, may start to realize that all it can do is to function according to its natural characteristics. It cannot not do so. And that brings about a tremendous sense of freedom. Until it happens you don't realize what a fantastic sense of freedom it is. The freedom, just understand, the freedom to do what you like. The freedom to continue living exactly as you have been doing, with the conviction that you cannot have any control over the consequences. So you continue to do what you have been doing, the same kind of work, unless a change happens to take place. The fact that you have *no* control over the results means you stop worrying about the results and concentrate on the work that is being done.

❏❏❏

The individual body-mind, when it is born, has a particular individuality in terms of genes. I'm the only one with my particular finger prints and I'm different from everything else. Does that continuity of being different carry on through my lifetime regardless of my being conscious of it? Do I have a particular path because of my genetic make-up? As I go through life, to what extent am I different in my actions because I am born differently?

This body-mind mechanism you consider yourself to be, when conceived, was stamped with certain characteristics: physical, mental, moral, temperamental... so that Consciousness or Totality could produce through that body-mind mechanism certain acts during its lifetime, the period between birth and death. And that is what is taking place.

So I would have to conclude then that Consciousness wanted an Adolf Hitler to happen and there is no way that it could have been circumvented?

Yes sir.

He had to be born to do what he had to do?

Yes sir. The Second World War had to happen. Millions of lives had to be lost. Therefore, a body-mind mechanism with those characteristics named Hitler had to be created. Hitler did not create the war. The war created Hitler.

And Consciousness created it all.

Yes. Consciousness has created all this dream within itself. Consciousness is playing all the roles via dreamed characters. Consciousness, Itself, is playing and perceiving this drama.

It's a big con game!

Yes, it is indeed a con game. And when you realize that it is a con game and the absurdity of it, that is enlightenment. When this realization is embodied totally, that is enlightenment.

It seems the only function of the illusion of an I is to create misery and suffering. How did it start?

It just started! You are not guilty of it. That is why the first statement is that there is no one guilty of anything. It is Consciousness which has identified itself. And Consciousness is living "a life" through this body-mind organism. You don't know how long. You don't know what it is going to achieve. All I am saying is why bother? Why bother? Just watch whatever goes on.

You bother because you think they are your actions. So consider them the actions of Consciousness or God or Totality, or whatever. And those actions are necessarily circumscribed by the natural characteristics of that organism. And when you see this you see the impersonality of the whole thing. And when you see the impersonality of the process, the individual "me" has to recede back. You don't push it back; you cannot fight your ego. But this understanding pushes the ego into the background.

What I think you are talking about is Grace.

Of course it is. Now look! You are here listening to this talk. There are thousands of people who are not interested in this subject. Isn't that Grace that brought you here?

Yes.

So if it is Grace that brought you here, why don't you leave it to that Grace that brought you here to proceed whichever way it wants to?

That is what I am trying too hard to figure out, is how to get out of the way.

You don't have to, so long as you don't get *in* the way. You don't have to get out of the way. Just watch whatever is happening and you are already out of the way. It is because you think you must get out of the way that the whole problem arises.

◘◘◘

You are saying that there is no free will and that there is no predestination either. Both are concepts. Why not just be?

Precisely! That is very well put! About predestination and free will, when do the questions arise? Who brings up those questions? The individual brings up those questions, but when you see the impersonality of the whole thing no questions can arise. If you see things from the individual viewpoint, problems can never cease. But as soon as you see the impersonality of the whole functioning, no problems can arise.

◘◘◘

– MANIFESTATION –

Does Universal Consciousness know itself in other spiritual dimensions?

Universal Consciousness is part of the human mind. Universal Consciousness is not concerned. Everything is spontaneous. All is energy. The universe goes on its merry, mystical, magical way until you start observing it and you, by observing it, create problems. The working of the universe has no problems. But the physicist, in observing, expects the universe to work in a particular way, according to common sense. Where he finds that the universe does not work according to common sense, he says, "How come a particle can behave like a particle and suddenly start behaving like a wave? We have a wave behaving like a wave and suddenly it becomes a particle." So he has had to accept the fact that a particle will sometimes act like a wave and a wave like a particle. Thus he coins the word, "wavicle." It is only in his observing and his problems that he must create solutions. But the universe goes on its own merry way. It has no problems. Problems arise only when you observe, so the individual creates problems saying, "This should/shouldn't be."

So, Gods and spirits in different planes all exist only when there is an individual observer to see them, conceptualize them and to interpret them?

Yes. Quite.

That would mean then that the Universal Consciousness doesn't know itself?

Universal Consciousness in movement knows itself. But it doesn't have to know each individual for the simple reason that it sees the whole plot as one whole plot. Ramana Maharshi was asked once, "Are the gods and goddesses in human mythology real? " His answer was, "Yes, they are as real as you are." If you accept that there has been no creation, no destruction, just an appearance in Consciousness, going on its merry way, the question of gods and goddesses just doesn't arise. They're as much a creation of the human mind as an individual.

◻◻◻

The difficulty for me in understanding the fundamentals of what you're teaching is not the moral objection, but the paradox that we are here as individuals and that our sense of who we are is determined by our physical body, our experiences, by our memories. And when you speak of the illusory nature of the individual, it's ex-

tremely hard to understand how Consciousness could exist, except within the boundaries of the self.

Oh yes. You see, Consciousness can only express itself objectively through organisms. If all organisms were dead at any particular point, there would be no question of the existence of Consciousness at all. Consciousness, when it manifests itself, is really the Subjectivity expressing itself objectively. That means any expression of Consciousness as subjectivity has to be through objects.

What is the source of Consciousness?

The source of Consciousness is Consciousness. Consciousness is all there is.

It is beyond all the elements?

Yes, it is beyond all the elements because all the elements are part of this phenomenality which is an appearance in Consciousness.

ㅁㅁㅁ

– THE FUNCTIONING OF MANIFESTATION –

When people have memories of past lives, is it just the spontaneous arising of thought at that moment, without any memory connected with it?

The arising of a thought is spontaneous. Anything, of course, can happen, but a thought which is likely to occur to a doctor is not likely to occur to a lawyer or a mechanic. The thought which occurs in a particular body-mind organism has something to do with its natural characteristics. This thought of the equation which arose in the Einstein brain could not have occurred anywhere else. The whole basic point is, the human mind tries to observe and understand something which is totally beyond its compass and therefore we find tremendous paradoxes. The entire life becomes a paradox because the mind cannot understand it.

Earlier, the Newtonian physicist's thought was that you could understand the world by understanding a part of it. Now it is accepted that the part is as much necessary to understand the whole, as the whole is necessary to understand the part, and this causes considerable confusion in the human mind. The limitation of the human intellect is never taken into consideration when we think of these bigger items. The question of free will versus predetermination is really not free will versus, or free will against, predetermination. The free will is *part* of this predetermination. You consider free will as something you have as a result of a certain thought. But that thought occurring, leading to what you think is your free will is part of the totality of functioning. So it is really a misconception to consider free will as opposed to predetermination.

I have a short paper which discusses all this difficulty that we are faced with. Let me read it very slowly, and you will be astonished how much confusion would be cleared if you accept that things occur in the universe which the human mind *cannot* comprehend.

Creating Order Out of Disorder:
The Theory of Probability—The Law of Large Numbers

One of the best kept secrets of the universe relates to the question of how the sub-atomic, micro-world of particles which are at the same time wavicles, which defy strict determinism and mechanical causation—how this ambiguous, "undulating carpet of foam" gives rise to the solid, orderly macro-world of everyday experience, of causality. The macro world, as we see it, is very determined, very clear, very precise, cause and effect, and yet the micro-world out of which this has come is, for the human mind, for the human intellect, total chaos.

Out of this chaos and disorder, how could the order of the macro world arise? The modern scientist's answer is that this seemingly miraculous feat of creating order out of disorder must be seen in the light of the theory of probability or the "law of large numbers." But then, this "law" cannot be explained by physical forces. The human intellect says ,"The natural law must have a certain physical basis." It need not. It's a wrong assumption. This law cannot be explained by physical forces. It hangs, so to speak, in the air. It is, however, not difficult to see the point through a few examples. The first two examples are classic cases from Warren Weaver's book on the theory of probability. One: The statistics of the New York Department of Health show that in 1955 the average number of dogs biting people reported per day was 75.3. In 1956, 73.6; in 1957, 73.5; in 1958, 74.5; in 1959, 72.4. How could the dogs know when they should start biting and when they should stop biting? A similar statistical reliability was shown by cavalry horses administering fatal kicks to soldiers in the German army in the last century. They were apparently guided by the so-called equation of probability. And then the murders in England and Wales, however different in character and motives, they displayed the same respect for the law of statistics. Since the end of the first World War, the average number of murders over successive decades was 1920-29, 3.8 per million of population; in the thirties, 3.7; the forties, 3.9; the fifties, 3.3; the sixties, 3.5. It's there in statistics. Why? The human intellect by nature wants to know "Why?" The only answer is "Why not?" These bizarre examples illustrate the paradoxical nature of probability which has puzzled philosophers ever since Pascal initiated that branch of mathematics, and which Von Neumann, perhaps the greatest mathematician of our century, called, "black magic." The paradox consists of the fact that the theory of probability is able to predict with uncanny precision, the overall result of a large number of individual events, each of which, in itself, is totally unpredictable. In other words, we are faced with a large number of uncertainties, producing a certainty, a large number of random events creating a lawful, total outcome but paradoxically or not, the law of large numbers works! The mystery is why and how it works. It has become an indispensable tool of physics and genetics, of economic planners, insurance companies, gambling casinos and opinion polls—so much so, that the" black magic" has been taken for granted. Basically, what the question boils down to is "By what agency is this controlling and correcting influence exerted?" How do dogs of New York know when to stop biting and when to make up the daily quota? How are murderers in England and Wales made to stop at four victims per million? By what mysterious power is a roulette ball induced after a time to restore the balance in the long run? By the law of probability, we are told. But that law has no physical powers to enforce itself. It is impotent and yet virtually omnipotent. The purpose and design of this acausal agency is unknown and, more likely, unknowable to the human intellect. But somehow we feel intuitively that it is related to that striving towards higher forms of order and unity in diversity which we observe in the evolution of the universe at large. As Feynmann has concluded, the order from disorder principle seems to be irreducible, inexplicably, just there. To ask why is like asking why the universe is there, or why space has three dimensions? If indeed, it has! As Prof. David Bohm has put it, "Thus, one is led to a new notion of unbroken wholeness which denies the classical idea of the analyzability of the world into separately and independently existing parts." One *Tao* master has put it very vividly, saying, "You pull out a blade of grass and you shake the universe." There is no event which is not connected to everything else that happens in the universe. You think you have pulled the blade of grass out of the ground. The real point is that the blade of grass has been pulled. By what hands is immaterial. The metaphysical implications of this principle are fundamental. It is a remarkable fact that in 1925, before he created his famous equation, Erwin Schrödinger stated in his *My View Of The World*[4], "This life of yours which you are living is not merely a piece of this entire existence, but is, in a certain sense, the whole. Only this whole is not so constituted that it can be surveyed in one single glance." This, as we know, is what the *Brahmans* express in that sacred mystic formula which is so simple and yet so complete,

[4] *My View Of The World*, Erwin Schrödinger (Ox-Bow: 1961)

"That thou art," or again in such words as, "I am in the east and in the west. I am below and above. I am this whole universe." The problem for the human being arises because we *seem* to have some control over our daily lives and yet we cannot avoid feeling that we're helpless victims to another Will, subject to some incredibly superior order, what Schopenhauer called a "metaphysical entity," a kind of universal Consciousness compared to which individual Consciousness is but a dream. If we realize the wholeness of the universe and accept the fact that there is a miraculous order being brought out of apparent disorder, a kind of certainty out of the uncertainty of the probability theory, if we accept this without seeking an explanation, then it will not be difficult to accept that situation. It is just there and why not? It is a self-generated process in which the human being is a very, very small part. We cannot make total order of our observations on the working of this world of paradox. There always appears to be something missing. There is paradox and yet there is an exquisite order to the paradox and utter confusion for the limited human intellect. We feel inadequate and helpless only because we attempt to observe and then discern the pattern. All we can really do is to go along with it. The human intellect likes order. It doesn't like this theory of probability and uncertainty. I came across this next passage by a physicist: "Why should we not have security? Why should we not have certainty? We cannot have this world. It is unacceptable, it is unworkable. A world of certainty is unworkable." The alternative to this uncertain world is a certain world. In such a world particles will follow well determined paths, with exact locations at each and every point. That is what the human intellect wants because that is something it can understand. But this alternative of a certain world is known to be unworkable. That tiny electron inside of every atom would have to radiate each and every instant in such a certain world. It would lose all of its energy and quickly fall into the nucleus. All atoms would disappear. All electromagnetic energy would vanish. All nervous systems would cease their activity. All life would stop, for life as we know it can only exist through the blessing of uncertainty. Security is a myth. So, for the seeker to expect that he will follow such and such path, follow certain disciplines, meditate for such and such a time, and feel that he has a right to expect to be enlightened... That kind of certainty, that kind of expectation is a myth.

So, what's the probability out of 50 seekers? (laughter)

Out of the millions of people, how many have had their minds turned inwards? How many have given up their "happy life" to be miserable seekers? They had no choice.

◻◻◻

Why does Consciousness want to observe itself or experience itself?

You see, once it has manifested itself, that is a spontaneous process.

That's spontaneous?

Yes. I Am, the sense of I Am. I repeat, all these are concepts. There is potential energy throbbing. If the energy were dead, like a void or nothingness, then nothing can come out of nothingness. But if that nothingness is the potential source of everythingness, then that potential void is throbbing, throbbing with potential energy, and that must come up, must activate itself. And when it comes up as I Am, or the Big Bang, or whatever, then the energy explodes into this manifestation and it functions until that burst of energy exhausts itself and goes back into the potential to come up again some other time.

I'm going to expound a little thing in parts, and then it will be followed by a question. There's a game played by biologists who study insects and specialize in beetles. These entomologists go to the Amazon jungles to the rain forests, and every year, among them, they discover a thousand new species of beetles, this is beetles alone, not insects in general. And they name these new beetles for each

other, and their friends, and so forth (laughter) and it's competitive.
I suppose the one who discovers the most new species of beetles is
the big gun in the field, you know, the god in that game room. I have
the feeling that these beetles weren't there already, that these beetles
were created by the game process. This really puzzles me. In all the
thinking about Maya, and the "me" is part of the Maya, and so
on, I can't seem to get it clear whether these things projected by
science exist as dreams of the Absolute, or whether the Absolute
simply dreamed the game player and the game.

The question that you have put is not dissimilar to the
question that Chuang Tzu put upon awakening one morning: "Was it Chuang Tzu that dreamt he was a butterfly, or
is it a butterfly that is now dreaming that it is Chuang Tzu?"

If you mean that the observer is himself creating something, the answer would be yes. Now, whatever I am saying
is subject to the fact that whatever *anybody* says, any Scripture, anything, is still a concept. The original concept, the
original thought, is I Am, the sense of presence. So long as
that sense of presence is there, everything keeps on changing. And my own interpretation of seek-and-you-shall-find,
is that whatever the beetle-seeker is seeking, he will find.
Whatever the astronomer-seeker is seeking he will find. So
seek-and-you-shall-find does not, I think, refer to that state
of paradise or heaven or whatever.

Did the galaxies and the whole big universe, as we see it today,
project out there conceptually somewhere between ten and sixteen
billion years ago or was it here all along in the projection of the
Absolute? Or did they begin to exist with Galileo looking at the first
four moons of Jupiter?

You see, at this point, the question that arises in my mind
is what Ramana Maharshi used to ask, and it was described
by one of his disciples as the ultimate weapon: "Who wants
to know?" (laughter)

It is the intellect, you see that won't let you be. The only
point is that, as in our personal dream, the dream arises
suddenly including everything, including the universe as it

is, including the astronomer, including the scientist who is seeking. What exists is the dream which has arisen spontaneously. We wake up from our personal dream into this waking dream with the identical questions, the identical problems, which never existed in deep sleep. So as long as there is a "who" asking questions, that "who" will continue to remain puzzled.

🮕🮕🮕

– THE WONDROUS DIVERSITY OF MANIFESTATION –

You know, I can't help but get back to that story of the tailor, who was always sewing and he kept asking himself, "Who is really sewing this cloth?" All of a sudden, his mind kind of blew open, and he felt very happy and free. He didn't know what happened, he wanted an explanation, so he went to a Zen Buddhist priest and the priest told him, "You have seen into your true nature, and you realize that 'you' are not doing the sewing."

And then he got himself all involved once again. "Who is it who saw the real nature? Who is real?"

So in a sense he may have had a realization?

There was indeed.

That he was not really the doer.

Yes, but that realization happened to a "me!" When true realization happens, the tailor will find no need to go to a Zen master or any other Master.

If it were deep enough and true enough?

Yes.

When there has been an understanding, and one is awake, woken up, is it true, that there is no more attachment to one's own body-mind than to the objects that one is looking at? All is seen as Consciousness?

Yes, that is the understanding, yes.

There is that awareness even though this body-mind is here and that body-mind is there?

Yes. But all body-mind organisms, all objects, are not seen as one object.

They are all seen as Consciousness?

They are all seen in the great diversity with a sense of wonder, that Consciousness could have produced such diversity and yet be the same, that Consciousness is immanent in the billions of beings and yet in each one that it should be so diverse, so separate that no two human beings are alike; even the fingerprints are different, pulse rate is different, the voice graph is different. So the understanding is that in that diversity there is Oneness which is immanent.

◘◘◘

– THE UNICITY OF DIVERSE MANIFESTATION –

Would you please make more clear to me the word, "unicity," what it means. And also the prana, the vital life. You refer only to it as breath, that is all?

Yes, *prana* is the breath.

And the unicity?

You see, unicity is a word that I use to indicate that it is neither duality nor non-duality. Duality and non-duality are the opposite interconnected aspects. Unicity is still a concept, a word, but the point I am making about unicity is that it is totally unconnected to the interconnected opposites of duality and non-duality.

Would you speak of unicity? Did Nisargadatta use the word?

No, it's an English word. But what he meant was, indeed, unicity. It is a word used by a writer, dead now, whose name was Wei Wu Wei. Noumenon and phenomena were not his words, they were used much earlier. I think unicity was a word he coined. I like it and use it freely without anyone's permission.

Why unicity? Why not unity?

Unity presupposes duality. Unicity, though still a concept, gives the idea that there can never be two. All there can be is Consciousness. Notionally then, Unicity or Consciousness brings about duality by identifying itself with each individual being, so that this process of the observer and the object observed, the *lila*, can go on.

◻◻◻

– THE INTERCONNECTEDNESS OF MANIFESTATION –

There's a Zen saying, "When you carry water, carry water."

Yes! Just as one Zen master said, "If you want enlightenment, go and wash dishes." Meaning, when you wash dishes, do not wash dishes with your hands while your mind is wandering all over.

With resentment.

That is not washing dishes. The sage, the wise man, has the basic working and living attitude of respectful trust towards nature and human nature, despite war, revolutions, starvation, rising crime and all manner of horrors. He is not concerned with the notion of an original sin, nor does he have the feeling that existence, *samsara* itself, is a disaster. His basic understanding has the premise that if you cannot trust nature and other people, you cannot trust yourself.

Without this underlying trust, the faith in the functioning of Totality, the whole system of nature, we are simply paralyzed. Ultimately, it is not really a matter of you on the one hand, and trusting nature on the other. It is really a matter of realizing that we and nature are one and the same process, not separate entities. You cannot omit one integer without upsetting the entire system.

In other words, the universe is an organic and relational process, not a mechanism. It is by no means analogous to a political or military hierarchy in which there is a supreme commander. It is multitudinous, a multi-dimensional network of jewels, each one containing the reflection of all others. That's how the universe has been described. Each jewel is a thing-event, and between one thing-event and another there is no obstruction. The mutual interpenetration and interdependence of everything in the universe. That's why the Chinese say, "Pick a blade of grass and you shake the universe."

The basic principle of this organic view of the universe is that the cosmos is implicit in every member of it and every point of it may be regarded as a center. The perfect understanding is a floodlight on the whole universe in its functioning, exhibiting it as a harmony of intricate patterns. Whereas, the spotlight vision of the split-mind of the illusory individual entity sees only each pattern by itself, section by section and concludes that the universe is a mass of conflict. It is a limited spotlight vision which would give a sense of horror to the normal universal phenomenon of one species in the biological world, being the food of another. The broad perspective, the floodlight which is the perfect understanding, would see things as they are.

Birth and death are nothing but integration and disintegration, the appearance and subsequent disappearance of the phenomenal objects in manifestation. True understanding, apperception, includes the understanding that there is no separation between understanding and action.

❏❏❏

– SPACE AND TIME –

Is there Consciousness in the physical space between you and I?

All there is, is Consciousness. You and I are mere objects projected in this space. All there is, is Consciousness. Space and time are mere concepts, a mechanism for objects to be extended. For three-dimensional objects to be extended, space is necessary. And time is necessary for objects to be observed. Unless that object is observed, it doesn't exist.

So space and time are merely concepts, a mechanism, created for this manifestation to take place and be observed. It is amazing how in the last few years, comparatively, science is bang-on. Science says the same thing, you see. It says space and time are not real. And I think it was Sir Fred Hoyle who said, "If you think that there is a past going into the future, or the future going into past, you couldn't be more wrong. There couldn't be such flow. It is all there, now."

The nearest metaphor I can suggest is this: If there is a painting a mile long and ten stories high, it is all there; but for you to see it from one end to the other, it will take some time. Because we can't see the whole picture in one glance, the human mind is not capable of it, we think in terms of time. But the whole thing is there.

And, as you said, we do not see the whole picture, we are just seeing a small part of it.

Part by part. So, by the time you go to the end, time has elapsed. The concept of time has elapsed.

So, in effect we are limited by time and space?

Correct. We are limited by time and space, and intellect!

❐❐❐

– POLARIC OPPOSITES –

Is this appearance a polaric opposite to the state of Consciousness-at-rest?

No, the polaric opposites are the sleeping state and the waking state. And...

Not the thing and the no-thing?

And that state which is prior to both the waking state and the sleeping state is the Nothingness.

Okay, but out of the Nothingness comes the thingness. Is that a polaric opposite?

No! Oh no. Out of Nothingness, which is really the potential energy, the potential energy activates itself, and once it has activated itself the dualities immediately come into being.

I see.

Love and hate. When the love and hate have been transcended, that which remains, which cannot really be labeled, is Consciousness or compassion or love or charity or whatever you want to call it. So that which *is*, is prior to the arising of the existence of the opposites, love, hate.

Would you please expand upon your usage of the terms duality and dualism or polarity? More on that little nuance of difference there.

Everything in the universe is based on opposites. Nothing in the world, nothing in the universe is static; the universe is moving all the time. The universe is always changing from one opposite to the other. The opposites are interconnected. In reality, we can only go along with them. But the human intellect compares the opposites, wants to choose between the opposites and it just can't be done. Opposites are interrelated polarities. One cannot exist without the other. The human being is unhappy because he seeks security. Security means no change, and nothing in the universe can remain unchanged. The human being's search for security must necessarily end in frustration. The human being has to accept that insecurity. The changing from one opposite into the other is the very basis of life and existence.

The basis of indeterminacy from the point of view of the physicist is even clearer. The basic particle has its own nature. Sometimes it is a particle, sometimes a wave. So the modern scientists had to come up with a new word called "wavicle." The dual nature of the electron, both theoretically and practically is impossible to pin down. If you have its velocity, then its exact position will not be known. If the exact position is known, its velocity will not be known. This uncertainty prevails all the time. This unpredictability can be more easily seen in what is known as a paradoxical cube. If you keep looking at a cube, the face suddenly changes. You do not know when it changes and it eventually changes back to its original face. Advaita Press has a logo which has a drawing of more than one cube. One moment it will look as if there are three cubes, but if you keep looking at it the three cubes turn into five cubes. This flip-flop, this change from one face to the other, is a clear indication of this basic duality. The human processes of perceiving are such that you cannot see both the faces at the same time.

So, it is really in how you look at the processes of life. Human beings compare, judge and prefer, they want to keep on knowing the why of it, always involved in the process of looking and interpreting. According to the physicist, this is misinterpretation. The question is, "If I don't see it and understand it, how can I accept it?" The mystic and the physicist both say, "accept it, and then you will see it," not with your intellectual perception, but from a different dimension altogether. In fact it's not really seeing. It will be felt, it will be experienced.

It is for this reason, failing to see the inherent polarity in life, that we seem to have a feeling of having some kind of choice. We feel that we can exercise our volition and yet, deep

down, we know that there is an order infinitely more powerful which seems to dictate our life. We have the deep
feeling, a deep intuitive feeling, that while our choices are
merely superficial, our lives are actually being lived by a
totally different power, an infinitely more powerful principle, a universal Consciousness before which the individual
Consciousness is like a candle compared to the sun. So the
metaphysical aspects of this understanding are astonishing.

ꗃꗃꗃ

In the Sutras, *which are translated many ways, it says in essence
that when the mind has troubling thoughts, focus on the opposite.
Is that another teaching that is directed at an ego? At the Absolute
level there is no chooser to choose to focus on the opposite thought.
At what level does that teaching apply?*

Frankly, I don't know what teaching you are taking about.

In the Yoga Sutras, *second book, it says when there is thought
of sin, focus on the opposite.*

I haven't read Patanjali but what you have said makes
sense in this way: there are no irreconcilable opposites.
All opposites are polaric. Neither of the two opposites
could exist without the other. Lao Tzu has put it so beautifully, "As soon as you talk of beauty, the ugliness is already
there, as soon as you talk of good, the evil is already there."
So when you remember this, then you will understand that
everything is interrelated, there is nothing which is totally
separate from its opposite. When you think of something,
don't forget its polaric opposite. Then you will understand
that there is nothing in the world which can stand by itself.
In other words, this *sutra* draws attention to the fact that
all opposites are interconnected, all opposites are polaric,
and one cannot exist without the other. It is in order to bring
this fact to our attention that the *sutra* says this. In other
words, when you think of beauty and you want beauty all
the time, understand that when you think of beauty, the
ugliness is already there. And in this change which is going

on all the time, there is beauty at one time and ugliness at another. What is considered beautiful today may not be considered beautiful at some other time. Modern art is considered beautiful, worth millions of dollars. A few years ago, nobody would have touched it. Abortion, a few years ago was a crime. Today, the third world governments are sponsoring abortion in order to check the population explosion. What is good? What is evil? What is beautiful? What is ugly? Who decides? On what basis do you decide? From the German point of view, Hitler's onslaught was very good. No doubt about it. For the Germans at that time Hitler was God, but not for the rest of the world. So the same event is good for some, bad for the others. We have eradicated certain pests, we have eradicated smallpox, good for the man, bad for the germ!

◘◘◘

– THE COSMIC DREAM - THE DIVINE PLAY –

Ramesh, you've quoted a couple of different people who said that there is no birth and there is no death. How much of this comes from your own experience?

One hundred percent! You see, there really is no question of experience. It is a matter of conviction and that is it, the deepest possible conviction.

At an experiential or intellectual level?

No, it is very much deeper than an intellectual level. I would hesitate to use the word experiential because the word can be misleading. But it is as much a conviction as the conviction that I am alive, I am present here and now. I don't have to ask anybody if I am alive, if I am present. Now whether you call that experience, I don't know. Experience of what? Just being, I frankly wouldn't call an experience. In that beingness, in that impersonal sense of being, there is no need of a "me." And if there is no need of a "me" there is no need of an experience, you see?

When you say that the final truth is that nothing has happened, is it also true that this fiction has not happened?

You see, what has *not* happened is that which appears to us to have happened. This manifestation is merely an appearance in Consciousness and in no way different from our personal dream. The mirage has "happened" and yet has not really happened!

So this has not happened?

All that has happened is this waking dream. And in the personal dream everything is very real, just as to us this life is very much real. But once we are awake, we are no longer bothered by what happened to our friend in the dream who was dying! What happens is that we wake up from our personal dream into this living dream.

When you say "no-thing" is happening, this dream seems like a happening, so I am wondering how strict you were with the final truth.

That *is* the final truth.

The happening that we see as a dream is an illusion. So, if you mean an illusion has happened; if you can use the word "illusion" with "happened," fine, you are welcome. But to the extent that an illusion cannot be real, this has not happened. When there is enlightenment or understanding, manifestation is seen as an appearance in Consciousness. You are aware that it is a dream. And, as a dreamed character, you're not concerned with how long your character lasts. Whatever you are supposed to do, whatever role you are playing, is all part of the dream.

🗆🗆🗆

If I think about the present concepts of the history of the universe, sentient beings did not arrive for several billion years after the universe arrived. Was the appearance of the I Am at the beginning of the universe, or at the beginning of the appearance of the first sentient being?

In your personal dream, you find rivers and mountains thousands of years old. You find a baby being born, and you find old men, all of different phenomenal age. But they are all born at the instant that your dream begins. In your personal dream, all these objects of different ages appear at the moment when the dream starts. Yet, in that dream, each has its own age.

Where does the dream start?

The dream starts in Consciousness. That is why in almost every religion there is the basic concept that life is a dream.

What about the chronology of the universe? When did the dream start?

It is the same as the chronology in your personal dream.

Is it true, then, that when enlightenment happens for an individual, excuse the contradiction in terms...

Yes, I understand, but you have to speak from your terms.

Does the dream stop only for a certain isolated part of the dream?

The dream doesn't stop, the dream goes on. After enlightenment, what is seen is that this body-mind mechanism is a character in the dream and will continue as a character in the dream during its lifetime. But there is no concern about it. There's no personal concern about what happens to what organism.

Is there a point when the dream stops for all characters?

It stops for all characters when there is total dissolution.

Then there must have been a time when the dream started for all characters.

Yes! This is what the dream character wants to know!

When was that? (laughter)

The element of time is only in phenomenality.

It's part of the dream.

Correct! The concept of time is part of the dream.

Then the nature of the dream is such that there's no waking up, no beginning, no ending.

Quite right. It's like a circle. You don't know where the circle starts and where the circle ends.

In some of the Eastern teaching they talk about reincarnation, about karma, about the wheel of life. If I understand you correctly, all that is a dream and an illusion.

Which continues from cause to effect. If it is easier to understand, think of it as an unwritten, unfinished, continuously ongoing novel or a TV series. Time goes on and on with cause and effect and it goes on like an unfinished novel, written by God.

But is that an illusion?

What is a novel but an illusion created by the novelist? We can call this the Divine Novel.

So, for "me," all this is a dream.

That is correct. And if you really and truly accept it as a dream, then there is no question of your accepting it as a dream. You accept that this body-mind organism is functioning as part of the dream and that you become the dreamed character. And once you accept yourself as a dreamed character, where is the individual? Where is the individual doer?

I think the problem we're running into is that calling this a dream is only an analogy.

That is correct!

Ramesh, could you explain the symbol of the lila?

The *lila* is the only answer to the question, "Why has God created this universe?" You can either say, "Why not?" or you say, "It was just a game God is playing." Just a game of hide-and-go-seek. Just a game of the observer and the observed, each considering itself the subject, and therefore there are human relations and the problems of human relations. Basically, it simply means it's a game that is going on. And we ask, "Why?" There is really no answer.

You can see this if you watch a couple of children on the seashore with a spade and a bucket. They create a castle or whatever and they spend a lot of time over it, a lot of trouble over it and at the end of the day, when the parents say that it's time to go home, they just kick it and go! You ask the child, "Why did you build the castle and then demolish it?" The child wouldn't understand your question! If you persist, he would say, "Because I like to create. I created a castle because I like to create the castle. I demolished it because I like to demolish it."

◻◻◻

Enlightenment in some sense, is the most natural state. Why is enlightenment such a rarity, rather than the rule?

You see, enlightenment is the original state. Enlightenment is the original state on which this identification with an individual has taken place. It has taken place because if it had not taken place then there would not be any life and living in this dream play. So for this dream play, *lila* as the Hindu tradition calls it, to take place, Consciousness identifies itself with each individual. Each individual has been conceived and created with certain given characteristics so that only certain actions, good, bad or indifferent, as society decides, will take place through that organism. And that is *karma*.

So in other words, what I'm saying is, new organisms are created so that the effects of the earlier actions will take place.

Organisms are not created with some old souls continuing, and new organisms are not created so that they can be punished or rewarded for past actions. Whose past actions?! It's an impersonal process; it's an impersonal play going on. It's like a novelist who begins with certain characters, creates certain actions, and those actions produce effects. So for new effects, new actions must be produced and the novelist creates new characters.

I've been talking about this novelist, the Divine Novelist, and the other day someone sent me a cutting of Schopenhauer's metaphor of the novelist. So no simile, no metaphor, can be claimed as one's own. Let me tell you what Schopenhauer said:

"In the later years of a lifetime, looking back over the course of one's days and noticing how encounters and events that appeared at the time to be accidental became the crucial structural features of an unintended life-story through which the potentialities of one's character were fostered to fulfillment, when this is noticed, one may find it difficult to resist the notion of the course of one's biography as comparable to that of a cleverly constructed novel, wondering who the author of the amazing plot could have been. The whole context of world history is, in fact, of destinies unfolding through time as a vast net of reciprocal influences of this kind which are not only of people upon people, but involve also the natural world with its creatures and accidents of all kind."

What is any action but merely the actualization of a thought which comes from outside? So whose action? And where does that thought come from? Why does a particular thought come? Only because that thought is supposed to produce a certain action through a particular body-mind organism which is conceived and created so that that kind of action has to take place. It's so programmed. So who is guilty of what?

ㅁㅁㅁ

I don't know why this question bothers me. You keep talking about the novelist.

Yes, and new characters being created by the novelist. Yes.

Is there any direction or purpose in the play?

Not from the point of view of the individual.

No, I mean from the standpoint of the Divine Novelist.

On the part of the Novelist, the whole purpose is just described in that one word, *lila*. It is just Consciousness, God, playing hide-and-seek. *Lila* just goes on.

Rather than cause and effect then, is it possible to say it's just indefiniteness?

Yes. Indefiniteness from the point of view of the individual. We don't know, we cannot know why. Therefore, you can say indefinite.

It's kind of like ignorance of the Divine? I mean on our part we don't...

We don't know! As one scientist has said, which I like very much, "Something, somewhere, is doing we know not what." (laughter) A scientist! I say perfect. That's it. We know not what. And he must have said it with great sincerity. That's the same thing as, we do not know, we cannot know.

How do you accept something you don't know? It seems like acceptance requires knowing that they are the same.

That's what the mind says. That is the difficulty that the mind feels all the time. In fact, you know, the mind says, "You talk of enlightenment. How do I know what that state is? You say it cannot be described. How do I know that I'm going to like that state of enlightenment?" You see? And nonetheless, when the seeking begins, you cannot avoid seeking something though you don't know what it is.

So the seeking starts with an individual and ends with the total annihilation of the individual.

❐❐❐

— ILLUSION AND REALITY —

After enlightenment are there still phenomena?

Yes, all that enlightenment really means is that the sense of personal doership disappears. All actions are taken as the actions of Totality.

But there are still phenomena?

Indeed!

Which is still illusion?

Of course it is! That is precisely what the sage has understood: that this body through which actions take place is part of the illusion. Precisely what the sage has understood.

What is the meaning of illusion in this context then?

Illusion is something which does not exist beyond time. Illusion is something that appears and disappears.

Then illusion and phenomena can be interchangeable?

Precisely, yes!

"Illusion" is also another "concept"?

Yes, Surely!

So everything changes.

Yes. That the mystic has been saying for thousands of years. Now the scientist is saying that the illusion of something being static is the illusion. And this illusion of something static, something unchanged, security, which the

human mind wants, is the basic illusion. If this firm understanding is there, that there is nothing unchangeable, then
this search for continuous security will not remain.

Ramesh, is the unicity an illusion?

Everything is a concept. Even this unicity, the background
of this manifestation, is still a concept. The individual wants
to know what *was* before the manifestation occurred. Only
that silence, in the absence of thinking, is real.

*When you use the word "illusion," I am confused because I see
it something like a bicycle, not like a piece of rope looking like a
snake. The rope mistaken for a snake was never a snake but the
bicycle* is *a bicycle. It's not an illusion of a bicycle.*

There's a primary illusion and a secondary illusion. The
classic case of this in Vedanta, is a rope being mistaken for a
snake. The rope, being mistaken for a snake, is a secondary
illusion that disappears when there is light and you find that
it is not a snake. But the rope itself is the primary illusion.
That you take the rope itself as an object, is the primary
illusion.

Is it a primary illusion because it is impermanent?

Basically, I would say, because it has no existence of its
own. It is an appearance in Consciousness. It has no independent existence. You go out into the sun and there's your
shadow. There *is* a shadow. It is real to the extent that you
can see it, but it is an illusion in the sense that it has no
independent existence. So the shadow is a secondary illusion. Your body itself, which seems so solid, is the primary
illusion within the total illusion which is this manifestation.

❑❑❑

*Ramesh, nothing is real, everything is illusion except noumenon
and that's like useless information.*

Yes! (laughter) A friend of mine has been coming for eight years and we talk of reality and he says, "You're telling me reality is a concept?" I said, "Yes, show me Reality."

Reality is a concept that is necessary as a complementary concept of unreality. If the concept of unreality was not thought of by the intellect, the concept of reality need not come. In your deep sleep there is no question of reality or unreality. But that absence of presence gets converted when you wake up into the presence of reality. Again, because of this concept you have to have the concept of the double negative. It is *all* a concept.

❏❏❏

– CONCEPTS TO IDENTIFY TOTALITY –

Can we know That which is before conceptualization, or can we only be That?

We can only be That, and even *that* is a concept. (laughter) In other words, what I am telling you is precisely what Ramana Maharshi said, "Nothing has happened; there has been no creation." Notice, if we accept that, what remains is silence, total absence of the working of the mind. And in that silence is all that is to be known. Everything else is a concept.

I'm finding a lot of things being said here are going over my head. Now, in a simple way, what I understand is that everything just happens. This body-mind cannot think, cannot talk, cannot do anything. Consciousness is what's doing it. And also, Consciousness makes this body-mind think that it can "think" and that it can "do."

Correct!

That simplifies it as far as I'm concerned.

Yes indeed. Therefore, what you are saying is that there is no one to really care whether enlightenment is going to happen in this body-mind or not! Why bother about it?

Which brings another question. Is enlightenment also a concept?

Indeed it is. Not only is enlightenment a concept, reality itself is a concept!

◻◻◻

– CONSCIOUSNESS AND AWARENESS –

Sir, in the matter of words, I remember that in some of the books it sounds as though there's a difference between Awareness and Consciousness. I've worried about that.

Forget it.

But if what we're aiming at is Awareness...

Maurice Frydman used that to distinguish between Consciousness-in movement, and that state of Consciousness-at-rest, noumenality, before the Consciousness arose as I Am.

So, they're separate.

In fact, the term "Awareness" gives you the impression that they're two separate states. They're not. It is the same state, at rest and in movement. They are not two different kinds of Consciousness. There's only one Consciousness, either at rest or in movement.

Awareness has been called the energy of Consciousness.

Yes, if you use the word "energy" then I would say, Consciousness-at-rest is potential energy and when the energy activates itself it becomes Consciousness-in-movement. So long as you see past the apparent difference. Basically, there is no difference. It is still energy, either in its potential form or in its activized form. It is the same Consciousness, either at rest or in movement. Once the understanding has happened, you really don't need words. You don't need concepts.

❏❏❏

– THE SENSE OF PRESENCE; OUR TRUE CAPITAL –

It seems to me that everything can be considered unreal except that I exist. There is a difference between "I exist" and the possessive "mine," because the "me" or the "mine" is like "my body," "my ideas," "my house," but the existence itself is incontrovertible.

Therefore, whatever we say, whatever we think is a concept. The only thing which is not a concept, the only truth, is the sense of presence. I Am. I'm alive. I exist. That is the only truth. But that truth, even that truth, is in phenomenality.

And that truth is also a concept.

That is right. Ultimately, even this I Am is a concept. But in the absence of all other concepts, the only thing that we know—everything else is a concept—is the sense of presence: I Am, I exist. If you imagine that you are the only sentient being on earth, then the sense of presence is all there is. And in that case there wouldn't be even the sense of "I exist." The sense would then be, "There is existence." There is awareness because there is something to be aware of and that is the rest of the manifestation.

And if you do not put that into words, then it's true.

Yes. That is Reality.

❏❏❏

Ramesh, "I Am." That's the only thing which we can know?

Correct. I Am, here and now, in this present moment.

How do we know that?

Don't you know it?

The way I know that is, I always have a thought that I am. I sense things.

No, no!

The sense of presence itself?

That is right. The sense of presence is always there. Therefore what I am saying is, *you* don't have to have the sense of presence. The sense of presence is there.

Without an object?

Yes. Originally that sense of presence is impersonal. When you get up in the morning the first sense of presence is impersonal. Then it dawns on you, I am so and so. The personal identification comes later. Originally there is merely the sense of presence, the impersonal sense of presence.

You're not really a "me" at all. There is no sense of being a "me"?

That is correct.

A sense of presence depends on there being a body.

Yes. The sense of presence arises only when there is a body. If there is no body, there is no instrument in which the sense of presence can make its appearance.

It's a very fragile instrument.

Indeed! But the only point is, there are billions of them. So if one goes, it doesn't matter. In this body there are millions of cells dying and being created all the time. Who ever thinks of that individual cell? "Poor cell, it hardly lived a split second and its dead!" Okay.

Are you talking about acceptance and sensing the presence of the present and seeing everything that is in front of us as what life is?

Quite so. Again, let me repeat, anything that I say, anything that anybody says, anything the Scriptures say, is all a concept. We need concepts in order to communicate until the mind has reached a stage where it realizes that what it is seeking is beyond its comprehension.

Then the mind will quiet itself and then the silence will reign. Until then, even this sense of presence that we are talking about is in phenomenality. You see, there is the presence of the sense of presence. In deep sleep or under sedation there is an absence of the sense of presence. So, there is the presence of the sense of presence and the absence of the sense of presence. This presence and absence of the sense of presence is part of phenomenality. In the noumenality, which is the potential, which is Consciousness-at-rest, there is the absence of both the presence of the sense of presence and the absence of the sense of presence.

Let me put it this way—though no illustration can ever be complete in itself because an illustration builds with objects—the subject we're talking about doesn't have the slightest taint of objectivity: You arise in the morning. You're awake. There is the presence of the beard. You shave it off. Now there is the absence of the presence of the beard. But in a boy there is *potential* presence and absence of the beard. There is an absence of the presence of the beard and an absence of the absence of the beard. Potential, yes—so I am talking about *that* state; that original state where there's an absence of *both* the presence of the sense of Presence and the absence of the absence of the sense of Presence.

◻◻◻

– DUALITY –

Isn't Consciousness-at-rest simply that basic concept upon which Consciousness-in-movement occurs?

Correct.

But the cessation of thought, the cessation of that activity, why postulate or conceptualize that it goes someplace? Why isn't it simply a cessation of movement?

Again, absolutely correct. Then no further question remains. I agree entirely. But, because this question persists, you have to have an additional concept. I was just going to talk about this.

This is what can be called a divergent problem. The scientist deals with a problem which is convergent. A hundred scientists performing the same experiment must have the same results. Where the problem concerns an inner experience of Consciousness, it becomes a divergent problem. In other words, divergent problems are created by the intellect, by splitting what is by nature whole and indivisible. The intellect creates the problem by dividing polarity. The opposites which exist cannot exist by themselves. There cannot be up without down, cannot be beauty without ugliness. But what the intellect wants is, this *or* that. By comparing and wanting to select, the intellect creates a divergent problem, and divergent problems can never be solved. A divergent problem can only *dissolve* by understanding the problem itself, that it really is not a problem, that it is created by the intellect wanting to choose between opposites which are not opposites at all. They are interrelated.

For example, in education one idea is that the student must have discipline. So a little discipline is good, more discipline is better and total discipline is perfect. The school becomes a prison. The other side says, "No, the student must have liberty of thought and action." So, if a little liberty is a good thing, more liberty must be better and absolute liberty would be perfect. Then the school becomes a chaos. So, this *or* that, wanting to choose between two opposites is creating a diversive problem. The two opposites are interrelated, you cannot have one *or* the other. When that is understood, when the polarity of opposites is understood, and that the whole universe is based on this polarity where you cannot choose, then the problem need not be solved. The problem gets dissolved.

There were two monks studying in a seminary and both were passionately fond of smoking. Their problem was, "Am I allowed to smoke when praying?" They couldn't come to an agreement, so each one said he would go to his superior. Upon meeting again later, one monk asked the other if his abbot said it was all right to smoke.

He said, "No, I was berated soundly for even mentioning it. What did your abbot say?"

The other replied, "My abbot was delighted with me. He said it was fine. What did you ask your abbot?"

"I asked him if I can smoke when I am praying?"

"Well, there you have it. I asked, 'Can I pray when I am smoking?'"

The same problem, depends on how you view it. Then there's the classic case of the dream of an Indian king. The king dreamt that all the leaves had fallen off his favorite tree and the tree was bare. So he sent for his dream-reader, who said, "Your majesty this is a terrible dream. It means that you are going to lose all your relatives." So the dream-reader was sent to the dungeon. Another night, again the same dream, and a second dream-reader was called. He said, "Your majesty this is a wonderful dream. You are going to survive all your relatives!"

It's all a matter of perspective! The basis of life is polarity and polarity comes about because of change. The universe and everything in the universe is in continual movement. And movement doesn't mean lateral movement as the human intellect thinks. It is not a lateral movement; it's a circular movement, or up and down. So changes must happen. If this is not understood, then that creates problems. And most problems of life are divergent problems.

When you say the nature of the universe is polarity, isn't it more that the intellect, in perceiving the universe, creates polarities?

No. Polarity is a principle on which the universe works. What that polarity simply means is there is a wholeness and that change between opposites is based on the interdependence of the opposites, one to the other.

❏❏❏

– DUALITY AND DUALISM –

I'm uncertain about the difference between duality and dualism.

You see, duality is the basis on which this manifestation takes place. So if duality is understood as duality, as merely polaric opposites, that one cannot exist without the other, that is understanding. That is enlightenment. It is Consciousness itself that has descended from the level of duality to the level of dualism and identified itself with each object and created these subject-object relations so that this *lila* may go on. So it is Consciousness which has identified with itself and continues the identification for a time. Then a certain body-mind mechanism, which may have been living its life in a perfectly reasonable, healthy and happy way, gets struck by that urge to find out, "Am I really separate from the other? What is life all about?" So, the mind turns inwards, and the seeker starts his miserable journey! The process of disidentification then goes on until the understanding is that this dualism is a joke, a cosmic joke. And that realization raises the dualism back to the level of duality. When that level of duality also becomes unbearable, then the "me" and the "thee" also disappear.

❏❏❏

– IMMEDIATE PERCEPTION –

I'm having a hard time trying to correlate a couple of ideas. First, that I am not the body.

This is where words fail. Language produces implications which are not intended. In the instance of pain, you witness the pain until at a certain stage you become the pain. The witnessing turns into the experience of pain without the panicked experiencer. The experience of pain is there. You are the experience. In that moment of experience, whether it is sheer terror or utter ecstasy, there is no experiencer. The next time it happens, test it. Any experience is always an experience in the moment.

And there is no witness either, so the witness turns...

It's the same thing: Consciousness, Understanding, Witnessing and Experiencing. The experience is all there is, in the present moment. The experien*cer* arises later, when the thinking mind thinks about the experience, saying "That was a terrible experience." But in the moment of direct experience it was sheer terror, you *were* the terror. Later, the thinking mind absorbs it and projects it.

This thinking mind retains the memory of that terror and keeps on projecting it. That is how our fears arise. They are based on memories. All our fears are merely projections of the mind, based on memories of the past. The experience itself is always in the present moment. The recalling of it in memory is always horizontal, in duration.

If you were in a situation and there was some danger, would you feel the danger?

Certainly. The working mind would *sense* the danger. The mind would not *project* a danger.

It could be dangerous not to be prepared.

Yes, indeed. It is the working mind which plans and prepares. It is the thinking mind which brings about the fears. The whole burden of the *Bhagavad Gita* is just this. Lord Krishna says to Arjuna, "You are born a fighter, you are trained to be a fighter, you must fight." That is the working mind which makes you fight. It is the thinking mind which brings in worries about what is going to happen. What is going to happen is not in your hands. So forget about what is going to happen and do your duty.

🔲🔲🔲

– SPONTANEOUS ACTION –

You mentioned yesterday something about when a person is totally involved in his work, I don't quite remember the exact wording, but I got the sense that you meant that they were one with Consciousness or one with the Absolute at that time.

Put it the other way around. The basic point is that there is no conceptualization going on. The split-mind of subject-object, the "me," is not working.

Does that mean that any time a person has their mind totally absorbed in some activity, mental or physical, that this is the state?

It is a good state, yes.

The natural state.

Yes, yes.

Okay. Now, extending that, you can apply that same situation to where a person is totally absorbed in sleep. So could you say also that sleep is the natural state?

Yes.

But what about when a person spends their life watching soap operas, or movies, or has their mind absorbed by these types of things? Or what if a person is committing violence and they're totally absorbed in that violence against another person? Could you say that this is also a desirable state?

For whom? That violence that is going on in which total attention is being paid is part of the functioning of Totality at that time. And there is no sense of...

So you can't say it's good or bad.

The good or bad is only from the personal point of view. Since you are asking the question, you are asking the question from the point of view of a seeker or a "me." So, from the point of view of the "me," it would be an undesirable state. And when the violence is being committed there will be no question of anyone asking whether that violence is a good state to be in. But *talk* of violence being committed and whoever is committing the violence will necessarily have the thinking-mind totally involved in it.

Yes. I guess I'm asking this question from a personal standpoint. When I'm totally involved in my work, I don't have any thoughts going on and you seem to be saying that is the desirable state to be in.

From the personal point of view, yes.

A lot of times when I have nothing to do I just sit around and think, which is not really a desirable state to be in.

Quite.

So does that mean that one should just try to keep oneself absorbed in activities, in order to avoid all this thought pattern? For instance, is it better to go to a movie or watch a soap opera or even commit some act of violence, so that you prevent yourself from having this discursive thought all the time?

You see, in this case there is a "me" choosing to do one or the other and in that choosing, the "me" is very much there. In that choosing itself, the "me" is there. But, when certain work takes place, and that intensity of attention happens, in that state the "me" is absent. If the "me" chooses to do something it will almost certainly be that the "me" will not be absent from that activity. You see?

◘◘◘

– THE AGGREGATES OF THE "ME" –

I have a glimmering of your statement that the "me" is merely a subjective illusion, but I don't have the clarity about it.

Yes, when we talk of "me" there is the body which appears to be so solid, but it isn't. Apart from the body, the "me" that we think of, what is it but a collection or a collage of impressions which you, yourself, have about you and which others have about you? The impressions you have may be a little more flattering to the "me" than the others, or it may be the other way around. Still, it is just a collection of impressions. Other than a collection of impressions, what is the "me"? That's what I mean. The "me" is merely an illusion.

◻◻◻

In the statement, "As ye sow, so shall ye reap" it sounds as though that's something that will happen to an individual, but might it be better said, "As it is sown, so shall it be reaped."?

Yes. Or, you can interpret the "ye" as God: as God sows, God reaps. That means action and reaction.

And there is cause and effect and reward and punishment but no individual has anything to do with it.

No, no. There is cause and effect but the question of reward or punishment is totally irrelevant. Reward and punishment refers to the individual doer, and in this impersonal functioning there is no individual doer to be punished or rewarded. In fact, this punishment and reward is the very basis of the misconception about reincarnation.

◻◻◻

– IMPRINTING AT CONCEPTION –

You said you had two notions from a very early age, that this is all illusion and that it's all predetermined. Do you know where those notions came from?

Yes. At the moment of conception.

Oh, from a really early age! (laughter) Those notions which you said come at the moment of conception, where are they engraved? In the mind? Where is the mind? In the body?

All there is, is Consciousness. And the mind is merely a reflection of that Consciousness. Mind is a collection of thoughts which arise and are not disposed of, they are collected. Mind is merely a collection of thoughts, or a collection of impressions which makes up this "me," this self image. That image is made up of various thoughts and impressions, not *all* the thoughts and impressions, but only selected thoughts and impressions. Therefore, the "me" as a self-image is an inaccurate image.

I understand that, but those thoughts and impressions which are gathered around the inaccurate image of "me," where do they come from?

Yes. They come from Consciousness and the brain reacts to those thoughts that come from Consciousness.

They are not imprinted in the brain? They just come...

Brain is inert matter. Brain cannot create any thoughts. Brain can only react to the thoughts which come from outside and then get involved.

◻◻◻

– SENTIENCE AND INTELLECT - THE HUMAN CONDITION –

Why do I experience so much fear and anxiety?

Human beings assume that basically, essentially, they are different from other objects. But they are different only in the sense that human beings, like animals and insects, have been additionally imbued with sentience. The human beings have sentience plus intellect. Therefore the human being, because of the presence of intellect, wants to ask questions.

By the same token, it is intellect which makes him miserable. The animal, when there is a sense of impending danger, is at once alert. But when the danger is gone the animal relaxes. In the human being, under those circumstances, the intellect makes him look forward. He says, "What do I do if something happens? What do I do if this doesn't happen?"

So intellect is what brings about the sense of fear, because it is intellect which wants security. It is intellect which rejects change and wants security. In the case of the animal, because that kind of thinking mind is not there, it's not bothered about security.

There's no anxiety?

There is no anxiety because there is no thinking or conceptualizing mind!

ΟΟΟ

– DREAMS AND DREAMING –

What is dreaming?

Dreaming? Dreaming is a state of the mind. In phenomenality, there are three states: the waking state, the dreaming state, and when both are absent, the deep sleep state. And when in this deep sleep state your personal dream suddenly arises, it is akin to this waking dream—what is called being awake—arising in Consciousness.

If there were only one sentient being on earth, then Consciousness is all there is, projecting itself through that one body as a sentient being. In that being there is bound to be a sense of impersonal awareness. When that sentient being wakes and sees this manifestation, it is not *seeing* the manifestation, it is *creating* the manifestation. So Consciousness, objectifying itself in that one sentient being, in the only sentient being, creates the manifestation.

In deep sleep the sentient being himself is not there. So the Consciousness in deep sleep not aware of itself, is the original state. Then in the waking state, the first moment of awakening *is* Consciousness becoming aware of itself. And if there are other sentient beings, then inter-human relationships arise. But if there are no other sentient beings, then there is only Consciousness observing the manifestation, and there is no sense of "me." There is merely a sense of awareness of the manifestation. No "me" and no "other" exist.

Back to dreaming. Scientists have conducted experiments in measuring people in sleep. They call the dream state, or the rapid-eye-movement, the "rem" state. Well, what they are saying is that the mind is working in that dream state.

That's it, yes. What you are talking about is the mechanics of the brain in producing a sleep dream. The basic objection to all of this manifestation being a dream is that in the dream...

Sleep dream?

No. In this living, waking dream there are rivers and mountains thousands of years old, and old people. How can it be said that this dream has appeared suddenly? That's the main objection. If the dream has suddenly appeared, how can there be chronological time? And the answer to that is, that is precisely what happens in your personal dream.

Rapid-eye-movement, and in a split second your personal dream has arisen. And in that personal dream everything that exists in this "life dream" is also present: rivers and mountains thousands of years old, babies being born, old people dying. You realize that it is a dream only when you wake up. In this case, waking up is realizing the unreality of it. You realize the unreality of your personal dream when you wake up from sleep. What really happens is, you wake up from your personal dream into this living, waking dream.

Personally, I can accept that the personal dream is a dream state. It is difficult for me to realize that my waking state is a dream.

Yes, yes. I know what you mean. But in your personal dream there are characters who talk to one another and have the same kind of problems as you have here.

I was afraid of this. (laughter)

You see, the problems that exist in this life also exist in your personal dream!

So when do I wake up from this world?

You wake up from this only when there is an understanding, a realization that this is a dream, when there are no more doubts.

Do you feel like you are awakened from the dream that I am still in?

Yes. Basically enlightenment means only *one* thing: a sudden realization that that which appears real, is really unreal. Then you have the experience of the unreal as being real. There is a sudden sense of transcendence, a vision of transcendence. That this is all a dream no longer remains a concept. It becomes a reality. Suppose there is a bereavement. There is a reaction of the body-mind to that bereavement, but deep down there is the understanding that that bereavement is also part of the dream.

When I wake up from my sleep dream, I am aware that I am the author of the "me" in the dream as well as all the other objects and people in the dream. But in order for me to be the author of those, I cannot be the object in that sleep dream. So, when I wake up out of this waking dream, it cannot be the small "I." It would have to be the large "I" that awakens.

Yes, that is correct. That is the whole point. Therefore, this realization that all this is a dream does not happen to a "me." In fact, the sudden realization is that this "me" that was all the time considering itself as a separate entity, is just part of the illusion.

I think I found a paradox here.

Indeed!

To go back to the dream analogy again, an enlightened man is a man who wakes from the sleep-dream and then chooses to go back into the dream to have a conversation with the people in that dream and then comes back, and goes in and out?

Yes. And your difficulty at the moment is that you are thinking in terms of the "me" being a dreamer of this waking dream and a "me" being the dreamer of the personal dream. Neither dream is the creation of the "me."

I see!

Your personal dream is a creation of Consciousness and this waking dream is also a creation of Consciousness. The only dreamer is Consciousness.

Yes, so I see. I really see then that anything, any individuality or any separateness is itself the obstacle to that.

That is correct. So it is only the Consciousness which is the dreamer. The concept of a "personal me" is so strong, that you say, "I dream." There is no "me" which can dream. So in this waking dream, as well as in your personal dream, the "dreamer" is only Consciousness.

Other than Consciousness, there is just nothing. The personal dream is created through the individual mind, which is the identified consciousness.

Now, when you are saying "personal dream," you are talking about the "life dream?"

No. Personal dream is what you dream when you are asleep. But, what I'm saying is that in both the personal dreams of billions of human beings and this one big whole living dream, in the case of both, the "dreamer" is Consciousness and we are all dreamed characters. The mistake or the illusion gets deepened when we think of ourself in terms of being "dreamers." We are not "dreamers," we are only dreamed characters.

Did you say dreamed? We are dreamed?

Yes. We are dreamed characters. We are only characters. We think we live our lives, but our lives are being lived. We are dreamed characters.

What is it when you are dreaming that you are aware of your dreaming?

I'm told that they call this lucid dreaming. It's one of those peculiar things. For instance, in dreams certain people say they have memories of a past life. What they mean is that they have memories of certain events of a past life which they misconstrue as *their* past life. But certain people are able to draw on certain memories. What you are speaking of is, I presume, something of this kind, lucid dreaming. But the technical aspect of the lucid dream I know nothing about.

◻◻◻

– DEEP SLEEP –

When I go to sleep, I lose consciousness. There may be some consciousness when I dream, but I have none in deep sleep. When I asked Maharaj about this, he intimated that he maintained a level

of consciousness in deep sleep. Ramana Maharshi's great enlight-
enment experience began with a description of going through the
death process. When I was with Maharaj, he intimated that he felt
he had similar experiences during his years of practice. So, as a way
of generating a conversation, I am interested in your comments on
this matter.

What both of them said, particularly Ramana Maharshi, was about the intensity of, "Who am I?" He wanted to find out what would happen to this body when the body is dead, so he lived that experience and he experientially came to the conclusion that it is only the body that dies. From then on the fear of dying individually never arose.

What is absent in deep sleep is the sense of "me." The identified consciousness is absent, but the impersonal Consciousness has to be present. And that is why Ramana Maharshi repeatedly asked, "Who is it that says when you wake up, I slept well?" It is Consciousness that has been aware during deep sleep but that Consciousness is the impersonal Consciousness. The personal identification is absent.

I think that is where the essence of my question lies. We wake
up and say, "I slept well." We are not aware of having been asleep
until we are awake. What I have understood from other sages is that
they remain aware even in deep sleep.

You see, that awareness, the personal awareness, has merged with the impersonal Awareness, so even when they are awake, there is no personal awareness. There is no sense of personal doership. So when the personal identified consciousness has disappeared altogether, or more accurately, merged, then the impersonal Consciousness is all there is, all the time.

🔳🔳🔳

– LOVE, COMPASSION –

I want to know how you define love and how love relates to
Consciousness.

What do you mean by love? When you talk of love you are talking of an emotion of loving something or somebody, isn't that right?

I am not talking about the emotional type of love at all. That is why I wanted to know your definition, because I think there is a kind of Divine Love.

Yes. Love, as I see it, is compassion. And love is something you cannot create. As I see it, love or compassion is something which arises with the understanding. So when the sense of personal doership leaves, then love and compassion automatically arise. When you understand that actions which take place through your own body-mind organism are not your actions, and thus the actions which take place through other body-mind organisms are not their actions, whichever way they may seem to affect you, then there is deep understanding that what exists in all organisms, that which brings about all actions, is the same Consciousness.

Compassion prevails when there is no judging and condemning. Understanding produces compassion or love, or charity, whatever you choose to call it. You cannot ask that love be created in you. You cannot turn toward God until the turning away from the self has occurred. So the turning away from the self occurs first and then the turning toward God or Reality or whatever. That is why I keep saying it is a matter of Grace. So you can say, when love or compassion arises, it is a matter of Grace.

ꀸꀸꀸ

– THE BODY-MIND AS AN OPERATING CENTER –

You spoke of the object-observer and of Consciousness. To me they appear as two things. In my own experience the stillness is here, all encompassing, but I still can't get away from a "me" observing it. Is that what you mean by being an object-observer, when you are observing Consciousness?

You see, the "me" observer thinks it is an "I," a subject observer. The "me" is usurping the subjectivity of "I," and that is bondage. When you realize that no "me" can be a subject, that "me" can only be an object, has always been an object, will never be any thing more than an object, as a body-mind mechanism, and that the only subject is the "I" which is Consciousness, that in itself is enlightenment or awakening. In that realization or understanding there is no comprehender. This is the significant point.

When all my desires have gone, it doesn't matter where I am or what I do?

Quite. It does not matter. That is the point.

🖝🖝🖝

– THE NATURAL FLOW OF THE TAO –

I know my ego is the problem. But I can't seem to get it to go away.

You can't fight the ego. Accept the ego, and let it go on. This understanding will gradually push the ego back.

I'll read a quotation by Yang Chu, a Taoist. It's enough to shock most people. It says the same thing. Let the mind think whatever it wants to think. If the mind has to worry, let it worry. To try and stop the mind worrying is to create further involvement.

Yang Chu says, "Let the ear hear what it longs to hear, the eyes see what they long to see, the nose smell what it likes to smell, the mouth speak what it wants to speak. Let the body have every comfort that it craves. Let the mind do as it will. Now, what the ear wants to hear is music and to deprive it of this is to cramp the sense of hearing. What the eye wants to see is carnal beauty and to deprive it is to cramp the sense of sight. What the nose craves for is to smell the fragrant plants of dogwood and orchids and if it cannot have them the sense of smell is cramped. What the mouth desires is to speak of what is true and what is false and if it may not speak then knowledge is cramped. What the body desires for its comfort is warmth and good food. Thwart the attainment of these and you cramp what is natural and essential to man. What the mind wants is liberty to stray wither it will and if it doesn't have this freedom the very nature of man is cramped and thwarted."

"Kill the mind!" Ramana Maharshi used to say, so that his visitor would understand. "Kill the mind." But he explains later that *you* cannot kill the mind; it is only understanding which will kill the mind. The ego or the mind cannot kill itself. The ego will not commit suicide. In fact, the ego will put up all kinds of obstructions. It will say, "This is what the master says, but where is the proof for it?" And, "How do I know that the ultimate stage is something I am going to like? I may not like it!" The ego will put up all kinds of objections.

It is only an outside force which will reduce the mind to impotence, which will reduce its capability of mischief. Such understanding is not the knowledge that the mind has. Knowledge which the mind accumulates is based in phenomenality. The true understanding comes from outside. It is not of the space-time dimension. Therefore we can only call it Grace. Keeping your being open and receptive to that other dimension is a matter of Grace. It requires tremendous courage to give up religious dogma which has come down from time immemorial. And most of those dogmas are misinterpretations. So it requires tremendous courage.

Again, they're all just words: grace, courage etc., but when the time is appropriate the required courage comes along to be receptive to whatever is available. This passage that I just read might easily be misunderstood if not considered in conjunction with another Taoist passage, "Let hearing stop with the ears and the mind stop at the thinking. Then the spirit of the void embraces everything and only the *Tao* includes the void."

What all this means is that the governing of the body and the psyche cannot be egocentric. The senses, feelings and thoughts must be allowed to be spontaneous in the faith that they will then order themselves harmoniously. Trying to control the mind forcefully is like trying to flatten out waves with a board. It can only result in further disturbance. Trying to unify yourself means trying to subject your organism to autocratic government.

It is said in the *Bhagavad Gita*, "The man who is united with the divine and knows the truth thinks, 'I do nothing at all,' for in seeing, hearing, touching, smelling, tasting, walking, sleeping, breathing, speaking, and opening and closing the eyes, he holds that only the senses are occupied with the objects of the senses."

As Saint Jnaneshwar has put it, "Senses, according to their nature, may run towards objects that satisfy them, but almost simultaneously there is the realization that the experience is not different from what the self-realized one himself is. Just as when the sight meets the mirror, almost simultaneously there is the realization that the image therein is not different from the face."

▫▫▫

– CHANGE, IMPERMANENCE –

I feel comfortable with the concept of a loving mother-Consciousness that wants me to grow through this. I'm having trouble getting that to fit with what you're describing.

Love and hate are interconnected opposites in phenomenality. In phenomenality, nothing in this universe can exist except on a dual basis. Nothing is single, nothing is constant, nothing. Everything is changing all the time. Change and the interconnected opposites are the very core of phenomenal existence.

The difficulty arises when the split-mind of subject-object doesn't accept that love and hate are opposites, that good and evil are interconnected. One cannot exist without the other. Beauty cannot exist by itself. The moment you talk of beauty, the ugliness is already there. The moment you talk of goodness, the evil is already there. How can you talk of beauty in the absence of ugliness? The human being wants to experience one and not the other. That cannot be done.

Nothing can be constant in life. Change is the very basis of life. So with happiness, unhappiness is automatically connected with it, because change is inevitable. The misery comes in because the split-mind compares, judges and wants happiness to the exclusion of unhappiness. The split-mind does not accept that change is bound to come.

When the understanding arises that, "This too shall pass," whether it is happiness or misery, that understanding will bring about a tremendous change in perspective. Then when there is some understanding, you don't consider that those who don't have it are undeserving, you don't consider yourself as the "favorite of Allah" because you know that this state of awareness will pass, and other states of awareness will come in. And when the other states of awareness arise, you will not be miserable because they were not totally unexpected. It won't bring about the depth of misery that it would have previously. So the basis of this acceptance is that everything is moving, and therefore change is the very basis of life and basically everything is illusion.

☐☐☐

Why would Consciousness cause identification with the body-mind and then bring up an individual entity like yourself to teach us? It seems like a paradox, doesn't it?

Why should there not be a paradox? Who calls it a paradox? The human mind. Something that the human mind cannot understand, it calls a paradox. In other cases, it might be called a miracle. For the human being which considers itself an entity to remain puzzled, Consciousness must produce new puzzles. And that is what it is doing, amusing itself. If it is kept in mind that Consciousness is all there is, everything will resolve itself. All that is happening is that Consciousness is amusing itself.

Meanwhile some of us are going through hell.

Who is going through hell?

I understand what you're saying, I'm following you quite clearly. Consciousness is all there is, and this is all just Consciousness amusing itself. But when I have kids and they are paralyzed, it's hard to come to peace with this impersonal way of seeing things. Those personal concerns are what really count.

Yes, but they count only to that individual. For the "me," reacting to events is what life is all about. That is why the human being wants security. But security is something which cannot happen, and thus the human being is unhappy.

For three hundred years Newtonian physics prevailed, saying that you can take a piece of the universe, you can watch it and you can understand that part. But now, since the theory of quantum mechanics has come about, a particle moves and the scientist can know only its velocity or location, but not both. If he knows the velocity, he cannot know the place where the particle will be. He cannot know both. The whole universe and its functioning is based on polarity, interconnected opposites: man-woman, subject-object, up-down, good-evil, unhealthy-healthy, happiness-unhappiness. In the entire universe there is nothing which is static, no planet, no galaxy. Everything is moving and movement means change.

The human mind thinks in lateral terms, but almost everything in the universe is circular. Anything that changes has to come back again. The scientist today says that a world in which everything is precise, constant and measurable is an unworkable proposition. In such a world the tiny electron inside of every atom would have to work every instant without stopping. It would burn itself out. All energy would stop. Everything would go back into a nucleus.

Life is uncertainty. That is what the mystic has been saying for thousands of years, and now the scientist agrees. We have to live with insecurity. We have to live with change. Security is a myth. You cannot live with security and attempting to do so means frustration. Deeply understanding this and accepting that life and living is based on change, whether one likes it or not, is a great step ahead.

🔲🔲🔲

– DESTINY –

Can you tell us your thought on destiny?

Some like the word, some don't like the word. About destiny and acceptance there is a very old Chinese story about a farmer in the years when there were always a lot of internecine wars going on.

The story starts with a farmer who had a horse and one day the horse ran away. The neighbors came together, (it was a small community), to offer him their sympathy, saying, "Bad luck." The farmer listened, thanked them and said, "Maybe."

Shortly thereafter the horse came back and brought a lot of wild horses back with him. The neighbors got together to congratulate the farmer, saying, "Good luck!" Again the farmer said, "Maybe."

One day, his son got on one of the wild horses, and in trying to tame him he fell and broke his leg. Again came the neighbors, saying how bad it was that the son had fallen and broken his leg. The farmer said, "Maybe."

Not long after, soldiers came to conscript healthy young men for the army. They found the farmer's son strong and well-built but with a broken leg, so they left him alone. The neighbors all came by and said what a good thing it was that he had escaped being conscripted. Again the farmer said, "Maybe."

Destiny is something like the story. We don't know. What seems at one moment to be acceptable may turn out not to be so acceptable. Something unacceptable at one moment could well turn out to be acceptable in other circumstances.

How did you happen to go to Maharaj? Was that destiny?

It's curious that the question includes the word "happen." How did you "happen" to go to Maharaj? The fact that I *happened* to go to Maharaj, that I did not *choose* to go to Maharaj, seems to be inherent in the question. It is a very meaningful word. How did we all happen to be seekers? What is that special urge or force which turns a person who is quite happy in a normal way, not concerned with heaven or spiritual seeking, into an unhappy seeker? In the case of someone who's been an alcoholic for years, what is that force which suddenly one moment gives him the profound feeling that asks, "What am I doing with my life? This is ridiculous!" He may have felt remorse all along but it never really turned him from alcoholism. Then, suddenly one morning, something hits him and he gives up drink, joins Alcoholics Anonymous and from that point on is totally off it.

My point is, do we turn into seekers, or is there a force which turns certain people into seekers and completely ignores many others? If it is a force which turns people into seekers, why should those people consider themselves responsible for the seeking?

If you have been turned into a seeker, is it not reasonable to accept that it is the responsibility of the force to take you where it will, to make you do that kind of *sadhana* which is necessary for you at that moment? Is it necessary to consider and wonder whether what you are doing at any moment is right or wrong, correct or incorrect? Who is it that can be improved?

ꗃꗃꗃ

– PREDESTINATION –

To what does destiny refer?

Destiny exists only from the point of view of the individual. The individual mind refuses to think that it has no control over things. The individual split-mind expects that there would be chaos in his life or her life if there is no free will. But on the contrary, if every individual of the billions of individuals on earth did have free will, can you imagine the chaos that would prevail?

In the concept, there is still an individual to whom destiny is occurring.

Yes. So therefore the word destiny applies only to individuals. If the individual were not concerned, the word destiny would not be necessary. Therefore, as Chuang Tzu said about his master Lao Tzu, "The master came when it was time for him to come. The master left in the natural flow of events." For him, destiny was not a word necessary in his vocabulary. The flow goes on.

That's the "Thy Will"?

Indeed that is the "Thy Will." But because the separate person is not prepared to accept "Thy Will," but insists on his own, he has to be told that whatever is destined will happen. Otherwise, the word has no meaning.

In reply to an earlier question, you said there is no predestination and no free will. A few moments later you said in regard to an astrological prediction, that there was predestination.

That is correct. There was predestination from the point of view of the individual but not from the point of view of impersonality. Predestination is from the point of view that a certain action has to take place. So a body-mind organism was created for that action to take place. Therefore, the organism and that action became related. For a certain action to take place, which was predestined, the body-mind organism was created. The creation of this organism and the creation of that action were aligned. So, the conceiving and creating of the organism was as much a part of that predestined act as the action which was to take place.

Is there some intelligence that chose?

Indeed yes! But that kind of intelligence, that intelligence which we call God, the human intellect cannot possibly fathom.

How is it that there is predestination for the individual but there isn't for Totality?

Where Totality is concerned, there is no past and future. It sees the whole picture. If you watch one ant going and another ant coming on the other side, (Ramesh holds out a book to show the two ants coming from opposite sides of the book toward one edge) with your viewpoint you can say, in a few seconds they will meet. But for the ants it is predestination. (laughter)

So in the instance of the astrologer, at that moment, he saw the totality but for us it is opening up from moment to moment to moment.

That is the point. For him it was the whole picture. Let's call it a gift, for lack of a better word. He saw the whole picture, where we see bits and pieces.

And we call it unfolding in time, whereas he is seeing it in the moment.

Exactly!

◻◻◻

– KARMA: IMPERSONAL CAUSALITY –

I have a theory that if we work very hard in our meditation we can prevent war.

If meditation could prevent war, have not people existed who meditated and wanted to avoid war? Why are wars not yet stopped? I'm not saying that wars need not be stopped. If it is to stop, it will stop. But if it is to stop, it will not be because *you* or any other organism wanted it, except as an apparent cause. It will be part of the functioning of Totality.

It's hard for some of us to accept that the negativity, what people call wickedness, the atrocities, are part of the functioning of Totality!

Of course! But the "negativity" is the interconnected opposite of goodness and both are part of the functioning of Totality. When this is accepted completely, no questions arise. I will go a step further and say, whether that acceptance happens or not does not depend on the individual. It's part of the functioning of Totality.

It seems to me that the person who is conscientious, sensitive about ethics, and responsible is just as much stuck with that as the fellows in the tavern that are getting beered up and ready to have a fight in the alley, are stuck with that.

"Stuck with that," is a good expression! You are stuck with being a seeker, which many others are not!

I don't necessarily like that. (laughter)

Exactly. The point is that when the mind turns inwards, the perfectly happy, contented man becomes a seeker and becomes miserable. (laughter) He didn't choose to be miserable. As Harry put it quite rightly, we're all stuck with what we are. Some seek a million dollars and some seek salvation. So if you had the choice, which you don't, I would suggest that you seek a million dollars because then there will be someone to enjoy those million dollars. (laughter) But when enlightenment happens there will be no "one" to enjoy anything. (laughter)

That's really stuck.

You *are* "stuck" in a way. That's why I say it's a beautiful expression. I repeat therefore, honestly and truly, this is such a simple matter. It's only the intellect which makes it into a difficult problem. Basically it is that simple. As individuals, we're stuck with it. But once we cease thinking from the point of view of the individual and accept that we are stuck with it, then we'll begin to think from the point of view of

Totality. We'll recede from the personal into the impersonal and then there will be no problems.

ロロロ

– DEATH –

Is death the noumenal state?

No, no. Death is an event in phenomenality. Noumenality is before time ever was, before duration ever was, before space ever was, and therefore before life and death ever were.

Is death equivalent to the kind of awakening that happens in the dream state?

No, death is merely an event interrelated to life. Death is merely the absence of life and life is the absence of death. So life and death are interrelated constantly.

But death is the end of the individual.

Death is the end of the individual body-mind organism, yes.

Ramesh, your body dies and my body dies. Is the end result identical?

Identical as far as the body and everything else is concerned. The breath stops, the brain stops working. The consciousness which is stuck within the body is released and becomes Consciousness-at-large.

Does it mean that Consciousness becomes realized, enlightened?

Consciousness doesn't *need* any enlightenment.

OK, then any ordinary person, any ordinary seeker, will achieve the same result as your body did?

The *body* cannot be enlightened.

Okay. You think you're not special because you know that there is no more you, there is no one there. Then there is the guy like me who is sitting and thinking, "There is 'me.'" But if the end result is the same, then it means that you and I are essentially the same and we would all get realized at the moment of death?

No. Realization, enlightenment, itself is a concept. And it is totally unnecessary. Unnecessary, but it happens. What made you a seeker? The seeking is part of the functioning of Totality. The animal is not concerned with seeking. The human being is concerned with seeking and begins seeking because that seeking is part of the functioning of Totality.

Okay, and if the body dies, does Consciousness realize itself as pure Consciousness?

Tell me, why should Consciousness have to realize itself?

Okay, then nothing happens, period. Nothing happens in my case, in your case, in any case.

Referring to the person, you are quite right. Nothing happens, because the process itself has nothing to do with the human being. If the human beings were not required as instruments, the question wouldn't arise. The happening of enlightenment is an event, and like other events, that event needs a human being as an instrument. The human being is merely an instrument for any event to happen and enlightenment is an event which happens as part of the functioning of Totality.

The Tibetans have tracked a course for the human soul after death. Is this nonsense to have a tracking of afterlife?

The scientist keeps tracking what he thinks he should track. The Tibetan mind is tracking what Tibetan mind wants to track. But that tracking is still part of the functioning of Totality. It is still in phenomenality. If you are concerned with phenomenality, there are an unlimited number of subjects. You can go into astrology, reincarnation, you can go into lots of subjects, but all those subjects are in phenomenality. If we are concerned with transcending phenomenality, we are really not concerned with such subjects.

◻◻◻

– REINCARNATION: THE CONTINUUM OF IMPERSONAL MANIFESTATION –

Would Nisargadatta deny that I have had previous births?

Maharaj did not deny anything.

But he denies rebirth.

He denies the concept of rebirth. If you insist on believing in rebirth, how can he prevent you from doing so? If you ask him, "Do you believe in rebirth?" he would say, "No."

Would he say, as Ramana Maharshi said, that if a person believes in rebirth, then that is the case for him?

No, for one reason. First and last, there is no "you." But if you think there is a "you" and that you were a previous person, you are welcome to believe whatever you feel.

Then why would Ramana Maharshi say that for those people who believe themselves as individuals to be reborn, that is the case?

I think that Ramana Maharshi said precisely what I am saying but he couldn't be going into the same thing over and over again. I do think that Ramana Maharshi meant precisely what I just told you.

Well, he probably did but that is not the way I read it.

About reincarnation and *karma*, the Buddha has clearly put it, "As there is no self, there is no transmigration of self, but there are deeds and continued effects of deeds. There are deeds being done, but there is no doer. There is no entity that migrates, no self is transferred from one place to another, but there is a voice attuned here, and the echo of it comes back."

It means that if we only look at this functioning of Totality without the personal motive, without the angle as an individual, merely seeing the impersonal functioning of Totality, then there are no problems. When things are viewed from the point of view of an individual, problems can never cease. But when you view things from the point of view of Totality, as an impersonal course of events, deeds being done with no individual doer, then no problems can arise.

If there is no self that reincarnates, it seems to me that an organism comes into this world by chance.

Yes, chance from the point of view of the individual, but not as far as Totality is concerned. The Totality has conceived and created an organism with certain definite characteristics, physical, mental, temperamental, so that with those natural characteristics only certain actions will happen through that organism.

But why to that particular person?

There is no person, it is an organism.

So why does a particular action have to take place?

Because it is the effect of earlier actions. Certain actions have taken place. From those, certain effects have to happen. So, for those actions to take place, Totality has to create new organisms with such inherent characteristics as will produce those actions.

It doesn't seem fair!(laughter)

Totality is not concerned with the fairness or justice to each individual. If you must think in such terms, it is mainly concerned with fairness and justice in the functioning that is on a scale and comprising factors that no individual man can possibly comprehend. The universe is continuous movement, yet always in balance.

ᑕᑕᑕ

– GRACE –

Ramesh, are Grace and Consciousness synonymous? Is it not Consciousness that brings up the healing all the way from the lowest level?

That is correct.

So it is all Grace?

It is. You see, Consciousness is all there is. Whether you talk of Consciousness in the impersonal functioning of Totality or you talk in terms of God, the point is the same. And actually, God's grace begins at the lowest level. For example, an addict who has tried hundreds of times to give up his addiction and is not able to do that and then suddenly finds he is able to stop. How does it happen? I mean, here he has failed hundreds of times, and at a certain point, something happens which ends his addiction. What else can you call it, except that his giving up this addiction had to happen because that was part of the functioning of Totality? It had to happen at that time.

␣␣␣

– WHAT IS REAL –

At one point Maharaj was asked, "Is there anything in this play that is real, absolutely anything?" He said something like, "The action of love." That's all he said, I think.

The action of love? Anyway, whatever he might have said, I'll tell you what he meant. (laughter)

That'll take another six months (laughter)

Thank God that it doesn't take six *years*!

So is there anything real?

The question is, "What is real?" That which is real is the inseparable connection between the real real and this false real. There has to be a connection otherwise there would be two. So, what keeps them together, joined? Notionally speaking, it is love. Call it compassion, call it charity, call it what you like, the best thing is not to call it anything. That is what he meant.

Would you say that again?

I can't! It's gone! (laughter) It's on the tape.

3

- THE ILLUSION OF BONDAGE -

- GENERAL DISCUSSION -

You often ask us, "Who is in bondage? Who is seeking?" I'd like to ask you the same question.

It is the individual or personal consciousness which is seeking its source. Consciousness, having identified itself into a personal "me," is now trying to recover its impersonality. That is all that is happening. And the process becomes quicker when the mind doesn't interfere, when the "me" is not present, only the I, the Subjective I, is present. The sage Ashtavakra tells us what bondage is, what liberation is.

He says, "It means bondage when the mind desires something or grieves at something. It means liberation when the mind does not desire or grieve, does not accept or reject, does not feel happy or unhappy."

Now, the human mind, trained and conditioned as it is, promptly says, "I must not desire anything. I must not reject anything." But the mind is incapable of realizing that that not-desiring anything includes desiring the knowledge of your true nature. Desire does not mean only desiring some object, but even the desire for enlightenment. The need to know, to have the knowledge of one's true nature, even that is a desire and that desire is by the "me."

It means bondage when the mind desires something or grieves at something. The mind desires enlightenment and grieves at the fact that it is still unenlightened. "I've been at it for ten, twelve, twenty-five years and still nothing is happening!" The mind grieves at this "not happening." The mind desires, or wants some happening and grieves at the not happening of this event. It means liberation when the mind does not want, desire, or grieve, when the mind is vacant, when the mind is open. The vacant mind is not the vacant mind of an idiot, it is an open mind, as alert as the mind can ever be, because it is not conditioned. It is not wanting anything, it is not filled with anything. Nobody's home. The mind is vacant. It does not reject or accept, does not feel happy or unhappy.

Next, Ashtavakra says, "It means bondage when the mind is attached to any sense experience. It is liberation when the mind is detached from all sense experience." This again, he has put in such a brief fashion. He has not demeaned himself to explain. The sage wants the supposed individual seeker to find it out for himself. He's not saying that the sense experience will not arise. He's not saying that the enlightenment prevents an arising of any sense experience. The arising of an experience, an event, is totally outside the control of any body-mind organism, whether enlightenment has happened or not. So, it is not that the sage refuses any sense experience; it's there. The sense experience is experienced but the mind is not attached to that sense experience. The sense experience happens, and it is over. And any experience is always in the present moment. Any experience, good or bad, pleasant or unpleasant, is always in the present moment. Every experience is an impersonal experience. The impersonal experience loses its impersonality when the mind-intellect accepts this experience as its very own, accepts it or rejects it as good or bad. If it's pleasant, it wants that experience to come more often. If it is bad it rejects it, it doesn't want it. So, the attachment to an experience is always in time, in duration. The impersonal experience, which is the experience of the sage, is always in the present moment, and when that experience is gone the mind no longer thinks about it. The mind is totally detached. The experience is seen as an impersonal experience and at that moment it's finished. It is liberation when the mind is detached from all sense experiences.

Lastly Ashtavakra says, "When the "me" is present it is bondage. When the "me" is not there, it is liberation. Knowing this, the sage remains open to whatever life might bring, without accepting it, without rejecting it"

◻◻◻

– ENTITIFICATION –

One of the chapters in your book which I found especially helpful and useful was on identification and disidentification. In this chapter, you use the word "entitification."

Yes, for the identification with the body as a separate entity, I've coined the word "entitification." Even after enlightenment takes place the identity has to remain if the body-mind mechanism is to continue in its ordinary life for the rest of its span. So the identity with the body continues, but not as a separate entity. The entitification drops off, but the identity with the body continues in this sense: not as a separate doer.

So the basic prefix for that word is "entity."

Yes, that's it.

Is this a word you created yourself?

Yes, yes.

Oh, this is your own personal creation.

Let me put it this way: the word got created. Otherwise I would have to use the words, "This identification is with a body as a separate entity"every time. Instead of that, I thought "entitification" would be shorter and clearer.

Okay. Thank you. That's beautiful.

You see, even after enlightenment happens, as with Ramana Maharshi, if somebody called him "Bhagwan" he would respond. If somebody called Maharaj, he would respond. So that means there is an identification with the body, a sort of operating element which functions in the body. The same kind of operating element which functions without the sense of a "me" as a doer, as for instance when you are driving a car on a highway. Quite often between certain distances the "me" is hardly present. You arrive and then you suddenly realize that you've arrived. But the operating element was the driving. The one who was driving was the operating element. What was absent was the identification of the operating element as the functioning element. So the identification continues, but not as a separate doer. What drops off is the entitification. There's no longer a separate doer. I'm afraid you won't find the word, "entitification" in the dictionary.

❐❐❐

– IDENTIFICATION –

Is subjective, potential Consciousness capable of identifying?

No. There is no "me." All there is, is Consciousness, either in one state or the other state. Who is to identify with whom?

Yes, where is this identification happening? Is it at the subjective or the objective level?

Identification occurs only at the phenomenal objective level of the individual and his split-mind, when the object assumes the subjectivity of God and then says, "I am the subject. I can think. I am intelligent." By thinking this, he separates himself from the rest of the world.

Didn't you say earlier that it was Consciousness that identified with being a separate person?

That is right. In this process of manifestation and its functioning, for that functioning to take place, for this game or *lila* to take place, for these love and hate relationships to arise, Consciousness identifies itself with the individual organism. Now, supposing you write a play, you create six characters and you play all six characters. You become one character, and when you talk to another character the spotlight is on you as the character that is speaking. Then the light goes out for a moment and you become the other character. The spotlight goes back on and you talk like the second character. But who is talking? The six characters are not there. *You* are acting different parts. It is still just you who is producing the play and playing all the characters. If those six characters were to be injected with sentience and intellect, they would begin to quarrel among themselves as to who is more important, who is more attractive. That is precisely what is happening in this dream play. When there is awakening, you would be only watching. You see, you would just watch and witness.

But still it is the subjective Consciousness that has identified with the characters.

It is intellect that makes all those characters think that they are on their own and compare and judge one another. And Consciousness is just watching the fun in its objective expression.

So it is really the intellect that does the identifying and not pure Subjectivity.

Impersonal Consciousness identifies with each body-mind and creates the "me." The animal is also a "me," but the animal is not concerned with all these problems. It is the intellect that causes all the problems, which the animal doesn't have. Basically all are objects, then in some objects sentience has been created. They become sentient objects: insects, animals. Then in some sentient animals intellect has been injected, so they become the human beings.

But even animals have "me."

There is a "me," yes.

Is not the sense of "me" the source of the problem?

It is the "me" plus the intellect which is the cause of the problem. Sentience plus intellect. Basically, the intellect.

Animals don't suffer?

They don't suffer psychologically.

There's no need for an animal to get enlightened?

You see, when an animal senses danger the entire body will be ready to act. But as soon as the danger is gone, the animal will relax. It does not think, "What will I do if the danger occurs again?" That is where the intellect comes in. In an animal, as soon as the imminent danger is gone, it relaxes again. It is the intellect that makes the human being think, "What can I do to prevent this danger from occurring again?"

In a way that sounds as if the animals are superior to us.

Superior or inferior? If you feel happier, I would be glad to say "yes." Essentially they are all Consciousness in different forms with different characteristics.

◻◻◻

In a way, even this dialogue gets turned into an ego trip.

It *is* an ego trip.

I ask you a question and if you say, "That's true," I puff myself up and feel great about it. Sometimes it seems the more I listen, the worse the ego gets.

Try to find out who it is that wanted to know anything. Who is this seeker? Is there a seeker at all?

It's "me."

Where is the "me"? The "me" is always associated with the body and the body as seen through the microscope is nothing but a play of cells being created and destroyed.

But the body is all I know.

Yes, and that is the basic subjective illusion. So long as this subjective illusion is there, the illusory misery is going to be there. And *when* that subjective illusion and misery are going to disappear is not in the hands of that subjective illusion.

But I'm going to keep that illusion until something happens.

Yes, and *when* that something will happen, nobody knows. It's only when God's grace happens. And that also, again, is merely a concept.

And if it never happens, I just go to my death with the illusion?

No, no. "You" can never go to death. The body will die.

But at the present time, I call the body "me."

Yes, but it is only because you are conscious that the illusion is there, isn't it? There is consciousness in this body. It is this consciousness in the body which says, "I'm going to die." The illusion of a "me" arises only because consciousness is there. And when the body is dead and gone, consciousness cannot remain. Consciousness needs an object in order to manifest itself.

But that's all a concept.

Yes. Now, consider the concept of electricity. Nobody really knows exactly what electricity is. Electricity is what electricity does. Electricity is thus a concept, an aspect of Consciousness.

You can't see it.

True. Electricity works through billions of gadgets. Imagine if gadgets had mind and intellect. The gadget would create lots of problems for itself. A kitchen gadget might say, "Why am I a kitchen gadget? I want to be an atomic power station. It is unjust. Whoever made me has been unjust, unfair."

You are comparing me with the electricity?

No, I am comparing you with the gadget. When the gadget is demolished, what happens to the electricity?

But I'm not a gadget. I am a concept. Why do you call me a gadget, an object?

My point is, when a body-mind organism dies the Consciousness which was functioning through that body-mind organism is precisely like the electricity functioning through a gadget. If the gadget breaks, electricity continues to function. You blow up the problem because you consider yourself a "me," and for "me" this body-mind organism is the biggest thing that has happened in the world. But for aeons objects have been created and destroyed as part of the functioning of Totality, as part of God's will. How many billions of human organisms have been created and destroyed? Why do you attach importance to one organism?

Because it's me.

But when you see it all in perspective, body-mind organisms have been created and destroyed for thousands of years. Where is the big deal when one more body-mind organism is destroyed? The whole subjective illusion that I'm talking about is that "you" think "you" are this body-mind and "you" are worried about what is going to happen to this "you" after this body dies. When you understand that the "me" is only a concept, how can a concept be concerned with what happens after the body-mind is dead?

Now, if this really works, eventually the "me" will be gone.

Correct.

But until that time there is a "me."

Yes. But if the understanding is that the "me" is only a concept, is not even an *object*, then where is the "me"? Where is the "me" that is so blown up in importance?

But there is a body sitting there and a body sitting here. I can touch that body and this body can be touched also.

Yes. But if you are not conscious and your hand is touching, will the body understand that touch?

But at the present moment those are just words.

These words exist because there is Consciousness. That is very clear. If you were not conscious, none of this would be happening.

That is also just words. When you say, "That is Consciousness," those are just words.

Yes, yes. Any problem that you have, any questions that arise, words are still just words, aren't they?

You see, I buy the whole thing, but it just keeps coming up all the time.

Yes, "you" buy the whole thing, "you" buy the whole illusion. But "you" don't put *yourself* as part of that illusion. And that is where the ultimate trouble arises. You accept that everything is an illusion, everything is a dream, but you consider yourself as separate from that dream or illusion. Therefore the problem.

Because I don't find it real. I understand it, but I don't find it real.

You don't find it real? How can you find an illusion as real? You accept that it is an illusion.

Uh - huh.

So if you accept it as an illusion, how can you find something real?

Because that is an illusion, right?

Yes.

Right, it can't be real.

It can't be real. And if everything is an illusion, then you and I, the listener and the speaker, are both part of that illusion. We are *both* part of that illusion. This event that is happening is still part of that illusion.

How do I find the reality in it?

Who has to find the reality? Who is it?

Me.

And the "me" is an illusion. You see, if "me" is an illusion, how can the "me" find anything? How can the "me" seek anything?

But there has to be a truth somewhere.

No.

No?

No. Truth or Reality is itself a concept. When you are in the truth or in deep sleep, which is only a pale reflection of the real, in that state of deep sleep is the Truth. And in that Truth there is no experience. In the waking state, the state of deep sleep is a concept. In deep sleep it is the Truth. But the moment you think of Reality, the moment you think of

Subject, the moment you think of the Absolute, the moment you think of Truth, it is a concept. It is only when the thinking totally stops that Truth exists.

You are conscious, you are in the waking state; now there is a sense of presence. The sense of presence is present. When you are in deep sleep, there is an absence of the sense of presence. In the waking state there is the presence of the sense of presence; in deep sleep there is an absence of the sense of presence. But this absence and presence are both in this state of illusion, in phenomenality. So, if you can imagine a state in which there are no opposites, that state is the absence not only of the presence of the sense of presence, but also absence of the absence of the sense of presence. In other words, the whole concept of presence and absence is not there.

When we talk of time and space, we say infinite space and eternal time. It is still a mental concept of total space and total time. But the mind cannot conceive of that state prior to the arising of the space-time. The moment you think of Reality, the reality is a concept. You are the Reality of which the split-mind makes a concept. You *are* the Reality, but not as the "me."

ꓱꓱꓱ

– EGO –

Where does the ego come from?

The ego comes from only one place, from the only thing that exists all the time and that is Consciousness. That is why Ramana Maharshi says, "Find out the source of the ego. Who is doing this? Who wants to know?" The mind cannot find an answer. The point of this questioning is not to find an answer. But when there is no answer, the mind settles down. The ego is not something to be ashamed of or frightened of. The ego is merely a reflection of that same impersonal Consciousness. This understanding takes the ego back to its source. It is mainly being afraid of the ego that is the problem.

Accept the ego, along with everything else, as part of the functioning of the Totality and merely watch what happens. Then there is no trouble.

How does one accept the ego?

The average person who is not a seeker is not worried about his ego. He's perfectly content to be the ego. The seeker has been told, conditioned for years and years, "The ego is the problem. You must kill the ego, you must do this, you must do that." So the seeker, in the very beginning, is told the ego is the bad guy. "You must get rid of him." Who is to get rid of him? The ego is not prepared to commit *hara-kiri*. It will resist. That is why, in moments of meditation or quiet, the ego is frightened and says, "Don't waste your time, this is ridiculous. Go about your business, *do* something."

Does the ego disappear completely when enlightenment comes?

Ego disappears completely after the enlightenment is complete, in the sense that the sense of personal doership disappears. Then for all practical purposes, the ego has disappeared. The identification with the body continues because the body-mind has to function. The identification as the individual doer disappears.

ㅁㅁㅁ

Is it the ego that gets in the way, or occludes the expression of pure Consciousness?

The ego is the identified consciousness. When the impersonal Consciousness identifies itself with the personal organism, the ego arises. The ego itself has no independent existence. It is merely a reflection of the Consciousness which has created the ego by identifying itself. Therefore to say, "Kill the ego, fight the ego" is rubbish. What is the ego? It is the individual expression of the same impersonal Consciousness. The impersonal Consciousness has created the ego which then is turning towards its source. Why fight the ego? Merely witness the antics of the ego. When the ego does something, it is the same ego mind that says, "It shouldn't be done." Once the understanding is that you don't fight the ego, you merely witness it, the ego is no longer an obstruction, an enemy. The ego is just a fiction. Why should you fight a fiction?

It is the same way with child-raising. If you fight children about their "terrible" behavior, in some sense putting limits on it only makes it worse.

Precisely. The ego wants resistance. When there is understanding that the ego is only a fiction, there is no fight. Understanding means an absence of expectation, accepting whatever comes tomorrow. "He who hath, even shall be added on to it; he who hath not, even that will be taken away." When expecting and wanting drops off, you're open to nature. The basis of the understanding is not to not want. Let things take their own course. With this understanding, things astonishingly seem to take a much softer, easier course.

◻◻◻

- FROM DUALISM TO DUALITY -

Do animals feel separate from other things?

Not as separate entities. They feel separate only as predator and prey. The human being also experiences this basic duality of the observed object and the observing object. But along with the basic split of duality, the human being functions in dualism, which is the mental split between the "me" and the other. It is in the mind that the separation between "me" and the other arises. That is where the separation from duality to dualism occurs.

The basic split of duality happens in Consciousness itself, as a part of the process of perceiving the manifestation. For any manifestation to exist, it has to be observed. For observing to happen requires an observed object and an observer object. This duality between the observer object and the observed object is the basic split. In the human, the split goes deeper into the dualism of "me" and the other. The observer object assumes the subjectivity of the Absolute or Totality or God, saying, "I am the subject, the rest of the world is my object." The moment the "me" and the other come into play, duality gets further subdivided into dualism. The observer object considers himself the observer subject, the experiencer, the doer.

Enlightenment is merely the reverse process where the pseudo-subject realizes that there cannot be a separate entity and the body-mind can only function as an instrument in the manifestation of Totality. When the sense of doership is lost, dualism is restored to its basic duality. Duality is an essential mechanism in phenomenality. Enlightenment is thus nothing but the reverse process from dualism to duality, the end of the sense of personal doership. There is the deepest possible realization that the individual human being is not a separate entity, but merely an instrument through which Totality or God functions. That is all it really means, a transformation from oneself as doer to an absence of the sense of doership.

I'm getting that involvement is the key point. What is involved with what? Is there some entity that is involved with another entity or a process? But how can that be? Where is the mistake made?

No, there is no mistake made.

Why did this "me" happen at all? Why was there this separation from the duality to the dualism?

In duality there is no subject, other than God or Totality. Whatever perceiving takes place, whatever the eyes see, whatever the ears hear, whatever the tongue tastes and the nose smells, all that is impersonal functioning. In other words, there is the total understanding that I do nothing. I am not hearing, but hearing is taking place through the ears attached to this body-mind organism. There is no dualism, there is merely an awareness. But, if instead of the impersonal awareness I see something as an individual, promptly there is judgment. What I see, I like or don't like. What I hear, I like or don't like. The sense of personal doership along with personal judging of what-is, is the basis of dualism between "me" and the other.

❏❏❏

– JUDGING AND COMPARING –

I go about my daily life not aware that I am breathing, not aware that I am walking, not aware that I'm drinking water.

When do you begin to wonder who is breathing? I'll tell you; when something goes wrong with your breathing! Then you are aware of the breathing. Something goes wrong with your digestive process. Then you are aware of the digestive process.

But I am not really breathing, I'm not the doer.

What I'm saying is, one is not normally aware of all these natural processes. The nervous system, the most complex system you can imagine, and the digestive and the respiratory systems, they go on all by themselves. You can say you are not really aware of them, until something goes wrong. My question to you is this: "Why are you so aware of the problem of life?" Because there is something deeply wrong with living! If living were natural, like the smooth working of the respiratory process and digestive process, living would present no problem. But living presents a problem because you are not living naturally. You are not living spontaneously. You are living from the point of view of a "me" and that's why living creates problems. I repeat, it is nobody's fault, nobody's guilt. Consciousness itself has identified with each body-mind mechanism so that that body-mind should usurp the subjectivity of Consciousness or God. Then the fun and games start.

❐❐❐

– GOOD AND EVIL –

I've spent much of my life trying to change people and institutions that were wrong. I don't know whether I can ever give that up. There are some things that are just basically wrong and need change.

The essence of this religious thinking is that you are good. The bad is not you. This is so firmly entrenched; that the purpose of life is supposed to be to seek the good. That just is not so. The good and the bad must exist together.

There's no such thing as evil or bad people or bad institutions or bad choices?

Yes! Quite so. Conditioning is so powerful. I can quite understand that it is extremely difficult. Yet it's so easy to see, there can be no up without a down, no backwards without a forwards: backward and forward, up and down are just relative terms. One has no meaning without the other. This polarity of opposites is such a basic, simple, obvious thing and yet our conditioning prevents us from seeing it. So the first glimmer of understanding is to see that that is so, that change is the very essence of life. The firm acceptance of that is a tremendously big step.

This suggests to me that good and bad are not permanent.

Precisely. Take an issue: abortion, for instance. A few years ago it was a crime. Now the developing countries have programs encouraging it. So the good and bad, crime and no crime, all depend on the circumstances of the times.

There are bad governments, there are bad policies, people in groups who sometimes do very nasty things that are very difficult for me to detach myself from. I can't see organizations and institu-

tions in an impersonal way. I can do this better with individuals, but when it gets to groups, the Third Reich, the cigarette companies or whatever, it's tough to see them as a manifestation of Totality.

Yes, I know. Ramana Maharshi stressed that there was no such thing as an individual, and that the whole thing was impersonal. And yet he had the compassion to see that the individual seeker can be extremely miserable. He has written eleven verses depicting the misery of the seeker. From the individual's point of view he says, the biggest encouragement should be the knowledge that the mind has already turned inwards, and thus "Your head is already in the tiger's mouth. There is no escape."

Today you find it difficult. Gradually, as the understanding goes deeper, I am sure you will be astonished to see that the understanding creeps up on you, that what you found difficult to accept yesterday will become clear to you tomorrow: all individuals, all groups are created by God or Totality with certain given characteristics so that they will bring about certain actions which they think are their own actions.

◘◘◘

– FORGETTING THAT WE ARE ALREADY HOME –

You were saying that as long as one has to keep remembering, then he's not home. Can you explain that?

Sure. Now when you are home, where your home is, do you have to remember that you're home? You're home! Do you see it?

Yes.

So if you have to remember, then it will be because you are not home.

Well, it may be you are at home but you have forgotten it because the mind is caught up in its thoughts.

But, so long as you have to remember, it means the mind has taken you away from home. In fact, it is always the mind which takes you away from home. Otherwise you have never left home.

But for many people, the feeling is that they are away from home.

Yes indeed. So therefore, when this feeling arises, or the conviction arises that you are always home, you'll no longer have to remember. There will be that conviction that you have never left home, you see. Therefore you won't have to remember that you are home. So really the injunction, "Just be," has only a limited significance. So long as you keep thinking in terms of "Just be," the question will always be, "Who is to be?"

Or, "How to do it?"

Yes, or "How to do it?" which is precisely what the mind keeps asking. That is the core of the problem.

4

THE MIND

– THINKING MIND AND WORKING MIND –

You said earlier that even in the jnani *there was a limited identification with the body-mind mechanism. Is there any sense in that identification of what we would call "will"?*

None at all. In fact, that is precisely what is absent in the *jnani:* the personal will.

Is there an impersonal or functional will that is part of the body-mind mechanism?

A concept which I found useful in speaking about this very point is to notionally divide the mind into the working mind and the thinking mind.

Thinking mind is a conceptualizing mind, the "me." What is absent after enlightenment is the thinking mind, the "me" distinguishing itself from the other. The conceptualizing thinking mind, the mind which draws upon memories and projects fears, hopes and ambitions: *that* is absent. The working mind is what remains.

So, the working mind couldn't have a set of, for lack of a better word, "ethics" under which it operates?

No, the working mind is merely concerned with what is happening, with what it's doing.

It does not differentiate, it does not make any judgment of what is good or bad?

That is correct.

Consciousness is speaking through you. Are you doing a thinking process at the time that you speak?

No.

Words just come out?

That is correct.

It's not a thinking mind, it's the working mind?

Precisely.

When I'm talking, now, I sort of have an image ahead of me. I'm formulating it as I go along from a whole lot of memories. You don't do any of that?

That is correct.

Is this the silent mind operating? Is the silent mind spontaneously talking?

Yes, or it is the working mind. The silent mind is when the thinking mind is not present. It is silent. But the working mind must continue; otherwise the body-mind couldn't do whatever it is doing. The thinking mind is what creates problems. The working mind goes about its job and the thinking mind comes and interferes and interrupts. It says, "Are you doing this right? Could it be done a better way? What if you fail? You'll lose your job." So all this thinking mind interfering with the working mind produces worry and obviously the working mind cannot function effectively.

When there is this conviction that I can have no control over the results, I can only work, then the thinking mind gradually gets ousted, the working mind has full charge and it works beautifully without the interruptions of the thinking mind. And the working mind at the end of the day is astonished at how quickly the work's been done, without any sense of tension, simply because there was no interruption from the thinking mind.

So, what this understanding produces is the prevention of the thinking mind from obstructing the working mind.

The thinking mind is very persistent though. It keeps bugging me. Even though I'm aware of the split between the thinking and working mind and want the thinking mind to shut up because I'm realizing it's interfering, it still is there.

Yes. Therefore...

How to deal with it?

Ah, you see. *How* to? (laughter) *How* to stop the thinking mind? *How* to get enlightened?

I'll take either one. (laughter)

Ultimately, to what extent in this spiritual journey the Consciousness is supposed to proceed towards the final enlightenment, depends on the extent to which the progress is being made through a particular body-mind organism. It cannot be a step behind, it cannot be a step further.

Aren't there times when you need to think, though? What if you were doing mathematics?

That's the working mind. If I have to catch a plane, the working mind must say, "The plane takes off at such and such a time, I have to be present at the airport at such and such a time. I must therefore leave my home at a particular time." All that planning has to be done. It is the working mind.

Thinking mind is what?

Thinking mind is that which creates worry for you. Thinking mind is that which creates anxiety. The thinking mind is that which keeps on interfering when you are working, "Is this going to be good? Am I going to be all right? Is this going to give me a promotion? Is this going to bring me profit or loss?"

All that rehearsing and chattering.

Chattering is the thinking mind. But when you're really absorbed in something, not necessarily working, you could be absorbed in listening to music, the thinking mind is absent.

Then, your working mind is in charge. At the end of two hours you will be surprised that you were working for two hours. There wouldn't be that physical or mental strain, either. Physical, maybe, but when your working mind is fully in charge there will be very little strain, very little tension.

So, underneath it all, that's Consciousness doing that, isn't it?

That is absolutely correct.

What is the relationship between the two, while the working mind is functioning?

While the working mind is functioning, there is no "me" there at all. Therefore the question of a relationship between the "me" and the working mind does not arise. No "me," no relationship.

A kind of a silent witness?

No, no. There's witnessing only if there is something to be witnessed. If I am talking to you, then all that is happening is that the working mind does the talking and the listening. There is no question of "me" talking to "you" and "me" listening to "you." That doesn't happen. There is just the working mind listening and talking.

There's not a field of awareness behind that?

No, no. There is no awareness of anything.

Is it an either/or phenomenon? When the thinking mind is operating, is the working mind operating on some other level? Like when I drive a car. Although I may be talking to myself with the thinking mind, the working mind is still going on underneath doing the driving?

Yes.

So it's not a complete either/or phenomenon.

No.

But they're both equally a function of Consciousness.

Yes. As the spiritual evolution is going on, the thinking mind gets less and less and more attention is paid to the working mind. The thinking mind, the "me," recedes further and further back, and the working mind takes over. It is all part of the spiritual evolutionary process that is taking place.

But the working mind has a function of judgment, deciding that those are tomatoes and are edible and those are stones and are not.

That is correct. Therefore, the working mind may do precisely what the thinking mind also does. But the thinking mind works either in the past or the future. It dwells in its memory and projects into the future. The working mind is concerned with the present moment. That is the big difference. The working mind is not concerned with the past or the future, except insofar as the present work is concerned.

I see, but it draws on memory.

Certainly. Now if it is doing something and says, "The last time I did that it went wrong therefore I must correct the mistake." That is still the working mind. The working mind has to draw on the memory but it doesn't project anything into the future. It draws on the memory only to the extent of the job at hand.

So, in a way, it is the animal mind.

You can say that, yes.

Because that's what an animal does. It thinks only in those terms, as far as we know.

Yes. As soon as there is danger, the animal senses that danger and reacts to it. Once the danger is over, the animal mind doesn't think "Such a thing might arise in future, what evasive action should I now take?" The danger is over and the matter is finished.

Is the identification with the body necessarily the thinking mind?

This is a good question and the distinction is most relevant and important. Merely saying, "I am identified with the body and therefore I am in bondage" is not correct. If you are identified with your body, with the sense of personal doership and think that you are the experiencer, that you are the doer, *then* there is bondage. Not so in the mere identification with the body. The identification with the body, with the working mind, is absolutely necessary. This is a notional distinction, but it is a subtle, most important distinction.

What about the arising of the self-image? Is that from the thinking mind?

Indeed it is. It *is* the thinking mind.

Can it ever be from the working mind?

It cannot be in the working mind.

So, if I respond to my name being called, it could be the working mind? But if I have an image of myself that comes up and then I respond, that would be the thinking mind?

Yes. And if you are really concentrating on something and some one calls you a damn fool, you won't even hear it.

There's a Christian book entitled something like, Self Abandonment Through Divine Providence. *Is that the same thing?*

That is beautiful!! Self abandonment through Divine Providence. That is precisely what happens. That means there is no "you" which can bring about self-abandonment. The self-abandonment can only happen through Divine Providence. There's no use my asking who said that. I don't care who said it. That is beautiful.

ᗒᗒᗒ

When one gets lost in a waking activity, such as lost in a task, is that witnessing?

It is. The understanding, the witnessing and the working mind are really the same thing. When the working mind is working, there is no need of witnessing, because the working mind, itself concentrates fully on what it's doing and that is precisely what I compare with total meditation. Because the "me" is not there, duration is not there. There is just the activity. Now, in that activity you often look at your watch and say, "Good Lord, two hours have elapsed!" In that activity the sense of duration was not there. At that particular time there is no memory, because there is no thinking mind.

Is that the same or comparable state as the non-witnessing state when you are not in an activity?

You may compare it, but I'd rather not. All I will compare is this: there is a tremendous difference when the working mind concentrates on the job at hand without the thinking mind interfering in its activity and obstructing it with such thoughts as, "Is this right or wrong? Is it going to effect my job? How will it effect my profit?" This trespassing on the working mind is what is absent and that is why, when the working mind is fully there, at the end of the day you find that there's much less tension, either physical or mental. There's a tremendous sense of something being achieved without an achiever.

I'll tell you a story about the difference between the working mind and the thinking mind:

Winston Churchill had a horse and he was expecting to win the Derby with that horse. He didn't win. When he was asked what happened, he said, "I made a mistake. Before the race, I talked to the horse and I said, 'You win this race and for the rest of your life you won't have to work anymore. You'll have the company of the best females and you'll have nothing to worry about.' That was the mistake. The horse then didn't have his mind on the job!" So, when you think of the possible consequences, good or bad, the working mind gets affected.

ㅁㅁㅁ

Would you say that the automatic habits that have been formed in life all belong to the working mind?

It depends. The working mind needs habits to do its work well. But most habits, I would think, are of the thinking mind. The worst habit—when I say worst or best, it must be understood that both belong to the functioning of Totality— the worst habit is to judge events from the personal point of view as they happen. Even thoughts are judged as acceptable or unacceptable. That is the conditioning. Conceptualizing is the worst habit. To conceptualize means to compare and judge.

There is a beautiful passage by Chuang Tzu in which he tells how the ancients had the perfect knowledge. They did not even know that things existed. Then they came to know that things existed, but they did not compare them. They did not view them as being different. Then they began to distinguish between things, and the *Tao* was lost. The *Tao* was lost when they started judging.

This describes how identification occurs in the process of evolution, starting with not knowing that things existed and ending with judging and comparing. Eventually the process goes full circle, from the arising of the *Tao*, through the moving of the *Tao*, to the *Tao* returning to its original purity. In this process, human beings are merely instruments through which the process takes place.

If you are doing something and you are completely there at that moment and you are not thinking about whether you are doing it well or not, is that the working mind?

That is correct, yes. And for that to happen, there has to be an understanding that "There is no way I can control the consequences. Life is an impersonal flowing and I cannot control either my life or anybody else's life." That is the understanding. That is the conviction which will allow the working mind to continue without the interruptions.

If I tell myself, "I better use my working mind," then I'm creating an obstacle?

That's right. Whichever way you look at it, it's only the understanding which can produce something. This understanding is that I can have no control, I am just a dreamed character and therefore all I can do is to function according to my natural characteristics. And even there, the understanding is that there is truly no "I" or "me" except the body-mind organism as a reacting agent.

All that a body-mind can do, is to react to an outside thought or event. So that reaction to an outside thought or event by a body-mind organism is the working mind.

When my working mind is working, do I get the feeling of my mind being blank?

No, not at all. Your mind isn't blank. You see this working mind and thinking mind are only notional differences.

When your working mind is there, there is the absence of the thinking mind. That means you don't worry about the future, your mind is concentrated on the work in hand.

Would you say that the working mind is the intuitive mind?

Yes, you can say that. And the efficacy of that working mind is diminished by the intervention of the thinking mind. In times of emergency, the thinking mind has no time to come in. Then it is all the awareness of the working mind.

Are you saying that the thinking mind is useless?

It is very much of use to Consciousness in order to bring about this life and living. It is this thinking mind which creates human relationships and the problems. Unless it did that, there would be no life and living as we know it. The thinking mind is the personalized individual mind with which the impersonal Mind, universal Consciousness, has deliberately identified itself so that life and living should go on.

Then the concept of the ego is the tool of the thinking mind?

Ego *is* the thinking mind.

Isn't ego a concept of the thinking mind?

The ego is certainly a concept. The thinking mind, the ego, the "me" are all the same. They are different names for the same thing, which is an illusion.

❏❏❏

I'm still confused about how witnessing is different from the working mind, because there's no observer of the working mind, either.

Now, this involvement is by the thinking mind. Everybody has had experience of the working mind. When you are really engrossed in something that you are doing—it need not be a doing, it may be just listening to good music; or you're working on a job which needs your full attention— at that time there is no thinking mind. It is entirely your working mind.

But in those situations, I would be just as involved in that as I would be involved in my own thinking mind.

Ah, you are quite correct. The confusion is caused here by the words "involved" and "involvement." The working mind, in order to be fully effective, has to be *totally* involved in what it is doing. So, the word "involved" is what is causing confusion in you.

Oh, so while I'm not in my thinking mind, even though I am identified with it and involved, maybe I'm not totally involved, just sort of mixed up in other distractions.

Yes, so, involvement of the thinking mind causes distraction in the involvement of the working mind.

Usually while I'm thinking, I'm also doing something else.

So involvement is indeed necessary. In fact, total involvement is necessary in the working mind to prevent the interfering of the thinking mind.

Yes, for that's that sense of timelessness.

When the working mind is totally involved, there is indeed the sense of timelessness, because the working mind can only function in the present moment. It is the thinking mind which always works either in the past or in the future.

You suddenly wake up and think, "Half-hour has gone by!"

Precisely.

If I'm crossing the street and there's a car bearing down, would it be the working mind that tells me that...?

The working mind does not tell you anything. The working mind will *act*.

And I'd run out of the way.

Yes! That running out of the way will be an instinctive happening.

But if I sit down and worry if I'm going to have rent money at the end of the month...

That is definitely the thinking mind.

A waste of time, really.

Of course it is!

I keep telling myself that. (laughter)

🔳🔳🔳

When daydreaming takes place is it imagination that takes over? Is there an importance to it? Why does it occur?

The daydreaming is really nothing but another kind of objectivizing and creating images by the thinking mind. It is still the thinking mind. Instead of drawing on the past memories and creating hopes and fears in the future, it goes along a different trail bringing about this daydreaming. But the point is, when the daydreaming happens the working mind is not present. The working mind does not have anything to do. Or, the working mind has something to do but this thinking mind wanders, interferes. It is just another aspect of the thinking mind interfering with the working mind and slowing it down.

Seems like the thinking mind is 100% speculation. The thoughts are really beside the point, not having to do with what is going on.

Quite correct.

Would the attempts to suppress the thinking mind interfere with your working mind?

Certainly. Attempts to suppress the thinking mind are the result of the thinking mind wanting to suppress itself. It will find that it cannot suppress itself.

It can, for a little while.

Yes, but then it comes back up with twice the speed and power.

I think it was D. T. Suzuki who said, "After enlightenment there is no difference except the enlightened person walks on the ground and the unenlightened person walks two inches off of it."

So those two inches are the actions of the thinking mind.

◘◘◘

Some of us were talking at the break and we're having a thinking mind, working mind quandary. If the working mind is working and a problem presents itself and there's a response to it, isn't image making occurring in that process? Image making of the finished product? Image making of the desired result? Image making about the consequences of that action?

In most cases, yes.

And doesn't that process of image making influence the result, or the direction that that work is taking? And isn't that an area of overlapping of the thinking mind with the working mind?

Oh yes indeed.

I'm having a very difficult time visualizing the working mind working with no interruptions of the thinking mind.

Until the final awakening happens and the sense of doership is totally lost, there is *always* an overlapping to some extent.

Okay, if a jnani were flying a 747 as a pilot, he's making calculations based on the working mind, and if one of those calculations begins to go awry and the plane begins to veer, doesn't the image come up in the jnani's *mind that the consequences of this veering are that the plane will crash and hundreds of lives will be lost?*

I would not think so. On the contrary, even if there is just limited understanding then the working mind would be working with the greatest possible intensity to correct the situation.

But if he doesn't project the thought, "This plane will crash if I don't take certain actions," then how will he know to take the action to prohibit the plane from crashing?

All those thoughts would be part of the working mind to decide whether what is being done at that moment is right or wrong from the point of view of the working itself, *not* from the point of view of the results.

But won't a projection into the future have to be made about what the results of this work may be, so that a correction can be made based on that projection?

Yes, but the projection will not include the image of a crash. There would be no worry or fear.

While driving a car, when I'm taking a curve, if I realize I'm not turning my wheel enough, I don't think, "Oh my god, I'm going to crash in the ditch and die!" What I do is turn the steering wheel a little bit more. Is that what you're talking about?

Quite right. That corrective action will be instinctive and intuitive. It is the encroaching of an image by the thinking mind which is likely to cause the accident.

Most of the time it is intuitive. There are times however when it's not a click-click-click situation. You have time for reflection upon the alternatives. I'm a surgeon. During surgery I can say, "Well, if I do this, then the patient will experience that, but if I do something else then there will be a different result." Alternative images of what might happen are considered and then applied to the situation. Now, isn't that the thinking mind influencing the work-ing mind, sometimes positively?

What you are describing is still the working mind. I'm not saying that such images will not be projected, but they will be images projected by the working mind and will relate directly to the task at hand.

So, image making isn't necessarily part of the thinking mind?

Quite right. As I said, drawing on the memory is done both by the working mind and the thinking mind. The thinking mind would draw on the memory of the past to project some fears in the future. But the working mind, drawing on the memory, will use those memories to make the job at hand a better one.

◻◻◻

– THOUGHT –

I just finished a book about thought-forms. It talked about how we can't afford the luxury of negative thoughts because thought-forms manifest in the outside world and then you meet your thought-forms as you move through life. Would you comment on that idea?

Quite frankly, a thought arises and the individual mind turns it into a negative thought or a positive thought. It is the mind that decides, "I don't want a negative thought, I only want the positive thought" and that is the involvement. When the thought is witnessed as it arises, it gets cut off. There is never any question of it being negative or positive.

So it's just another concept?

Yes, indeed it is a concept! Once we start a discussion everything is a concept. That is why the ultimate teaching is silence. Not just quietude. Not the silence where somebody says, "Oh I will have a day of silence" and then he writes out his questions and gets written answers. That is not silence. That is giving the throat a rest. It is not silence.

It is noise. It's the mind in activity.

Quite so. It is the nature of the monkey-mind to jump about and chatter.

As they say in Buddhism, it is the mind that is noisy.

The mind *is* the noise! It is not that the mind is noisy, the mind *is* the noise.

It's the mind talking to itself.

Yes, that is its nature. Therefore, trying to control it, by any means, is merely suppressing it.

When will the mind not be noisy?

When there is understanding. Then it will be time for the mind to be silent.

◘◘◘

– CONCEPTS –

I think it's a useful concept that there is no "me," but do you think there is much use in the concept that there is no "I," as in God?

The concept of "I" comes in because there's the concept of "me." Because there is the concept of the individual, the concept of God comes in.

Can you comment on the saying of Maharaj, "Consciousness is like a leach which happens to you?"

He said many things. Whatever he said is a concept, make no mistake, whether Maharaj said it or Buddha said it or Christ said it.

Is it like a koan? I couldn't break this koan.

I believe the best explanation of the value of concepts, is that given by Ramana Maharshi. He said, "A concept is useful only so long as you use it as you would a thorn to dig out another thorn which is embedded in your foot. Then, when the embedded thorn is removed, you throw both thorns away." That is all a concept is good for; to remove an obstructing concept.

When the understanding happens, these words and concepts are discarded. If you hold on to them, these words and concepts become like cancer. They gnaw at your insides.

So, we are to extract the essence from what you are saying, and not hang on to the details?

Absolutely! Quite often the people who come to see me in Bombay, after we talk one or two hours, say when they are leaving, "I've understood it, I really have! Now, when I leave this place, what should I do?"

I tell them, "It's very simple. Don't think about what you have heard here. Just don't think about what you think you've understood. And then that understanding will have a chance to flower. But the more you think about what you have understood, the more it's wasted."

I'll throw out my notes. (laughter)

Good.

◘◘◘

– EGO –

Is ego absolutely essential for this whole thing to happen?

You mean for the normal living of the individual?

I was thinking that the ego is an unavoidable, inevitable thing. And it's such a terrible thing. It's the source of all the problems. Yet isn't it supposed to be there in the overall scheme of things?

That question arises because you confuse the word ego with the thinking mind. In the cases of Ramana Maharshi, Jesus and Buddha, their bodies continued to function for many years, even after enlightenment happened. So the body-mind organism certainly carries on its functions both conscious and unconscious. For consciousness in that organism to happen, there had to be some ego identified with the body. If any of these people were called, they would turn and respond. So, the ego is certainly there.

The word ego has been much maligned. That is because we don't understand the word. Ego, identified with the body, is the working mind and it is necessary for the body to function. What is absent in the case of enlightenment is the thinking mind which never lives in the present moment. The working mind always lives in the present moment and does whatever is necessary. The thinking mind always lives either in the past or the future.

You must really understand what you mean by the ego. Ego as the operating element, as the working mind, has to be there. It is only the ego as the thinking mind, thinking of the consequences, thinking as the doer, which is the cause of misery.

5

ENLIGHTENMENT

– GENERAL DISCUSSIONS –

It's very rough on us people who are attached to the idea of ananda.

And it's tougher on those who get attached to non-attachment. It's still a...

It's still a concept?

That's the point. You see?

They use the analogy of enlightenment as like being in the deep sleep state while awake. Does that mean the person is no longer aware of himself?

Yes, no longer aware as a separate entity, as a separate doer, as a separate experiencer.

There's just awareness of the functions of the body-mind?

That's right. There's witnessing of the actions which take place through this body-mind mechanism precisely as if they were those of any other body-mind mechanism. There is no sense of a separate entity.

There's no continuity of one who went through a series of actions or events over time. In a sense, it just disappears?

Therefore, as I said, if someone were to ask Maharaj, "Why did you get angry?" he'd say, "Who got angry?" There is no sense of personal doership.

He doesn't have that psychological memory of "me" being the one who was angry for a certain amount of time?

Quite. Precisely. Not the sense of guilt that he should not have been angry.

◻◻◻

– THE END OF THE SUFFERER –

When enlightenment takes place in a particular body-mind, does it become like a clear window for the Divine Self to be in the dream? Does the Divine Self have a certain kind of enjoyment through that enlightened body-mind, a certain kind of involvement? Or, is it like nothing is happening?

The witnessing means there is no involvement. So, how can the Pure Consciousness or Awareness have any interest in any enjoyment?

But isn't there still a difference between the enlightened body-mind and the original sleeping awareness before the I Am arises.

All that happens is, when enlightenment takes place, the worries and doubts and problems of life disappear because the personal "me" is not there. And the sense of personal doership is not there. That the Totality or God or the Absolute functions through the organism is a fact whether a particular organism believes it or not.

So from that standpoint, there is no difference between one or the other?

As far as the organism is concerned, yes! But the only difference is that the involved individual organism believes that he or she is the one who is functioning. After enlightenment, it is known that all are instruments through which Totality functions. Totality functions whether there is this understanding or not.

So the only difference is to this individual.

Yes!

The suffering is gone?

Yes, but, "Suffering is gone" needs a certain explanation. Buddha said, "There is suffering, but no one to suffer. There are deeds, but no doer." The suffering may be there but the reaction is not "I" am suffering. Rather, the reaction is that there *is* suffering, there *is* pain. From the ordinary man's point of view, when enlightenment takes place the body doesn't suddenly become perfect. The body is still liable to ailments, or whatever.

I'm trying to understand the difference between disidentification and attachment.

The best way to understand it, I think, is from the point of view of your pain. There's an immediate experience. If it is pain, the ordinary individual says, "I am in pain." But when there is pain after enlightenment, the feeling always is, "There *is* pain." When asked if he were in pain, Maharaj's immediate response was, "Yes there *is* great pain." In other words, the great pain is witnessed.

It's not felt?

Oh, indeed, it *is* felt!

By whom?

By the organism. Therefore the organism groans. The pain is witnessed, the reaction of the organism to the pain is also witnessed. The pain is there and the reaction of the organism to the pain is there, which may result in a groan or scream. The whole thing is witnessed; the pain and the reaction in the organism.

◘◘◘

– THE ABSENCE OF DUALISM –

The body-mind is disintegrated at death and also disintegrated before death through enlightenment, is that so?

No, enlightenment does not bring about disintegration of the body.

I meant, detached from duality at enlightenment.

Let me make it clear. What enlightenment does is to disassociate the entity from dualism. The entity cannot remove itself from duality. So long as the body-mind continues, duality is still there. Whatever the body-mind does in duration, in space-time, is in duality. What is absent in enlightenment is dualism, "me" as a separate entity and you as another separate entity.

That's what I was thinking, that that part would be disintegrated or detached.

Correct.

And at death the same thing happens together with the death of the body and any other attributes of this particular existence.

Quite so.

◻◻◻

– THE VARYING EFFECTS OF ENLIGHTENMENT –

When this enlightenment was happening to you, did you lose interest in your work?

On the contrary! I did not lose interest. But let me be clear. You ask in my case, "What happened?" In some other case it may happen that all interest may stop. What will be the result is impossible to say. I was not a writer before, but the books started coming. When *Pointers*[5] started coming Maharaj knew about it, and he said, "Not one, seven, eight books will come."

Writing is not my profession or my hobby, it just happens. You should see the manuscript of these books: page after page of writing in longhand, with hardly any alterations. You write a letter to someone, a one-page letter and you see how many alterations you make. It is the thinking mind. So this page after page of spontaneous writing has been coming, and I think six or seven books have come in probably seven or eight years, along with some other work. So whenever I have to say "my" books, it makes me cringe a bit. Deep down, I know they're not my books.

Also, I have never been a speaker. In fact my wife has always complained, "You go to social parties and everybody talks. Why don't you talk?" I have nothing to say! I cannot make small talk. So, here I am.

After the experience and the understanding of the oneness of all things, some people appear to be God-intoxicated or in a state of bliss. Some masters seem to be in that God-intoxicated state. Is that a stage? Is there anything you can say about that?

Yes. That is precisely what I just talked about. When the impersonal event of enlightenment happens, what the result

Ramesh S. Balsekar, Pointers From Nisargadatta Maharaj (Bombay: Chetana, 1982)

of that event will be or how that body-mind organism will behave or what will happen through that body-mind organism after that event can be very different, of tremendous variety. So those who were talking and writing may stop writing and talking. Those who never did that may do it. And some don't do anything at all. Some may actually leave whatever they are doing and go into seclusion.

What I'm talking about is, they seem to be in a state like rapture.

I have a feeling that that kind of rapture is probably of a very short duration. But again, these words carry a great misconception. There could be a sense of rapture, but it doesn't remain, it quiets down. A drug could produce that state of rapture, but it settles down. Frankly, bliss is a word which I don't particularly like because it creates a misconception. Real bliss is the absence of the wanting of bliss. That is the real bliss. Peace, tranquillity, are the words which I prefer. In fact, the enlightenment state is not wanting either bliss or anything else. It is total acceptance. That is the state.

So if one were to have a one-word mantra, might it be the word, trust?

It could be, yes. But my own two words would be acceptance and surrender which mean the same thing. Mind you, you can use "trust."

◻◻◻

– A CONDITION IN PHENOMENALITY –

I am trying to bring this together, the difference between enlightenment and Consciousness-at-rest.

The state of Consciousness-at-rest is a subjective state.

Does that mean there is nothing?

It means that there is everything in a potential state.

But does that mean that awareness recedes? In other words, it sounds to me like enlightenment is the dissipation of awareness.

Enlightenment is only a condition in phenomenality. Let's not get away from that. Enlightenment is an understanding in phenomenality of what the position is. There is no question of any "one" being enlightened. The question of enlightenment is still a concept in phenomenality.

Then the impulse to be enlightened is just to be unaware, permanently?

An impulse on whose part? That is where the mistake occurs every time. We think in terms of an individual. You are thinking in terms of an individual thinker. Impulse can only be from the point of view of an individual, but enlightenment is merely an understanding in which there is no comprehender. It is a surrender in which there is no one to surrender anything. So the understanding is an impersonal understanding, a flash of understanding not in horizontal duration. It has nothing to do with the triangle of an understander, the process of understanding, and the object that is understood. It is an understanding pure and simple, in which there is no comprehender.

Yes, but there is someone aware...

No! That is just the point. That is *precisely* the point!

That makes no sense to me.

Exactly! Precisely! (laughter) No sense to "me"!

That's just a play on words. Why practice then? I've spent my whole life practicing and basically when I was with Maharaj I felt profoundly that he was confirming the practice that I had adopted very early on...

Then what is the problem?

I am just addressing what I have responded to in your teaching. I am just trying to clarify what you are saying.

All I am saying is, this understanding is a vertical understanding in which there is no comprehender to comprehend anything. There is just a flash of understanding, in which there is no comprehender. And if you say that you cannot understand it, my only answer is, I don't mean to be unkind, I can only say that "you" are not yet ready to have that understanding. That understanding can come only at the appropriate time, and no one can say when. All that can be said is that the understanding cannot come so long as there is expectation, so long as there is a "me" wanting it.

◘◘◘

– THE CONTINUED FUNCTIONING OF THE BODY-MIND –

What do you mean by disidentification of the "me"?

Enlightenment means the removal of the identification of Consciousness with the individual body-mind mechanism as a separate individual. Or, the removal of identification as a separate individual means enlightenment.

How then does the body-mind mechanism in which enlightenment has taken place function for the rest of its life?

The disidentification as an individual is the disidentification as a separate doer, but the identification with the body-mind mechanism as an individual must continue for the rest of his life. Otherwise, how will the organism function?

For instance, if someone called to Ramana Maharshi or Maharaj, they would respond. To that extent, the identification has to be there. So, the identification with the individual body continues, but what is discontinued is the identification as a separate doer. The acts which take place through that body-mind mechanism are witnessed precisely as are the acts which take place through any other body-mind mechanism.

When you say that there is still identification with the body but non-doership, who is identifying with the body?

The functional center is Totality or Consciousness or God, which uses each individual mechanism as an instrument through which to function. The operating center is considered the psychic part of the psychosomatic organism. The heart or liver is part of the somatic or the physical mechanism. This operating center is part of the psyche so that the body will function. Let me give an analogy, which is of course subject to its natural limitations:

There is a chauffeur who has a car and is able to take the car anywhere. For him to think that he owns the car simply because he is in a position to drive the car, is a misidentification. The functional center is the owner; the operating center is the chauffeur. When enlightenment takes place, there is an owner-driver who knows precisely the two different aspects of ownership and drivership.

❑❑❑

– PREREQUISITES OF ENLIGHTENMENT –

Can it happen that you have only a slight understanding of spiritual matters, and then enlightenment happens?

Absolutely! In fact what you mean is, in the spiritual evolution can there be a quantum jump from only a minimal level of understanding to the total understanding? Yes, there can be a quantum jump.

I have to beg the question, "How?"

"How" is more than I can say. All I can say is that's what happens, and I go along with it. This is precisely the biggest obstruction: the "How." The only answer is Ramana Maharshi's, "Who wants to know?"

So there are no prerequisites, no types of people that it's more likely to happen to?

Many years ago, there was a Dr. Sheldon. He was not concerned with the spiritual aspect. He was concerned with finding out if organically, the human organism could be divided into certain classifications. He and his associates came to the conclusion that there were three types. One type was physically soft but temperamentally very outgoing; this they called the viscerotonic. Another type was big boned, muscular, keen on competition; this they called the somatotonic. The third type was not concerned with competition. He was an introvert with small bones and weak muscles; this they called the cerebrotonic.

When the seeking begins, it can begin in any of those three. Then the seeking will take that organism to the path for which it is best suited. Hindu tradition describes three paths or *yogas* that correspond remarkably to these types.

The viscerotonic is an organism that will most likely be led to the path of *bhakti*, of devotion. The somatotonic will be led to the path of action or *karma yoga*. The third one, the cerebrotonic, will most naturally tend towards the path of knowledge, or *jnana*. But though the paths are notionally separate they can merge, and very often they do merge; the *bhakti* and *jnana* especially, often come together.

❏❏❏

When you say there is a body-mind organism and enlightenment takes place in that, and then that organism continues, could that happen in a psychopath?

No, because the organism of a psychopath would not be ready to receive an event called enlightenment. What I meant was that it can happen in any type of organism. It can happen in a viscerotonic who is a *bhakta*, or a devotee, or it can happen in the case of a somatotonic who is an achiever, or in the case of a *jnani*, which is the cerebrotonic. In any of those types it can occur. But within each type the organism has to evolve to an extent whereby it can receive this event called enlightenment. During Einstein's time there were many scientists, but it was only Einstein who was capable of receiving the theory of relativity. His was a brain highly evolved enough to receive the equation "from outside," as Einstein himself has said.

◘◘◘

You mentioned that the body-mind organism or complex has to be prepared to receive this so-called enlightenment. What I really want to ask is, where is the importance or the value? Is it the physical preparation, or is it the mental preparation?

It's both. You see, you really cannot separate the mind and the body. That's why I keep saying "psychosomatic organism."

Well, is it not that the mind is complaining about a pain rather than the body?

Yes, it is really the mind complaining about the pain in the body and therefore you feel the pain.

Because the body couldn't give a hoot.

Quite. So, in the preparation that you are talking of, you cannot separate the body and the mind. The mind gets ready to accept this understanding. And the mind gets ready to accept this understanding only at a certain time. Even the necessary earnestness is a matter of evolution.

So it's just a matter of mental conditioning?

A matter of mental conditioning is the beginning of the search. The thought enters, for instance, "There must be more to life than just physical pleasure." That thought could come into ten organisms. Only one may respond. The other nine, at that moment, are not ready to respond to that thought. So only a certain organism will respond to a thought from outside of this kind, and then the mind will turn inward. So ultimately it is a matter of the mind or the organism responding to a thought from outside.

◘◘◘

– THE RARITY OF ENLIGHTENMENT –

It is my impression that Nisargadatta taught in his loft for something like forty years, and must therefore have spoken to thousands of people. Some of them may have become either near enlightened or enlightened, but to our knowledge, only one person has emerged in whom Nisargadatta had the confidence to encourage to speak up. It seems to reflect the enormity or the loftiness of the accomplishment, and the rarity of it.

I think the importantly misused word is, *accomplishment.* Nobody has accomplished anything. That is the point.

Suppose we say the rarity of the occurrence.

Yes quite so, the rarity of the occurrence.

That would suggest that our outlook should be modest. (laughter) Have you yourself wondered about that? So many people went through that loft.

Not too many people, really. Certainly not thousands. Actually, when Maharaj spoke to me there was only Maharaj and myself, as he was resting before I took him for the usual half an hour ride along the seashore. As he was getting ready, out of the blue he put his hand on my shoulder and said, "I am happy that there is at least one instance in which there is total understanding." I didn't really need his certificate. Quite frankly, I knew that it had happened. And I knew that, speaking relatively, it had happened purely by his grace, so there was a tremendous sense of gratitude. But nonetheless, an acknowledgment from the *guru* was really overwhelming. I looked at him with tears in my eyes, questioningly, and he said, "Well, maybe one or two others." So yes, it is rare. But the basic point is that the rarity is accepted and once the rarity is accepted, the personal wanting disappears. So the rarity of the occurrence can be both frustrating and also yield total freedom. It will be frustrating as long as the "me" is wanting something. And I keep repeating: whether the "me"

wants a million dollars or enlightenment, qualitatively there
is no difference.

6

FROM THE ENLIGHTENED VIEW

– GENERAL DISCUSSIONS –

How *does the enlightened body-mind organism view the world? What does he see? What does he mean when he describes the world as being unreal?*

Shankara described the phenomenal world as unreal, so he was dubbed an atheist. The context in which he used the word "unreal" is a point of much misunderstanding. By describing the phenomenal world as unreal, he meant that it is like a shadow which cannot exist without an object to cast it. It is dependent on something else for its existence. It has no independent existence. In this sense the phenomenal world is unreal, as it is a reflection of the noumenal.

In other words, Subjectivity or Noumenon transcends the phenomenal manifestation. The Absolute Subject and the manifested object are not two. This identification between the Unmanifest and the manifest is one of the first basic aspects of the understanding. There is no question of identifying with the world. If you ask, "Is there identification with the world?" then the two are still there. The understanding then is: all there is, is Consciousness, which manifests itself as this total manifestation in which there are objects with an astonishing amount of divergence, astonishing amount of individuality. I'm told that not only fingerprints are separate but that individual voices can be identified by sensitive machines and the heartbeats of particular individuals can be identified. Yet, with such diversity there is still this unity in the diversity. That Unity which functions as the Totality, the subjective element, is common in all sentient beings. Understanding removes the separation. The diversity of the diverse is seen but only on the surface.

ꗋꗋꗋ

Who are you?

I am Consciousness and so are you. And Consciousness is what constitutes and what functions through every single body-mind organism, every sentient being, whether it is an animal or a human being or an insect.

If this exchange were not going on, would any concepts arise in your mind of the subject matter of enlightenment or Consciousness?

No. You see, the happening of enlightenment means all concepts cease. All doubts have ceased. There are no more doubts, there are no more concepts. There is no need of a concept. Concepts and doubts can only be there if the "me" is there. In the split-mind of subject and object, of logic and reason, in the thinking mind the "me" is this collection of doubts. When this "me" is gone, who is to have any doubts? What I started to say today I don't think I ever said before. It just happens. The answers are not formulated. When the questions are put, the answers just come out. They are not formulated. There is no mind interpreting and thinking up the answers.

So, you live naturally and spontaneously all the time?

In fact living is always natural and spontaneous. But the ordinary person thinks he is acting and therefore feels responsible. He believes he can change the world. Eventually he finds that the control he thought he had over events just doesn't exist. In the process of understanding he comes across a lot of difficulties and changes, what he calls unhappiness. In those times of unhappiness, instead of realizing that things have happened spontaneously by themselves and that change is the very basis of living, he thinks that in order to be happier he must improve himself. So he goes through a lot of self-improvement courses. Of course, when those self-improvement courses have only limited results, further frustration ensues.

So, you believe that you have no control over the way your life goes?

Events happening through any body-mind mechanism are always beyond the control of the separate entity. But the average person doesn't realize this. He is used to believing that he is doing the choosing. He believes that he has choice of decision and action and therefore continues to be miserable. Enlightenment simply means that all of this is realized. Then, instead of being involved in whatever actions take place, not only through his body-mind organism, but through those with whom he comes into contact, he accepts *all* actions as part of the functioning of Totality. All that has changed is the attitude, the perspective, the understanding. The world goes on and will continue to go on in the same way.

The result of enlightenment comes up in various ways. Spontaneous living is described by Lao Tzu in such beautiful terms. Incidentally, I'm sure Maharaj never heard of Lao Tzu. He couldn't have heard of Lao Tzu or Taoism. But it is absolutely amazing how parallel the teachings are. They have to be, because the kind of life that begins after enlightenment, whether it is in China two-thousand years ago or in Ramana Maharshi one hundred years ago, has to be the same. When you read Lao Tzu, you are struck with wonder. There was Maharaj in a tiny room in the busiest part of Bombay, with the red light district within a stone's throw. And there was Lao Tzu, living in the mountains in China, both with identical attitudes to life, that attitude which brings about a kind of shining that affects those with whom they come in contact.

The sage's life is a life courageous from the viewpoint of the average person. What I mean by "life courageous" is living not in confrontation with life, but in the full acceptance that change is the very basis of life. Living life courageously means reconciling discipline with understanding, unity with diversity, order with spontaneity, sociability with individuality. The variety of experience and perception is seen in its wonder of diversity, together with the unity. The sage doesn't reconcile discipline with understanding, or combine order with spontaneity. It just happens, and therein lies the magic and wonder of it.

Life courageous does not happen in the case of an ordinary person because he's saying, "I must be disciplined." And when he finds that discipline has to be tempered with other people's freedom, he considers it a conflict. He wants to be individual, saying, "I want to live my own life. I want to have a particular way of life, diet, exercise. I want to live by myself." But in life you cannot be a recluse. You have to live with others. When the adaptability towards living with others and the desire to have one's own individual life are seen as opposites and conflicting, there's misery. But when it is understood that both work spontaneously together, then there is an automatic natural order of conciliation between them. A life courageous does not mean confrontation with nature, but a joyous cooperation with the working principles of nature. In actual living, this takes the form of a willing participation in the events which constitute the what-is in each moment, living without concepts and formulas, naturally and spontaneously. There is the deepest possible conviction of, "Thy Will, oh Lord, not mine." Such an attitude needs the spontaneous absence of personal doership, whatever the activity. Such living, then becomes naturally virtuous, though not in the sense of a deliberate exercise of moral rectitude.

❏❏❏

Your enlightenment, was it given the purpose to teach? Is there another enlightenment that gives the purpose to heal?

Yes, precisely. Once enlightenment happens, what will happen further through that body-mind organism is impossible to say. There is no hard and fast rule. Nothing may happen through that body-mind organism. It may continue to do precisely what it was doing earlier, or it may change. Someone who had never written a word before will write books. Someone who was terrified of giving an after dinner speech will give talks. It's a miracle of a kind.

I am amazed at how your words just flow.

To say they "just flow" is correct. The same was true when the books were written, the words just flowed.

❏❏❏

– RAMESH'S ENLIGHTENMENT –

Perhaps you could tell us something about your enlightenment and how it came to you.

Well, you see, enlightenment is an extremely obtuse word. The word enlightenment somehow seems to suggest a sort of occurrence where there are lights blazing and bliss coming out of the ears, you see. But it isn't, at least not in my case.

I've heard that it can be a very mild but distinctive occurrence and particularly when I read a story about Lao Tzu and his disciple, it struck me that that was so. Some of you perhaps know it, but I don't suppose there is any harm in repeating it.

One of Lao Tzu's disciples went to him one morning with his eyes blazing and his face glowing with a sense of achievement, and he said, "Master, I have arrived." And Lao Tzu with great compassion put his hands on his shoulders and said, "Son, you have not arrived anywhere." So the disciple went away. He came back after some time and then, with great quiet composure, said, "Master, it has happened." So Lao Tzu looked in his eyes, embraced him and said, "Now tell me what happened."

He said, "I accepted your word that nothing had happened. But I also knew that I could not have possibly put in any more effort. So I gave up thinking of enlightenment, I gave up all effort towards enlightenment and went about my normal business. Then it suddenly occurred to me that there was nothing to be achieved. It was there all the time!"

The understanding had dawned that there is no individual to want anything. The state is already there. The ultimate state, before it can happen, is the absence of the "me" wanting something to happen.

What you are saying then is, the arrival at that place will happen when it is time to happen.

Yes! When it is His Will. When it is *time* for it to happen, is correct.

In the meantime there is nothing we can do to encourage it?

Correct again. (laughter) So, in my case I know the specific date when it happened. There is one day in the year which is called the Divali Day, the festival of light, which is a common festival throughout India. This festival of light is supposed to signify the victory of right over wrong, of good over evil, the victory of Rama over Ravana.

Normally in Maharaj's place that used to be the day of cleaning up his loft, sort of a "spring cleaning," and no talks were held on that day. This happened in the year I first went to visit him. That was in 1978. The following year, on the day previous to Divali, when the announcement was being made that there would be no talks the following day for this reason, a colleague of mine suggested that if Maharaj agreed he could hold the talks at his own place which was very close to Maharaj's place, and known to most people who used to attend. The result was that the next day we had the talk at this residence of the colleague. This colleague used to be one of the translators. So on that day he said he would look after the people coming in, would I translate? I agreed.

The moment Maharaj started to talk, something peculiar happened. Maharaj's voice seemed to come to me from a distance, very, very clear. In fact, clearer than it used to be normally. Maharaj didn't have any teeth, so I needed some time to get used to his words. But that morning his voice seemed to come from a distance, yet much much clearer than it ever was before, needing no concentration on my part. I found that the translation began to come so spontaneously that in actual fact I was not translating, I was merely witnessing the translation taking place. It was as if Maharaj was translating into English and I was merely sitting there, a witness.

At the end of the translation I felt quite ill. I didn't know what was happening and the body had reacted in a certain way for the simple reason that it was not used to that experience. My colleague later said, "Ramesh, you were in great form today!"

"How so?"

He said, "You were talking louder than you normally do, you spoke with great authority and you were making gestures that you never did before." So I just accepted that. It was confirmation that something had happened. But the something that had happened was internally a complete change, a total change. Outside, the only change that I could find was that my body felt a peculiar kind of weightlessness. I couldn't name it and I think that was noticed for a day or two before it settled down. But if you ask me when it happened, this is how and when it happened. As I say, it was a very quiet event, sudden of course, as sudden as anything could be...totally unexpected...totally spontaneous.

After that, the translations were always that way and Maharaj noticed it too. Maharaj didn't understand English, but he could sense when the translation was not strictly accurate. When the translations were taking place, Maharaj would often ask whoever was translating, "What did you tell them?" He would make him repeat and then he would confirm it or he would say, "No, that is not what I meant. You see you have got it wrong. You often get it wrong." (laughter) But after that day I noticed I was no longer paying attention to what was being said, so the translations came out smoothly and spontaneously.

One morning when I was waiting for Maharaj to get ready for me to take him out for the usual car ride, he was in a particularly calm mood and he said, "I'm glad it's happened." He also knew at that time the book, *Pointers*[6] was coming out, so he said, "I'm glad it's happened. It's not just one book. Several books will come out. And what the books will say will not be a parroting of what I have said. How it will come about, I won't know. Even you won't know."

Ramesh, you had said when the awakening happened that there was a peculiar sense of the body, some sense of discomfort and disorientation. Is that because Consciousness is no longer identified with the body?

Yes.

When you were talking about the experience of enlightenment, you spoke about Maharaj and that particular moment when he said, "So it's happened." Was there a particular moment when you made that comment to yourself, "So it's happened?"

After a day or two, when I came back to normal, physically, then I knew it had happened, and there was no doubt

_____
ibid.

at all. Quite frankly I did not feel any need for certification from Maharaj, but when it did come it was welcome. But the basic fact is that I did not need any certificate from anybody.

It sounds like that moment for you came at the end of this two or three day period.

The feeling that something had happened, yes. The awareness of what had happened, the consciousness of what had happened.

◘◘◘

– ENJOYMENT OF LIFE AS IT IS –

I noticed the sunset this evening, and it was really beautiful. What I wanted to ask you is, when you look at something like the sunset and then you experience the noises caused by all the automobiles, to me, the noise is not as beautiful as the sunset. Do you make the distinction that one is pleasant and the other is not?

I can't have this sunset for any length of time, nor can I avoid the noises. That I'm aware of. So there is no wishing that the sunset should continue forever, or that the noise wouldn't interfere. In other words, there is an acceptance of whatever "is." If there is a beautiful sunset, it is enjoyed. There is no wish that it continue forever, you see.

When an ordinary person enjoys a pleasure, that enjoyment is invariably concerned with a certain fear that that enjoyment would not last. At the moment of enjoyment, questions arise: "When did I have such a good meal like this? When will I have it again? Am I ever going to have sex like this again?" The pleasure for the *jnani* is more intense because he's not worrying about when he'll have it again. If it comes again, fine, if not, it doesn't bother him. Therefore the *jnani* is often described as a *mahabhogi*, a super-enjoyer. He's far from being a vegetable. In that enjoyment there is no enjoyer, there is pure enjoyment.

Then he turns his whole being into that.

That is natural spontaneous living. There is no live*r* of spontaneous life, only spontaneous living.

🞒🞒🞒

– FROM WITNESSING TO SAHAJA –

When you are in those moments of rest, when Consciousness is at ease, as Ramana Maharshi says, that is what it is all about...those moments of total lack of "me." When you are out of the "me," is that the closest to satori?

This *satori* or *samadhi* or *salvikalpa samadhi*, where consciousness is temporarily absent would be the nearest, but Ramana Maharshi has made it clear that it is not the natural state in the sense of non-witnessing which is the natural state. From the non-witnessing state you go to the witnessing state and back again, very, very smoothly, like the automatic changing of gears. You are in the non-witnessing state when there is nothing to witness.

Someone calls you, or somebody comes, or there is a door bell, then you are back in the witnessing state. But there is no disturbance, you don't feel any disturbance. It is natural from one to the other.

Sir, could I refer to that process as chittah, *that mind stuff running? That is to say, when we are caught in illusion, that this is the nature of* chittah, *this is what the mind does, this is its job, just as lungs do certain things and so on.*

Yes.

So, it creates illusion.

Quite so.

But we can be objective and just watch what it does, just as watching the lungs.

Quite so. Let's take the word, "sat-chit-ananda." "Sat" is beingness or be. "*Chit*" is Consciousness, conscious of being, and *"Ananda"* is bliss. Existence, Consciousness, Bliss. That is mistakenly taken to be the description of the Subjective state, *Nirvana*. It is not so, because it cannot exist in that state, cannot be in that state where the Consciousness is aware of its own existence. No words can describe it. It is not in the noumenal but the phenomenal state. Any description is in phenomenality.

As Lao Tzu says, "If you can name it, it is not Tao."

You name it and it is gone. You chase it and try to catch it and it is gone. I keep referring to this because it is such a lovely piece: "It is only when you hunt for it that you lose it. But then you cannot get rid of it. And while you cannot do either, you remain silent and it speaks. You speak and it is gone. The great gate of charity is wide open, with no obstacles before it."

◘◘◘

Witnessing is just being.

Yes, witnessing is just being, not observing by an observer.

Someone once said that the highest state of Consciousness is when the witness in what's witnessed collapses. Is that what you're talking about when you talk about just being?

Yes, witnessing is the state of Consciousness, when there is something to be witnessed. You witness the birds or people coming and going or whatever. When that stops, when there is nothing to be witnessed, that state goes deeper. Ramana Maharshi calls this the "natural state."

When you are the birds, or the people passing, right?

If you want to put it into words, but I'd rather not.

It really can't be put into words.

There's no need to.

The place you're talking about now is beyond witnessing?

Yes. In the ordinary case, there is involvement. With a certain amount of understanding, the involvement gets hazier and the state is merely witnessing. What happens is, when I'm talking and doing, that is the witnessing state, but when there is nothing to witness then the state goes deeper into non-witnessing. In that state the consciousness is present in the sense that you smell the smells, hear the sounds in a very passive, unconcerned way. This is the natural, non-witnessing state. If the non-witnessing state continues for a while, then it goes deeper into the state of *samadhi*.

Does witnessing always recur then?

Witnessing happens all the time. Witnessing is what Consciousness is.

But after witnessing stops and you go into the deeper state, do you always come back up again?

Oh yes, of course. Non-witnessing to witnessing. It's like the changing of gears on the highway. It happens automatically. You don't even think about it. One to the other is natural, spontaneous.

Is the deepest nonwitnessing state the same as deep sleep for the ordinary person, except that for the jnani *there is this awakened sense?*

Yes. In the deep sleep state for the ordinary person what is absent is the identified consciousness, the "me." But the unidentified, impersonal, universal Consciousness has to be there because when you wake up it is not as if you are reborn. Impersonal Consciousness is what is present in deep sleep that provides continuity. What is absent in deep sleep is the identified personal consciousness. But the understanding that what-is-present always, in any state, is the impersonal Consciousness, is what happens after enlightenment.

ꗣꗣꗣ

– WITNESSING –

Earlier you were talking about thoughts coming to you, that you are a kind of puppet. Then you referred to the sage as the witness of the thoughts. How can that be?

That is a very good question. The sage does not witness the thoughts. The thought *gets* witnessed.

That is Consciousness?

That is Consciousness. And if the mind thinks, if the average person thinks, "I am witnessing" it is nothing but self-deception. It is the mind watching the working of the mind. It is not witnessing. The mind watching the mind is horizontal in phenomenal time, comparing and judging the reactions all the time.

◘◘◘

Even when there's no "me," there's still the body-mind process. When you talk about witnessing after enlightenment, after there is no "me," is there any sense of separation between that which witnesses and that which appears as phenomenon?

The witnessing is a noumenal functioning. There is no "witnesser" witnessing anything, which is precisely the absence of the mind. If there is a mind, there is a "me" witnessing an event and therefore there is judging and comparing. In this case, there is no comparing. It is pure witnessing in which there is no witnesser as an individual. Therefore, *the* witness is a misconception. There is never *the* witness, or *a* witness. There can only be witness*ing*, as in noumenal functioning. In discussions with Maharaj, when someone would say, "I witness," Maharaj would stop and say, "That is not witnessing."

◘◘◘

– THE CONTINUED FUNCTIONING OF CONDITIONING –

You spoke of the conditioned mind, and that an enlightened being has no conditioning. But Maharaj was conditioned to your arriving fifteen minutes early and was upset when you came only five minutes early. Wasn't his mind conditioned?

Yes, that's a good point. When Maharaj was asked, "Do you have thoughts?" He said, "Not only thoughts, but desires and emotions arise. But they are not taken delivery of. Thoughts or desires may arise but they are merely witnessed." Even after enlightenment the organism continues to function and it can *only* function according to its inherent characteristics. One of the characteristics of Maharaj was impatience and this was a symptom of impatience.

He was conditioned, however, to expect you fifteen minutes early, regularly.

There were visitors waiting. So because of his nature, his impatience came up. In a *jnani*, thoughts and worries arise and are merely witnessed. They do not leave any remnant. You could see Maharaj get violently angry with someone, but literally the next minute the man would say something and Maharaj would be delighted. There was never any remnant of any reaction. The reaction was spontaneous and it was accepted. But if the understanding had not been complete and true then that organism would have thought, "I'm supposed to be a *jnani*, I'm not supposed to get angry. I must remember not to get angry." Maharaj couldn't care less. Anger arose and that was it. Even after enlightenment, the range of differences between the body-mind organisms to which enlightenment has occurred is enormous. Maharaj was full of fiery temper, whereas Ramana Maharshi was placid, rarely getting angry. That was the difference between the original characteristics of the respective organisms. They continue to function more or less according to the same characteristics. So it is not that enlightenment produces a clone of an enlightened being.

◘◘◘

– CAUSALITY –

If there is no longer a person in a jnani, *are there still causes and effects? Does the law of causality still affect the* jnani?

Oh yes, the whole drama is based on causation. Certain acts take place and have their consequences. Those consequences become acts for further consequences. Cause and effect goes on all the time. That is causation, which is evolution.

For the jnani, *though...*

The *jnani* is not concerned with this causation. Causation happens and the *jnani* merely witnesses it. All that goes on is merely witnessed, including his role.

But for the body-mind of the jnani *the causation still goes on?*

Certainly, the body-mind of the *jnani* is part of the causation and functioning. Whatever happens through that body-mind happens precisely as do acts and their consequences in any other body-mind mechanism.

So the spontaneous actions that happen through the jnani *still have repercussions that may return upon him.*

"That may return upon him." Who's "him"? The actions that take place through the body-mind mechanism of a *jnani*, even after enlightenment, will certainly have consequences on the body. If the *jnani* talks and certain people listen, then that talking/listening event will certainly have repercussions, hopefully beneficial! Such talking could certainly bring exhaustion to the body. But the *jnani* is not concerned.

◘◘◘

– THOUGHTS, DESIRES AND EMOTIONS –

If you get angry, what do you do with that?

I will come to me, but let us first take you. What really happens when you say you're angry? Basically, tell me, when you say you're angry, what do you really mean?

I would say I have some kind of attachment to something, or I'm misperceiving...

No, no, no, I'm not talking about the cause of the anger. I'm not asking about the *reason* for your being angry. When you say you are angry, it can only be at the present moment, you see? There was no anger earlier. Anger arises in the present moment, is that right?

Yes.

So, when you say you are angry, what you really mean is, in that present moment, there is anger, is that right?

Yes.

So, what arises is a sense of anger, whatever the cause. What arises is an experience of anger in that present moment. Then, when you take delivery of that anger and say, "I am angry," what happens is that you get horizontally involved with that anger. The arising of the anger is a vertical thing. You have no control of it. The arising of a thought or emotion is beyond your control. It is an event from outside. It can be anything. There can appear a sense of joy for no reason! A sense of fear arises, then you go into "Why am I afraid?" That thought, or a feeling of anger, is something which arises over which no one can have any control, whether there has been enlightenment or not. So when the feeling of anger arises you get involved in it horizontally and say, "I am angry. Why am I angry? For this reason or that reason I should not have gotten angry." But all of it is horizontal, in time. The original arising of this anger is vertical, in the present moment. The *jnani* does not get involved horizontally, in time. In your case, you get angry and annoyed and decide to try to find out what the anger is and how to get rid of it, what you can do to take revenge, or whatever. (laughter) That is horizontal involvement.

And you don't recommend that.

Recommend it?! If you are happy with it, by all means, enjoy it. Now I'll come back to what happens if I am angry. The point is, "I" am not angry. I have no control over an arising of a thought or an arising of fear, or anger or whatever. Arising of any thought, emotion or feeling is independent of the organism. The question is, "What happens to the organism when in the present moment anger arises?" You get involved. I don't. The feeling of anger must arise if I have no control over it. Then that feeling of anger is witnessed. There's no involvement. That anger arises vertically, it gets witnessed and cut off. There is no horizontal involvement.

You mean, you witness it and you let go?

No. *I* don't let go. That is the whole point.

You accept it?

No, *I* don't even accept it. *I* neither accept it nor reject it because that would mean...

You recognize it immediately?

It is witnessed. Without the agency of a witnesser.

◻◻◻

Would you say enlightenment is a way of playing the game in which there is no suffering or frustration?

No. For example, there is grief and you see that, you play the game but you do not respond to it. It's not that there are no thoughts or emotions in the body-mind organism after enlightenment. That is not correct. After enlightenment the body-mind continues to be an organism, and the organism reacts to an outside thought or event according to his own natural characteristics. But the moment a reaction arises, it is witnessed and gets cut off. There is no involvement horizontally.

Take pleasure, for example. I was once asked, "If you find somebody really understanding, and you see the transformation, do you not feel gratified?" A sense of gratification arises. It *must.* In an organism, any thought, feeling, or emotion *must* arise. But it is witnessed and then it gets cut off. If there is a bereavement in the family, grief arises but it is not carried over in duration. The body-mind organism doesn't live with that grief. Overwhelming grief can arise and then the organism continues to behave as before.

Is that true with fear also?

Yes indeed, it is true with fear. And particularly when there is a negative emotion like that.

I'm still thinking about this concept of functioning and desire. Would it be correct to say that desire continues on an impersonal level even after the "me" disappears?

Thoughts, desires, emotions may arise. Maharaj used to use the expression, "They are never taken delivery of," meaning there is no horizontal involvement. They arise, they are witnessed, they get cut off.

But the functioning itself...I have a hard time understanding functioning without desire.

Desires may arise, but they don't necessarily lead to involvement. In an ordinary person, desires most often lead to involvement.

For instance, Maharaj was addicted to smoking. If he had a desire to smoke, he lit a cigarette. His body-mind mechanism was addicted to that.

If he felt hungry, he ate, if he felt like walking, he walked.

But isn't such addiction the same as desire?

Precisely. Desires arise, because they are part of the consciousness. But the individual organism, after enlightenment or understanding, whatever you call it, merely witnesses the desires. They are not taken delivery of.

So they do lead to action nevertheless.

If the desire is something like hunger or thirst, that thought is actualized into action.

Without the mind participating?

Correct.

ロロロ

Forgive me if this sounds a little personal. Toward the end of what you read to us earlier, I noticed that you had what I would call an emotional reaction. There were tears and hesitation in your voice, a noticeable change in your demeanor. May I ask what movement that was?

It just arose! It was a movement in Consciousness over which I had no control.

Was thought or imagery associated with it?

A body-mind organism in which enlightenment has happened doesn't become a vegetable. Thoughts will arise. Emotions arise. But those thoughts or emotions or desires are not taken delivery of. They just happen. There's no personal reaction like embarrassment. Nor would I feel, "See how sensitive I am."

How about pain? Body pain. There is some kind of suffering at some level?

Oh, you mean *this* body? Of course there is. Certainly.

But because "you" don't exist, you sort of have nothing to do with it?

That is correct.

Ramesh, you said that the jnani, *the Self-Realized person, will identify with his body but not as the doer. Does the same thing apply to the emotions and to the thoughts?*

Yes! Precisely. He does not identify with whatever arises. It is merely witnessed. And one more thing: the *jnani* is never ever aware that he is a *jnani.*

There is no need to be a jnani?

That is precisely the point. There is no need. It's there! Whatever is happening is just happening. That is the point which is often not really understood. Once the enlightenment has happened, there is no further need to remember that enlightenment has happened! If there is, enlightenment has not happened.

Unless I ask you what state you are in?

Ah, yes. Then there's a question and an answer, but in the normal behavior there is never any need to question, "Am I doing this right or am I doing wrong? I'm supposed to be a *jnani,* I'm not supposed to do that."

When an individual considers himself a jnani, *he's separating himself from others, which is what the* jnani *does not do. Correct?*

Correct.

Ramesh, when it happened to you, did you feel that you lost interest in worldly things?

No, the only difference was that the sense of doership left. It so happened that in this organism there was always this sense that the organism is not the doer, that whatever happens is part of the functioning of Totality, and that that's the destiny of this organism. So the transformation was not as

momentous as you might think. At least in this body-mind
mechanism, the transformation was more or less spontaneous but not a momentous transformation. I always had these
two convictions: one, that this is an illusion, that nothing
really matters, and two, that whatever is happening is happening by itself and I cannot change it.

Did it happen that you found yourself losing desires for things?

No, no, desires don't disappear. Desires happen, but desires are just a thought. An emotion is a thought. Emotion,
desire, thought, they just arise, but they are not taken delivery of. Whatever arises, when it is witnessed, just disappears.
But the arising of that thought, emotion or desire is something beyond the control of the organism. The nature of the
mind can be either to "take delivery of" and get involved in
it or when the "me" is not there, the arising of it is witnessed
and it disappears.

*And sometimes acted upon, if it is to be, but without involve-
ment, right? Sometimes you act on the desires and sometimes you
look at it and it just disappears?*

A thought arises and the ordinary mind gets involved in
it; this is good or this is bad or something, and then decides
to act. But that action would be the same in any case. The
individual thinks he has decided, but the action was already
decided in Totality. Interference of the thinking mind doesn't
happen in the case of the *jnani*. A thought arises such as "I'm
hungry," and if that thought needs action I go and eat.

If there is no food, would you get angry?

There has rarely been an occasion when I had nothing to
eat.

(laughing) That is the best answer.

It is the best possible answer. I'll tell you why. You are
asking me, as an individual to an individual, what this
individual would do in certain circumstances. What I'm

saying is, I do not know what will happen in certain given circumstances, in certain hypothetical circumstances. If there is someone who is active and whose basic nature is to acquire something, then in that case that organism would probably snatch it from someone else who does have something to eat, enlightenment or no enlightenment. But where the organism is more passive by nature, he would probably not bother.

So you might *get angry?*

Yes, the anger could arise. Maharaj was once asked, "Maharaj, why do you get angry?" He said, "Who is getting angry?" He was not playing with words. The anger arises and then is gone. It doesn't keep sizzling.

Could you not act on the anger?

What I'm saying is that the anger *could* result in an action, yes. And that anger could result in an action which could lead this body-mind organism to be punished. Certainly.

Even in the case of a jnani?

Yes. There really is no *jnani*. After enlightenment happens, whatever event happens, the arising of the anger, the resulting action, which action gets punished, all that is witnessed. Not as my action but as part of the functioning of Totality.

So, really, anyone can become an enlightened being even if they're imperfect, even if they have desires, even if they do wrong, as long as there is the conviction they are not the doer, that they are just instruments?

When enlightenment happens, the organism does not become perfect. It is whole and the whole includes both opposites. Seeking perfection is the basic, primary folly and the *jnani* understands that. That is the basis of the understanding. Whatever happens is part of the functioning of Totality.

And that brings inner peace?

Inner tranquillity, or peace, it's just another word.

❏❏❏

– ACTION –

It would seem that the jnani *is not actually involved, that the* jnani *himself is the Consciousness that is not involved, but the functional relationship goes on?*

Yes, that's why there is no involvement. There is merely witnessing an event so long as there is something to witness. If there is nothing to witness, the state goes into a non-witnessing state.

In that state then, what would motivate an enlightened person to do anything? It sounds like they are reacting to their circumstances.

When I say "an enlightened person," there is no such thing, no such thing as an enlightened "person" at all. So the question of motivation does not arise. All actions which take place through such a body-mind mechanism are spontaneous. The mind has not intruded before an action takes place. That is what I mean when I say that the actions of a *jnani* need not necessarily stand to reason or consistency.

Is there ever a confusion in action when this awareness takes place as to what to do, instead of this spontaneity? Would there be a confusion?

No, the inherent aspect of this spontaneity is the absence of confusion. Confusion is a state of the mind. In spontaneity the mind is totally kept out.

So action is happening. Is there misjudgment happening also?

No. In the action and the spontaneity of it there is no confusion, and there is no judgment or misjudgment. Confusion and judgment are really alike. In the judgment of this or that is confusion.

I think you said compassion or love are ways in which a jnani *might respond to a human need, but that he might appear to take care of the need at one time and in another situation he might appear to ignore the need. If there is one thing that I thought was consistent it was love, but evidently it is not.*

The state of compassion is prior to the affective conditions in duality; love-hate, sympathy-lack of sympathy. An underlying state of compassion is always there. In duality, whatever event takes place is *not* the act of a *jnani*. If an act is supposed to help someone, then what is apparently conceived as compassion will take place. But where another person is concerned, if he is not to receive the help, then the inaction will be an apparent ignoring of the need. In neither event is the enlightened person concerned as an individual. The misconception lies in the act being related to the enlightened person. There is no relationship between the act that happens and the body-mind mechanism that is enlightened through which it happens or does not happen. The organism is merely an instrument.

◘◘◘

– REACTING TO EVENTS –

You said that when one sees clearly, the thinking mind will have less scope to do damage. Were you speaking of someone who is living in phenomenality? Does the jnani *have less scope?*

The thinking mind of the *jnani* has long been destroyed. Thinking mind *is* the "me." Thinking mind *is* the ego.

A jnani *can experience terror?*

The *jnani* does not *experience* terror. Terror can happen. Terror can arise in Consciousness.

Because of the jnani's *inherent characteristics?*

Correct. The organism reacts. If this enlightenment has happened in an organism which is of the somatotonic type, where the organism is ready to fight, the reaction to an event may not be terror, the reaction may be to resist it. But if the organism is a softer kind like the viscerotonic, then the terror might spring up and this organism might act in another way. What I am saying is, in hypothetical circumstances how the organism in which enlightenment has happened may react is unknowable. But from the standpoint of the *jnani* there is no *one* to be concerned, whatever is the reaction.

"What will the reaction be?" is the thinking mind, which projects, "What will 'I' be doing in such circumstances?" See? That hypothetical situation is purely the creation of the thinking mind, and that won't be there in the case of the *jnani*.

At Maharaj's, one of the infrequent visitors, a Hindu, thought that all this passive attitude of the Hindu had made him a weakling, so he changed his religion to the militant Sikh. He once said, "Maharaj, again you are saying the same thing: 'You have to accept what-is.' I cannot accept it. If tomorrow I come with a group of other militants and I start beating up these people who are here, what will you do?"

Maharaj said, "I don't know." Everybody laughed. Big joke. But Maharaj found me staring at him. He said, "What's the matter? Don't you think it was a good joke?"

I said, "It might have been a joke or not, I don't know. But you could not have uttered words which were more accurately correct." He looked at me. He knew what I meant.

Another visitor said, "What's going on between you and Maharaj?" We talked, of course in Marathi. I looked at Maharaj. Nothing was said or done without Maharaj's express sanction. He was a strict man! One of his injunctions was, "Nobody discusses my teaching except in my presence." He didn't want a Maharaj Club, where people met and discussed the subject like politics.

After Maharaj gave his approval, I told the visitor that the way I understood Maharaj's words was that the question was asked by an individual to another individual but here there was no individual. So the accurate response to "What will happen in these circumstances?" is "I don't know." The individual says, in such and such circumstances I would do such and such things. Here, there was no individual. Tomorrow if this happens, it may be that Maharaj will do nothing but some other people in the audience will resist. In identical circumstances, another day, exactly the opposite may happen, Maharaj may suddenly pick up a staff and resist.

Even when the thinking mind assumes that in such circumstances it would know what it would do, it may not happen as it predicts. A soldier, for instance, with three generations of military records behind him would say, "That's easy. In such circumstances I would do this or I wouldn't do that." And yet in the heat of the moment this soldier with three generations of soldiering behind him may run away. On the other hand, someone who was always rather timid could perform fantastically heroic acts.

In the last World War, the person who had the maximum number of medals was a comparatively small man, not even an officer, just a corporal I think, who in the spur of the moment acted with such bravery that he was the most decorated man. To think of what will happen in hypothetical circumstances is a waste of time. But that doesn't mean that the working mind, in doing its work, does not project. The memory is drawn upon by the working mind as much as by the thinking mind. The working mind does draw on the memory. In fact it *has* to draw upon the memory so that its working can be more efficient. But worrying is not a part of it.

🌑🌑🌑

– "WHO AM I?" FOR THE ENLIGHTENED –

I believe you said that when enlightenment happens and you no longer identify with the individual body, that your body becomes the Totality.

No, no, no, not the *body*.

No. I'm saying, when Consciousness no longer identifies with the individual body...

As the *doer*. But identification with the body must continue. Otherwise, how will the body function? That's why I said, "Jesus or Buddha or any master, if called would respond." The identification with the body *does* continue. And what is more, once this understanding is there, that he is not the doer, it is still necessary to use the words "I" and "mine." If I kept saying "Ramesh" all the time, it would look silly and it would be silly. Why should I not prefer to use the words "I" and "mine" when referring to the body? Once I know that Ramesh is not the doer, why should I not use the words?

Maybe I'm phrasing this wrong... If I were to ask you or someone who is God-realized, "Who are you?" the immediate reaction would be, "I am the Totality of space," right?

I would rather be inclined to say, "I am not this body-mind apparatus that you think I am."

The way I understand the literature is that when Consciousness is no longer confined to the identity of the ego-mind-body, it becomes Totality.

Yes.

In that situation, I'm just trying to imagine, if I identified my body as being the Totality of space then all phenomena, all bodies are within my body.

No. The body is totally different. Once you disidentify yourself from your body as the doer, you don't have to identify yourself with anything else. That is the point.

The closest thing would be space, though. The constant of space that contains everything.

Yes, but the fact is that you think you are Totality. Who thinks he's the Totality? There's no need of identification with the Totality.

But if Consciousness were conscious of itself then obviously all phenomena would be within that Consciousness. Like the analogy of the aquarium: in the aquarium is part of *the aquarium. I'm just trying to imagine. If Consciousness identifies itself with the Totality of space, then I could see where Consciousness would be no more attached to this body than it would be to that body, or to that body, because all bodies are within that Consciousness.*

Yes, quite so, but it is not that the differences are not seen. The difference, the variety is not only seen, but then really understood and appreciated, with a sense of wonder that there would be such tremendous diversity and yet in that diversity there is the one unicity prevailing throughout. The thought doesn't even occur that "I am the Totality." There's no need of that thought. Once identification with this body-mind organism as the individual doer disappears, then no further conclusion is necessary. Everything in this magnificent diversity is understood. I'll tell you a joke about this "Who are you?" A friend of mine in San Francisco was keeping track of me, so he rang up Ray to ask if I had arrived. Ray said, "Not yet, but who are you?" and Adrien replied, "*That*, my friend, is a very, very deep question."

But a jnani *would not consider that a deep question. As I understand it, the only answer a* jnani *would give would be...*

He would say, "Ramesh here."

◘◘◘

– VIRTUE –

Is the jnani *virtuous?*

It is the unselfconscious living of a sage, with a totally uncontrived skill in dealing with social and practical matters, which may be referred to as virtue. Lao Tzu says about such unselfconscious living, "Superior virtue is not intentionally virtuous, and thus is virtue. Inferior virtue does not let go of being virtuous, and thus is not virtue. Superior virtue uses no force, but nothing is left undone. Inferior virtue uses force but achieves nothing."

The ordinary man wants to be virtuous, wants to be known as virtuous. Lao Tzu would say that this is not virtue. The naturally virtuous man goes about his business and the things which happen through him are virtuous because there is no personal intention. There is nothing personal he wants from anybody. Courageous, natural living is thus based on an inherent feeling, as distinct from artificial virtue, based on adherence to a certain set of rules of conduct. Such artificial adherence to rules is necessarily accompanied by the fear and guilt of misinterpretation in given circumstances. The virtue and unpretentious naturalness of the sage often goes unnoticed because of its ordinariness.

Perhaps this is because it involves a sort of spiritual anonymity that works like the natural and unintentional coloring of a bird or animal. To quote Lao Tzu again, "The greatest perfection seems imperfect, yet its use will last without decay. The greatest fullness seems empty, yet its use cannot be exhausted. The greatest straightness seems crooked. The greatest dexterity seems awkward. The greatest eloquence seems stammering."

The virtue and unpretentious naturalness of the sage is not deliberate self-effacement, not punishing oneself like a masochist. Nor is it an assumed humility in the presence of something greater than ourselves. In an office, it's astonishing how extremely humble a man is in front of his superiors and how arrogant he can be in front of his subordinates. Humility is often a cloak that is worn and removed. In the case of simple, spontaneous living, humility is part of the living. The truly virtuous man doesn't have to ask himself, "Should I appear humble or not appear humble?" It is more like the innocent practicality of a cat.

The sage, or the wise man is well aware of the artificialities of the world of men.

How does this naturalness arise? Can it be acquired?

The question is based on the same desire as to learn the secret of the expert of any skill, either in a step-by-step method, or by being told in words. How is it that people ask for dancing to be explained to them instead of just watching and following? Why is there formal instruction to teach something so natural as swimming? Why do human beings have to read books to understand copulation?

The mythologies of many cultures contain the theme that man has fallen from grace or has separated himself from nature and has had to replace it with technology. As Lao Tzu said, "When the great *Tao* was lost, there came ideas of humanity and justice. When knowledge and cleverness arrived, there came great deceptions. When familial relations went out of harmony, there came ideas of good parents and loyal children. When the nation fell into disorder and misrule, there came ideas of loyal ministers."

◻◻◻

– MORALITY AND SOCIAL VALUES –

Socrates and Jesus Christ were condemned to death for offending against the moralities of the societies in which they lived.

That is correct. For offenses against the standards of morality prevailing at that time.

That seems to answer, for me, most of the concerns that people seem to be having about the relationship between morality on an everyday level, on a political and social level, and the state of Consciousness that you're trying to get at. They don't relate.

That is correct. In fact, you see, Jesus Christ was crucified not without reason. The reason was based on criteria which prevailed in society and law at that time. But that didn't prevent Jesus Christ from doing precisely what he did.

I'm not thinking of good and evil in terms of society's laws. I'm thinking of it in a different sense.

From the enlightened person's point of view, this question wouldn't arise at all. All action is spontaneous. He never decides. It is not possible for him to decide, since the sense of personal doership is not there. "Should I or should I not do this?" does not arise.

There is no malice and forethought in the actions of the enlightened?

That is correct. There is no malice or forethought. And if you consider that as goodness, of course it is goodness. But, how that goodness will work out in a spontaneous action nobody can tell.

Are there loving forethoughts in this understanding?

There is no forethought.

Not at all?

Not at all! (laughter) Either to do good or to do ill.

But merely to be the instrument of...

That is the inherent understanding. At the moment of action it is not as if the mind says, "Should I or should I not do it?" and then says, "Oh, what does it matter. I'm not the doer either. I'm only an instrument." All this is still the mind working. And that is just not there, you see. The thinking mind is just not there. The thinking mind is the mind of the doer.

Once the sense of "me" and separateness falls away, doesn't love flow forth?

Yes. But then what do you mean by love?

A sense of oneness.

You can call it love, or a sense of compassion, or whatever. You can call it compassion, you can call it love, you can call it tolerance, you can call it equanimity, you can call it tranquillity. They're all labels and it doesn't matter. There's no need to give any labels at all.

But would you say that an enlightened person wouldn't plan to kill?

Yes. Yes I would say that.

In Jesus saying that God is love, that would then be an incomplete statement?

Yes. But a statement which the individuals he was addressing could understand, you see.

So, in other words, Jesus himself may have had the understanding?

Indeed! He said it quite often, "I and my father are one. The kingdom of God is within." There is no question of it, Jesus had total understanding. But in conveying that understanding he had to come down to the level of his listeners.

ꓷꓷꓷ

– DEATH –

Would you say there is no difference between Consciousness-at--rest and Consciousness-in-motion?

There is no basic, essential difference.

What's being perceived is Consciousness-in-motion in all this beautiful variety?

That is correct, yes.

So the idea of death, then, is only a cessation of the movement of the perception part? With death, the perceiving ceases?

Perceiving would cease at death in any body-mind organism, whether enlightenment has happened or not.

But, with the understanding that perceiving is an impersonal activity, there would be no sense of anything being lost, it would just...

You mean at the moment of death? Once death happens?

No, prior.

Ah!

So there would not be the fear of any loss, no attachment.

None at all. That is why the deaths of many saints are described as beautiful events. Death is not seen as something happening to a "me," because the "me" does not exist. The process of death is merely witnessed. And for witnessing to happen, the "me" is no longer there.

And there is no fear?

Basically, you are quite right. There would be no sense of fear or loss.

Is there any difference between the death of the body-mind organism of an ordinary person and a jnani?

None. Absolutely none. A terrible confusion is created because of this considering a body-mind organism as a *jnani*, as an individual, as an enlightened *person*. You think that the organism suddenly gets transformed into something. Nothing of this sort happens! After enlightenment, or awakening, the body-mind organism continues to function, more or less as it did earlier. The body-mind organism will function according to its natural characteristics.

So the sense of doership has been eliminated. But the same thing happens when the body-mind organism of the ordinary person dies. The sense of doership is eliminated then also. So there's no difference?

None! After death, as far as the body-mind mechanism is concerned, there is no difference. And no difference in the Consciousness either. In one case the Consciousness has ceased to identify before the body-mind organism dies and in the other case the body-mind organism has ceased to identify when death occurs.

That's the only difference between the jnani *and the ordinary person?*

That is correct!

◼◼◼

7

THE IMPERSONAL PROCESS OF DISIDENTIFICATION

– A BROAD OVERVIEW –

What is it like to experience a sudden *dissolution of everything?*

The direct and immediate answer is, "Who wants to know?" But look at it in this way. It would be precisely like being in deep sleep. Everyone knows what deep sleep is, but when you're asked to describe what it is like to be in deep sleep, what can you say?

The significance of the question is really not the question itself, but the fact that the "me" wants to know what it is like. The event, as an event, is not accepted. Always there's a question, "Who?" For example, the word accident means something happening without premeditation, without cause. And yet we always ask who caused an accident? The mind always wants to know who is responsible. It is this question of "who" which is at the basis of all human problems. If the event is accepted and it is accepted that the instrument through which the event occurred is not of the essence, it is so much simpler to be transformed from personality to impersonality, from individualism to the universality.

There's a story of a beautiful Buddhist text being read by a master. At the end of the story the question promptly arose, "Who wrote it?" The master said, "If I told you that the Buddha wrote it, you'd worship it every morning with flowers. If I told you that it was written by a patriarch, you would still honor it, but not venerate or worship it as you would if the Buddha had written it. If I told you that one of the monks had written it, you wouldn't know how to accept that information. And if I told you that the cook had written it, you'd laugh at it."

Really, the "who" is not material, You see a beautiful painting and promptly ask, "Who painted it?" There is not acceptance that the *event* is what is significant. In order that actions should take place, the instruments, the "who"s are created. The "who"s are merely instruments through which events happen. I always felt that the easiest way to understand this would be to accept the whole world, the whole functioning of the Totality, as the work of a novelist. Certain actions are created through certain organisms. Those actions have results, effects. So fresh characters are created by the novelist through whom those events could take place. Deeds are not created for the instruments, the organisms. The organisms are created with certain given characteristics so that certain actions can take place. When this understanding is the base of everyday living, you can say and do whatever is appropriate.

When Christ says we should not have any anxiety about the morrow, he is not suggesting that we should be completely irresponsible. Lack of anxiety about the morrow is to be combined with "earning one's bread with the sweat of one's brow." Combine the two and you have the *mantra* for beautiful natural living. It is the anxiety for the morrow which brings about tensions. We find our ordinary life full of tensions. How true is the quip, "I've had a terrible life. Thank God most of it never happened."

The entire burden of the *Bhagavad Gita* is, as Krishna tells Arjuna, "You have been given a certain role in this dream play. You must play that role without any anxiety about the consequences. All you can do is to act your role to the best of your ability. The consequences are not in your hands."

If this one simple message goes home, there's nothing further to be done. This understanding is that change is the basis of life, that the opposites are interconnected polarities and not irreconcilables over which we have to make a choice. Then the thinking mind does not intrude or oppress the working mind and the working mind is free to concentrate on what it is doing.

When this understanding takes place, it is not an exception, but the rule that at the end of the day your work has been completed more efficiently, in much shorter time, with almost no tension.

"So, what will it get me?" the "me" asks. If you expect something of it, it will get you nothing. Without expecting anything, and the basis of this understanding is that the expectation itself is stopped, then the understanding works in its own magical, mysterious way. The working mind works without the oppression of the thinking mind. The work gets done more quickly, efficiently, without tension. So there *is* a benefit.

Understanding and living are not separate. The understanding brings about a definite change in one's life and living and that change is so natural, so spontaneous that very often it will not be recognized. That change will be recognized, curiously, only by others. Because you act naturally, ordinarily, most basically, you do not expect a change. Therefore the change occurs. The change occurs and is seen by others. How would you know it? You keep on doing precisely what you are doing without that sense of anxiety and wanting. Somehow that gets communicated to others with whom you come in contact. People say, "There's been some change in John." The change is, he is no longer anxious to please somebody and he is no longer anxious that the world satisfy him. He finds people coming to him, discussing their problems freely, asking his advice, and since it is not tainted by self-interest that advice is usually open. It would hardly be advice. It would be more, in effect, analyzing the problem itself. He himself would not realize why this increase in his popularity. The obvious fact is that that popularity has come about for the simple reason that he didn't *want* to be popular. He just carries on with his normal life.

So the understanding does have an effect, a very good effect, not only on your own physical and mental health, but on those with whom you come in contact. But there is a danger! If the understanding is not deep enough, this being considered as the wise man in the group can be very heady stuff. If the "wise man" wants to continue being the wise man the spontaneity will be lost and it will not be long before he is found out.

Why are we here today?

Obviously, you're all here seeking something. What is it you are seeking? What you're seeking is certainly not something you can see, nor is it something you can hear or taste or smell or touch. That means what you're seeking is not an object. So that which is sought is not an object. And who is seeking? That which is seeking, has to be the subject. The subject seeks an object and that which you seek you think is an object. But what is it that is seeking? That which is seeking is basically an object. When you think *you* are seeking, what is it that you think is seeking? We think in terms of a "me" that is seeking, but what is seeking is really a body-mind organism, an apparatus which is seeking and calls itself "me." Something is identified with a body-mind organism and says, "I am seeking." That something is Consciousness.

So that which you think is seeking is really an object, an object which is part of the totality of manifestation.

There is no difference between any objects in this manifestation. All objects are merely appearances in Consciousness. What you think is the subject, "yourself," is really an object perceived by another object who himself thinks he is the subject. Someone else sees you. For him, he's the subject and you're the object. But basically, both the observer and the observed are objects.

What is this paradox? Who is seeking what? The only satisfactory answer is, that Consciousness is seeking itself. It's the Subject seeking itself. Consciousness, which has identified itself with each individual human organism, then calls itself, "me." The "me" is merely a concept. It is impersonal Consciousness identified as personal consciousness. It is the personal consciousness which seeks its source, the Universal Consciousness. Consciousness, as the subject, seeks itself.

It is this peculiar game which the Hindu philosophy calls *lila*. There is no explanation for it. The mystic has long been saying that this manifestation is an appearance in Consciousness, perceived by Consciousness, and that the entire manifestation has been an impersonal process. Today, the scientist says the entire manifestation is a self generated process, meaning it's just happening by itself. This impersonal process is the seeking with which we identify ourselves. We believe that, "I am seeking something," meaning the "me" is seeking something. The seeking then becomes a tremendous misery.

Why does the individual consider himself a separate subject?

This part of it, that all there is, is Consciousness and the entire manifestation is merely an appearance in Consciousness, is intelligible at least to the intellect. But it is not *acceptable*. That is because this is a solid body.

Right, so how can I consider it as a mere appearance?

Identification with the body is so total that it gives one a sense of a separate identity. Now, this separate identity is merely a concept, a concept based on the individual body appearing solid. Is the body really solid? The mystic has always said that the body is merely an appearance, it is an emptiness. But the scientist today, has come to the conclusion that the body is merely the vibration of energy in a particular pattern. Cells are constantly being destroyed, new cells are being created, the energy continues but that energy is ultimately without substance.

ꓘꓘꓘ

– SUDDEN UNDERSTANDING –

Are you saying that the seeker and the ego are different?

No. They are the same. And therefore the seeking must begin with the individual. The seeking begins with the individual, and ends when the individual seeker realizes that all this time what he has been seeking is what he actually *is*, that the seeker *is* the sought, that there never had been an individual seeking.

But it begins with an individual and finally can cease only when this "individual me" is totally annihilated, when there is an intuitive insight in which there is no individual comprehender. That is why they say, it is a *sudden* understanding.

So then the seeker drops off.

Yes, the seeker drops off. When the seeker drops off, when the duration drops off and when the time drops off, this understanding is sudden. That understanding can only be in a different dimension. Not in time duration.

Is seeking inevitable?

Seeking is inevitable. That is correct.

Is not enlightenment therefore inevitable also?

Yes, yes indeed. But it is inevitable as an impersonal process for which there has to be an end. Now, in which body-mind organism it will happen you are not concerned. That is the understanding. In whichever body-mind organism it happens, it is not the body-mind organism that is going to be enlightened. It is merely an object through which this impersonal happening will occur. And therefore you are not concerned which body-mind organism it happens in. This notion of "me" is not being evolved. A physical organism is being evolved so that ultimately this impersonal happening can happen through that physical organism.

◘◘◘

I don't understand. It seems as if I have choice. I chose to come here rather than go to the beach today.

Supposed volition and freedom of choice of action are only concepts. What is so difficult to understand? The very curiosity concerning the true nature of the universe and the role of the human being therein is itself an intended part of the original objectivization. Wanting to know our true nature is itself part of the functioning of Totality. We are supposed to find out our true nature. In finding out our true nature, we come to the realization that we are not what we seem to be as individual objects. We are that of which the entire manifestation is merely a mirrored objectivization.

Still, it's frustrating.

The search, reaching all kinds of frustrations, is part of this process. The "me" wanting to know the "I," its source, is a game of hide-and-seek. Ramana Maharshi once said to a disciple wanting in great distress to know his true nature, "When you *do* understand, you will recollect this frustrating wanting-to-know incident with great amusement."

Until that moment this joke is an extraordinarily tragic one. Until the search, which begins with the individual and ends with the annihilation of the individual, until this fruit-less search is realized as being fruitless, it's truly tragic.

◘◘◘

– AN IMPERSONAL FUNCTIONING OF TOTALITY –

Ramesh, in manifestation Consciousness identifies itself with the mechanism that is labeled as a "me."

Yes.

The process of life is taken personally.

Yes.

As the disidentification occurs, identified consciousness is real-izing that it is an impersonal process.

Yes.

So, all "my" choices are being made by Consciousness.

Yes. The choice from Consciousness might be to eat a pound of chocolate chip cookies, but the effect would be to not feel that great. Other choices are made to eat certain foods or maybe to meditate and the effect is that the mind-body mechanism feels good.

If the process is approached as impersonal, as just the watcher watching the impersonal events, the choice being made through Consciousness, whatever is done, whether it's eating this, sitting here, or meditating, then it's okay. If it's approached another way it reinforces the "me."

You see, whatever action happens, whether you eat ice cream or meditate, at that moment you could not have done otherwise.

Whether that mind-body mechanism is still meditating, not meditating, going to retreats, or not going to retreats really doesn't matter.

Quite so.

I have a desire to eat chocolate. But I was told that it is not good for me, so it's a conflict.

Yes, so what happens is precisely what is going to happen.

But my mind wavers.

The mind will waver, but ultimately you will decide—you *think* you will decide—that you will not eat chocolates and therefore be healthy. Or if you are destined not to be healthy then you will think you will decide to eat chocolate!

So I could not get away from it.

That's the point. You're stuck with it. Let me put it this way: you say, "I made a bad investment and therefore I lost money." Or someone else says, "I made a good investment and therefore I made a profit." What I'm saying is, if you were supposed to lose money the thought will come into your mind to invest in what is a bad investment. If you are supposed to make money, a thought will come and because of it you will make what you think is a good investment.

It is not my choice.

It is *not* your choice. You think it is your choice, and you are *supposed* to think it is your choice, that is the joke of it, you see.

That's the problem, you know.

It *is* the problem, and what is more, you are supposed to have that problem until the process of disidentification reaches a certain point.

❑❑❑

Mr. Balsekar, is not this asking, "Who wants to know?" like a poisoning against any other concepts? Doesn't it bring you to a state of complete stillness of your mind?

You're quite right.

Because when I ask who I am, I'm coming full circle.

That is the point. Precisely.

I cannot get out of the loop. I'm stuck there.

Yes. That is the mental stick with which you hit yourself.

Yet sometimes asking "who," takes me to the stillness of my mind, which takes me to the Source.

How beautifully said. That is so.

So this is the essence...

It *is* the essence! It is *indeed* the essence.

But shouldn't this asking be made in a certain manner?

This asking will be made in precisely the manner in which it is destined to be made. And if it is to be made at a certain time in the "wrong" way, it is going to be made in the "wrong" way.

Is it really destined, predestination?

Absolutely.

By?

By? (laughter) You see how the "who" and the "what" and the "how" arise!

So there is this ancient, impersonal process functioning through this body-mechanism.

Quite so. And in that evolutionary process, whatever is to be achieved, will be achieved through this body-mind mechanism. Nothing less. Nothing more.

So this "me" is dealing with someone else's property?

Precisely. Yes indeed. And it is also at the same time taking on someone else's problems, someone else's responsibility. Why take on someone else's guilt, someone else's responsibility? So don't worry, be happy. I can't sing it, but someone else can.

There is a very innate beauty in that, and reverence. I'm sure it brings tears. There's a happiness.

There is indeed. And this happiness, as you said, is nothing but acceptance. You can call it surrender if you like, but it is acceptance.

My mind asks, "Where do the tears come from, where does the laughter come from?" It seems that if I could lose the preoccupation with that "where from," I would be really free.

Put that in the passive tense and you'll be accurate.

You mean, "If it was lost?"

Yes. But if you say, "If I didn't have that preoccupation," it's not right.

Yes, I see. Then you're giving it a person.

Yes.

If there was no preoccupation with the source, there would be freedom.

That's it! And that situation can arise only at the appropriate time, at the appropriate place, and with the appropriate body-mind mechanism.

And until then we are always asking who or what...

Yes. Until then, you're stuck with it.

◻◻◻

Why is everybody chasing enlightenment? It seems to be literally much ado about nothing. And when you get into it, it doesn't seem to be any big deal. Next to sex, it's the most over-rated thing I ever heard of.

Yes, neither sex nor enlightenment is a big deal. I say with sex and enlightenment, take it as it comes. Why make a big deal of it? The whole life and living is a flow and if we accept that flow and get into that flow, life can be tremendously simple. Life presents problems because we fight life, we don't accept what-is in the present moment. We want to become something other than what we are. We want something other than what we now have.

Will you comment on the "still, small, voice"?

Yes. Hitler also reported the "still, small voice" which made him do things. He honestly thought that he was God's messenger on earth, sent to create the superior German nation. The small still voice can be misunderstood. This misunderstanding arises when there is a turning towards God, or Reality, without the appropriate turning away from the self. That's when the still small voice turns into hideous loud noises.

How do you know if it's valid or not?

You don't! So, any actions that had to take place through Hitler *did* take place because they had to take place. Hitler had nothing to do with it as an entity. Hitler was merely the instrument through which the horrible events that had to take place, took place.

As you just said, you cannot know, and therefore self deception is part of the functioning of Totality at that time. It is not created by Satan. All there is, is Consciousness. All there is, is God. So, whatever happens is according to His Will. But, because we have been conditioned to think of God only in terms of good to the total exclusion of what is considered evil, we say, "Why should this happen, why should there be a Hitler at all? Why should there have been religious persecution throughout history?" The answer is, "Why not?"

All of it is part of the functioning of Totality. The Totality is not concerned with good or bad. So, whatever happens in the working of the universe at the present moment, has to be accepted. Not accepting it means human misery. Until this acceptance happens, until there is Grace or whatever you call it and this acceptance or surrender happens, until then you are destined to be miserable.

Last June, an Armenian American came to me in Bombay. He had been traveling in India during March, April and May, the worst possible months to travel. He said he had traveled north to south, with great hopes of finding something precious, and all he found were *ashramites*, parroting Scriptures and greedy priests putting their hands out for money. He was terribly disappointed. He raved like this for twenty minutes. I brought him a bottle of chilled water and a glass. He drained it in a gulp, so I brought him another. When he had both literally and spiritually cooled down, he said, "Do you have anything to say to me?"

I said, "If you give me the chance!" Then he quieted down.

His story was that he was a successful engineer with one daughter, settled comfortably. One day he began to wonder what he was making more money for, since he had enough. He sold his business and started reading up on this subject and something drove him to come to India. He had just been to the Ramana Maharshi *ashrama*. While there, he had told someone his tale of woe who then gave him my address and telephone number, and so he had called and come by.

I said, "I'll give you one question to think of an answer to. You get an answer for that question, and you will have your answers for all your problems."

He said, "You mean it?"

I said, "Certainly I do! Just think what turned you, a perfectly happy engineer, into this miserable seeker? Did you give up your work and choose to be a seeker? What turned you into a seeker?"

We talked about it for a while. Then I said, "If some power turned you into a seeker, don't you think it is the responsibility of that power to take you where you are supposed to be taken? Why are you so intense? Why do you want that thirst to end at a particular time?"

◘◘◘

We like to think we are driving this body-mind, but the controls aren't connected are they?

Children playing in an amusement park steering toy cars are very serious. They think they are driving. What's more, they're supposed to think they are driving. They are *entertained* because they think they are driving.

Conversely, when you are driving a car on the road, you'd better think that you are controlling it.

Yes. But even there, at the real moment of a crisis, are you really in control of the car or does it *get* controlled?

◘◘◘

You say there is no method that can be used in this. But with some things that I do, I try to disidentify with whatever is in front of me and look at the possibility of just seeing it without being involved in it. Is that a way that Consciousness has of trying to give something to me?

Yes, but not to *you*. Through this body-mind organism the evolutionary process is going on, and in that process whatever is supposed to happen in this body-mind organism will happen. Whatever "progress," if you like, that is supposed to be made *will* be made. And for that to happen, such disciplinary practices as are needed will also happen. Therefore you find certain people going through various practices almost as a matter of compulsion, because that is precisely what they are supposed to do. And when they have done a certain amount of these practices, a moment may occur where there is a sudden understanding that all these practices "have not gotten me anywhere." Then those practices may cease. If the practices cease, that is also part of the functioning of Totality.

Are you saying that God is something outside, or is God the inherent nature underneath what we call our individuality?

What I am saying is all there *is*, is God. So, the question of whether God is outside or within is really irrelevant.

I'm saying that it's God, or Totality, or Consciousness which is functioning all the time through the billions of human organisms and all other organisms, as instruments. All the billions of human organisms are merely instruments through which God, or Totality, or Consciousness is functioning. It is the only power that has been functioning all these thousands of years, and it is that power that is functioning now, and that power that will continue to function. It is an illusion for us to think that we are doing whatever we are doing.

Ultimately, it all boils down to a matter of surrender?

Yes. Unless the "me" is absent the "I" cannot enter. Furthermore "you" cannot drive the "me" away. Who is to drive the "me" away? The "me" will not drive itself away. Therefore the ultimate happening, Buddhahood, enlightenment, is an impersonal happening. The acceptance of this fact is the biggest step. You cannot chase God. At the right time and place God will chase you. Then you will come to a stage when you will say, "Please God, I'm tired. Let me go or take me."

Ramana Maharshi says in his eleven verses: "You dragged me here now why do you keep me dangling? Why do you keep me in such misery?" When I first read them I thought they were Ramana Maharshi's own predicament, that he was still on the path. I was surprised to learn they were written after enlightenment. When his compassion welled up these eleven verses came out, embodying the misery of the seeker.

Seeking God is like a wisdom tooth. So long as it doesn't bother you, leave it alone. When the wisdom tooth starts hurting you naturally go to a dentist.

Seeking begins not on your volition, and seeking God *ends* not on your volition. Seeking God begins with the individual and ends with the end of the individual, with realizing there is no volition.

You said that the individual doesn't exist, yet you address us as individuals.

It is the individual who needs the push, the glance, to suddenly realize that there is no individual. Seeking starts with the individual and ends with the annihilation of the individual.

Because of the sense of individual entity, praying to a Divine entity developed. It was all right years ago, but now especially, the Western man is not prepared to pray and beseech an entity, Divine though it be. He is not prepared to surrender. Now, I've found the Western man prepared to accept the words, "Reality" or "Consciousness." But somehow, the moment I use the word "God" there's a feeling of uneasiness. Look what religion has done to revered words. Same thing with the word *"guru."* The *guru* in India is a revered personality. When the disciple finally understands what it is all about, he knows that there is no difference between him and the *guru*. And yet phenomenally the *guru* is still of tremendous importance to him. In India particularly, the relationship between the disciple and the *guru* continues even after enlightenment. But look what the word *"guru"* has come down to... a dirty word.

What I find most difficult is when you talk about it being a game, or a novel with characters, because in spite of all its difficulties, life seems to have a lot of beauty and meaning in it. The feeling that I have is that you take it away. That it gets lost.

If you are happy, live your life. Accept nothing said here. Make no changes. Who is to make any changes? If change happens, it will happen by itself. I'm being perfectly serious. You, as an individual need make no changes. Continue with your life. If you like reading, do it. If you're meditating, continue to meditate. If you've heard something here, fine. If not, fine. If some change is to occur as a consequence, let it take place. If the understanding at any level has any value, any worth, it must work its way out.

◻◻◻

Even when I think I'm making the progress, it's part of the...

Yes, it is part of the impersonal process.

There's no use fighting it.

Correct. There's no use fighting it. There's no use trying to hasten it. The basic understanding has to be that it is an impersonal process. And if it is an impersonal process in duration, you keep climbing.

Why should I keep climbing?

You cannot *help* climbing! You cannot *not* climb. You have been wound up! There is no way you can get out of it.

Like a puppet?

Yes, but that is again an important understanding: you cannot hasten the process, and you cannot stop it either. So this climbing keeps on happening, and as I say, you do get glimpses of the progress. And when there is at least a glimmer of the understanding that *you* are not making any progress, that the progress is *taking place,* then a certain amount of freedom takes over, freedom from the "me" that wants to hasten it. Then you know that it is an impersonal process. It must take its own time.

If the number of steps you have to climb is one hundred and thirty, then from the one hundred and twenty-fifth to the one hundred and twenty-ninth step you may see the light coming in. But at that moment you also have the understanding there is no "me" involved. So the sense of freedom has already started. The step from one hundred and twenty-nine to one hundred and thirty is always sudden, because you did not know there were one hundred and thirty steps. That is why awakening is always sudden. The ultimate understanding is always sudden.

If we knew how many steps there were it would take the charm out of it, I guess.

That is one way to look at it.

You said yesterday, "We've all been created for a certain pur-pose." I have a little trouble with that because Maharaj seems to imply, and I could identify with this, that there's no purpose, no meaning, that even those terms are human concepts.

Wait a minute! I think this confusion will not arise if you don't think in terms of "we" having been created. Who is "we"?

I understand that, but you made it sound like those body-mind organisms were created with certain characteristics for a certain action to take place.

Yes, that is correct. At any specific moment in time, certain actions take place. Those actions are also produced by Con-sciousness in this functioning. Those actions will produce certain effects. Then for there to be subsequent actions, which are the effects of the present actions, certain body-mind organisms will have to be created with given charac-teristics which will produce those actions.

Sounds a little like a prepared script. I have a lot of trouble with that.

Yes, it is a prepared script. But the individual does not realize it until there is enlightenment.

But why does it have to be like that?

Can you tell me why not?

Why couldn't it just be that evolution started and then because of things being the way they are certain things happen, but not the other way around?

The "Why?" and "Why not?" It is precisely for this reason that in Hindu philosophy the term, *lila* is used. It is one of those very few words with such tremendous significance that you'll find it very difficult to substitute any other words. The nearest I'll come to explaining the word *lila* is this: "Why the *lila*?" the only answer is, "Why not?"

Why can't it be total randomness?

You think this is a chance happening? There is no chance in this at all!

Ramesh, didn't you say that every effect has a cause? Is that what you mean?

Yes.

But not that there was any originating plan?

No. Everything has occurred now, simultaneously. Whatever was, *is.* Whatever is, *is.* Whatever shall be, also is*!*

◻◻◻

You're saying there is no point in effort in that our mind-body mechanisms receive experiences when we are ready to get them. Well then, why do we come here to hear you and why do we read books? Why did you go and spend time with your Master? I mean, if it is just going to happen anyway and we're just unfolding, are we just here because we like to be here and we enjoy hearing this?

You couldn't *help* being here! I couldn't help being here. This-which-is-talking and that-which-is-listening have to be here for the talking-listening to take place as one event. You think *you* are listening, but the listening is taking place through the body-mind mechanism and that is part of the process of disidentification, of enlightenment, that is going on. And in that process of disidentification, in that evolution-

THE IMPERSONAL PROCESS OF DISIDENTIFICATION   201

ary process, this is an event. This is a specific event. So this listening is taking place through this body-mind mechanism because it *has to be so* at this moment, at this place. That is part of the functioning of Totality.

Then do I just let go of this feeling that I am trying to get something and just show up where I show up, without thinking about going there, without wanting to get something?

Yes. But the point is, your wanting to let go and the letting go are two different things. The letting go will happen only when you're not wanting to let go.

But I can't...

It's a bit of a paradox. (laughter)

Right. And I can't try to not want to...

You see, that is the double bind. That is the double bind in this seeking. You will get it in perspective if you try to remember what made you a seeker. You didn't decide, "I will be a seeker" even if it might have happened on a particular day at a particular moment. But what is it that happened at that moment, on that day, which made you a seeker? Some thought, some urge, some force, turned this body-mind mechanism into a seeker. Let me put it another way: why should it be that you are the seeker and thousands of others are just not interested in this kind of thing? It's not something you did. It has just happened. That is the point.

And as the process continues, the seeker, whichever path he's turned onto, knows there are other ways. He says, "Should I go here, should I do that?" The choice is not really his. The choice is made for him at birth, at conception.

◻◻◻

– THE IMPORTANCE OF INTELLECTUAL UNDERSTANDING –

If an enlightened person was being chased by a tiger, would he feel duality at that point?

Have you heard of the sage, Adi Shankaracharya? He was once going down the road when the king asked his *mahut*, the person in charge of the elephants, to charge at Shankaracharya. So Shankaracharya ran and took shelter in a house. That evening, the king asked him, "If all this is an illusion, why did you run away from the elephants?" Shankaracharya calmly explained to him that this body-mind organism called Shankara was part of the illusion, and his taking refuge was also part of the illusion.

This is precisely where the difficulty arises for most people. At a certain time the human being may say, "Yes, I can understand this. I can really understand this. In fact, I have always had a feeling that this was some sort of illusion, and now I am convinced." But he has certain questions. He understands that it is an illusion, but he or she has certain questions. What does this mean? It simply means that he or she who thinks he has understood that all this is an illusion wants to investigate something within that illusion. That means he accepts everything as an illusion except himself. That is the whole problem.

He wants an explanation that he thinks is not a part of the illusion, but wouldn't any explanation have to be a part of the illusion?

Yes. And any explanation would confirm his belief that he is separate from the illusion. If he really understands the whole thing as illusion, he would understand that he as a body-mind organism is part of that illusion. And whatever happens through that organism is part of the total illusion. So if everything is an illusion how can there be any questions?

Is there any point in reading all of your books?

None at all. None at all if you don't find the need for it. But if there is a need for it, you will read them. And having read them, if you have really understood the point, you will have come to the conclusion that you don't need them any more. Having read and understood the concepts, you come to the conclusion that they are then no longer necessary. But while you are reading them they *are* necessary. Otherwise, quite frankly, you would not have been reading them. You really don't have any choice in the matter.

On the other hand, thinking about them made them necessary for a long time afterwards. (laughter)

Yes indeed. That is quite true because *not* thinking is not in your hands. When you begin to think on this, that is involvement. When that involvement is witnessed the thinking will get cut off and gradually stop. When the witnessing becomes more or less continuous, this thinking will be less and less until it stops.

– IMPERSONAL UNDERSTANDING –

What about the merging of the individual soul with God?

You see it is all a concept. There is no need of these concepts if you just believe in one thing. That is, whatever has been happening, whatever is happening, and whatever will happen can only happen according to His Will. That is all that is necessary. If you believe in His Will and only His Will, none of these concepts about rebirth, soul or anything will bother you. These concepts bother you because the "me" entity wants perpetuity, and the "me" not being an individual entity, cannot have perpetuity.

One has to learn not to insist on knowing. I like to insist a lot. Maybe I should learn...

Madam, you will keep on insisting for knowledge until the time that you are supposed to give it up. And then you won't give it up, it will dissolve by itself. Until then keep on doing it.

I know. (laughter) I am really trapped in the search.

You have said absolutely the correct thing. The seeker is trapped...until you begin to think "Who is the seeker?"

The seeker is the ego.

The seeker is *not* the ego! That is my point. The seeker really is the impersonal Consciousness which has identified itself with the body, created the ego, and now is in the process of being disidentified. It is an impersonal process of the impersonal Consciousness. Having identified itself with the individual body, the identification continues over several lives. Then in a certain body-mind organism the mind turns inwards, but the ego still thinks he is the seeker. The process of disidentification continues until the seeker suddenly realizes that he is not the seeker, the seeker is the impersonal Consciousness. Therefore he decides that there is no point in seeking. That is the moment when the "me" begins to disappear.

Is this surrender?

It *is* surrender. And the finest, total, absolute surrender is when it includes the acceptance that enlightenment may not happen in this body-mind organism. Accepting that it may not happen in this body-mind organism is the ultimate surrender.

Very beautiful, I find what you have just said very beautiful.

❑❑❑

What is it that experiences freedom?

No "one."

I asked "what" not "who."

What or who makes no difference! You're merely playing with words. So long as there is a "who" that says, "I feel a great freedom," it's an untruth. You see?

Yes.

When understanding arises, a sense of freedom will arise by itself. And there will not be anyone to doubt it because the condition will be such that no one will want to know "who" or "what" experiences. When understanding arises the mind has no room to ask the question. That is the difference between this intellectual comprehension and the intuitive understanding, the intuitive conviction.

So understanding is really a still state?

Yes. That is correct.

It's not doing anything, just being!

Yes. And that is why true impersonal understanding can only *happen*. But the intellectual understanding is a step which may lead to the happening of the true understanding.

What happens? What's the transition from the intellectual understanding to total understanding?

Grace.

So I don't have to worry about that.

Precisely. There is no "one" to worry about it. And that is the true understanding which leads to the total understanding, impersonal understanding, understanding without an individual comprehender.

In deep sleep, and in the waking dream, the hardest thing is to recognize yourself. You usually see other people, other things.

That is what I mean by being transformed. The Hindu word is *paravritti*. It means the whole viewing gets changed. The Greek word is *metanoesis*, meaning a transformation, a transformation of the point of view. The seeing, from the personal seeing, becomes a perfect seeing, the impersonal seeing. The impersonal seeing means seeing this body-mind organism as part of the total life and living, part of the total dream.

So it is not that after enlightenment there is total disidentification with the organism. There cannot be, because the organism still functions. There has to be a working mind, an operating element. But the understanding is that the operating element is part of the mechanism of the organism and that the functioning element is the Consciousness making the operating element operate. That is what makes sentience operate the senses. With that understanding, what is disidentified? It is the sense of personal doership.

"Perception itself can be an effort," Buddha said.

No Sir! Perception is not an effort. Perception is what *happens*. And perception happens simply because there is consciousness. If the consciousness were not there, what would the body-mind organism be? Just an object. So the perception happens because in that object there is consciousness. Perceiving is what *happens*.

Is it because only Consciousness can perceive?

Yes, it is only Consciousness that can perceive. The human being is merely an instrument through which Consciousness functions.

You said that the human being is only an instrument, but earlier you said, "If the human being exerts an effort, most probably results will come."

I said, "The result will come at a certain level." If I take exercise I will develop muscles.

Most probably.

Quite.

If it is meant to happen.

You're quite right. If it is meant to happen.

It would happen?

If it is meant to happen, I would begin to take physical exercise. But if it is not meant to happen, I may intend to take physical exercise and never get around to it! You see? But if I *do* get around to it, and I do it correctly, then certain results must follow. So, this cause and effect is part of what happens in phenomenality. That which transcends phenomenality is a totally different dimension, of which the human being despite all its efforts cannot control.

Would that object that I've been thinking myself to be disappear then?

The object will not disappear until it is time for it to disintegrate. But your idea, your *concept* of what the individual is, that will change. Instead of thinking the "me" is doing whatever you're doing, the understanding will be that it is not the "me" who is doing it, but that everything that happens through this body-mind organism is part of the functioning of Totality.

God functions through this body-mind. Just as actions which happen through this body-mind are not my actions, by the same understanding, I must also understand that actions which take place in other body-mind organisms are not their actions. Therefore, even if actions taking place through your body-mind mechanism are not beneficial for me, I would still not consider you, as an individual, my enemy. That is the basis of this understanding. It means that the difference between "me" and the "other" disappears.

So, it's Totality's actions happening.

Correct.

If I understand correctly, we are not the ones to understand, because there's no "we" to understand.

Correct. That is a substantial part of the understanding, that there is nothing one can do about it. That leads to a further understanding: "If there is nothing I can do to be enlightened, I don't care if enlightenment happens in this body-mind organism or not!"

(laughing) But I do!

Someone asked me, "Phenomenally speaking, conceptually speaking,"—he was keeping his options open, you see—"assuming all that, what is the last stage before enlightenment happens?"

I said, "That's easy. There is this real, genuine feeling of not caring if enlightenment happens in this body-mind organism or not." It is practically the penultimate understanding. There's no longer any "me" wanting enlightenment.

◻◻◻

– THE DEEPENING IMPACT OF UNDERSTANDING –

Isn't there a paradox in the realization that we have no volition? You see that you don't have any freedom, yet you feel very free.

Yes! That is the point! Precisely. It is a paradox, but when the sense of freedom arises with a truly deep conviction, it is enormous, it is fantastic, truly enormous! It doesn't prevent you from doing anything, it doesn't prevent you from not doing anything. Actually it is the other way around. You neither do anything nor do you not do anything. What happens is not inaction. It is neither action nor inaction. What happens with that sense of "I am not the doer" is non-volitional non-doing, spontaneous action which is merely witnessed.

The tremendous advantage of that understanding is not so much that actions which take place through this body-mind organism are not my actions, as the more important fact that actions which take place through your body-mind are not your actions. Therefore, in no way can I consider you my enemy. It is only this understanding which brings about the admonishment, "Love thy neighbor." You may not love him, but you won't be able to *hate* him when you know that those actions are not "his" actions.

It seems you're saying most of us have no choice but to do what's in the cards for us, good or bad?

There's no question of good or bad. It just happens. Some organisms are constructed to do something, others are more passive. No question of good or bad. That's the way they are. I repeat again that even at the intellectual level this understanding is so powerful that it *must* produce some effect. As the understanding goes deeper, the effect is much greater. Only in the beginning, you are in a hurry. You tell the understanding, "Get on with the job!"

Perhaps as the understanding goes deeper the energy at the thinking level can be channeled into the working mind?

Not, "Can be channeled," but *gets* channeled. Please, it's important.

Okay, gets channeled into the working mind, so that you can be more effective.

Yes, quite so. Because you understand that there is nothing you can do about the consequences. The energy that was formerly dissipated in worrying about them will now be conserved.

Is it not only in the psyche that the energy would be conserved, but also the muscular energy?

Yes! That is why I said that once this understanding goes deeper, whatever work you are doing, mental or physical,

you find an astonishing lack of tension at the end of the day.
There's not that tiredness you used to feel before. What is it
but conservation of energy?

*Is it true that the individual cannot choose to meditate or not
meditate?*

Consciousness directs you through the ego to whichever
place you're supposed to be.

*Wouldn't the thought, "I want to meditate" still be coming from
the Absolute through personal consciousness?*

Yes! Therefore the seeking must begin with the individual. The seeking ceases when the ego, the individual, is
demolished.

*So all that mind stuff, "I want to be liberated from ego, etc.,"
has to happen?*

Of course, except in those cases where all that's needed is
a gentle push. Otherwise it is perfectly normal. The seeker-
as-an-individual has to happen, until there is that understanding that the ego cannot be enlightened.

*Often, in meditation, I get so damn frustrated, I say, "This is
not working!"*

Yes, absolutely! So this process of enlightenment is to a
certain extent in duration, but in duration there is no particular speed at which it is to happen. Quantum jumps can
happen at any stage.

*In I Am That[7] Maharaj said, "That must happen suddenly and
it is permanent. If it's not permanent it is not enlightenment."*

The ups and downs, elations and depressions, are at the
phenomenal level of the ego. The confusion arises because
the ego seeks enlightenment and doesn't realize that enlight-

[7] Sri Nisargadatta Maharaj, *I Am That*, trans. Maurice Frydman (Bombay: Chetana, 1975)

enment means total annihilation of the ego. So the "me" wants this bliss of Totality as an individual. That's the whole problem. When there is this basic understanding, that enlightenment means the total absence, annihilation, demolition of the ego, it becomes obvious that this understanding cannot happen *to* the ego. So when this enlightenment suddenly happens, at that moment the ego is already gone.

The understanding cannot disappear once it happens?

The understanding cannot disappear because it has not appeared! The understanding is What-Is. Understanding *is* Consciousness. Understanding has *always* been there. What has appeared is the misunderstanding. The misunderstanding will go and the understanding will remain exactly where it has always been.

But the misunderstanding can always come back, can't it?

Yes, until this conviction is complete, the misunderstanding comes and goes. That is why you have elations and depressions. Those periods are quite normal until the enlightenment, the understanding, the conviction, is total. Enlightenment is a state where all doubts have disappeared permanently. No doubts can arise again. That means the misunderstanding has totally dissolved.

Could you speak more of the coming and going before the final truth? What takes place before that final state. Well, it's not a state really, is it?

Enlightenment is the original state.

Right, the Ground of all states.

Yes.

What takes place for there to be no more doubts?

The right time and the right place and the right organism, and that's it. Until the right moment and the right place happen, the ups and downs will go on. Since the process *is* in duration, in phenomenality, in duality, the ups and downs, which originally are very violent gradually become not so violent as the understanding deepens.

You said that this looking within will happen, that it has already started and looking without would become less. What did you mean? I interpret the words "looking without becomes less" as meaning that we have less interest in this subject. Is that what you mean?

No. It is the thinking mind which looks without. So, with the understanding the working mind becomes more and more operative and the thinking mind becomes less and less operative. It is looking within. So looking within is happening. And the basis of all that is just the understanding, which comes by reading, or thinking, or attending seminars, or listening to someone. All that is part of the process which brings about, and deepens, the looking within.

Looking within is the absence of the thinking mind. It is the thinking mind which looks out, looks in the past and projects the future. When the thinking mind becomes less and less operative, the looking within is automatic. There is no "you" who can look within. As the thinking mind, looking out, becomes less operative, the looking within happens spontaneously. It is the same thing really, two sides of a coin.

◘◘◘

One doubt that persists for me is, if the understanding is without the comprehender, where does the mind/intellect come in?

Ramana Maharshi, the most non-violent person you can imagine, used to say, "Kill the mind!" The question was asked of him, "You say, 'Kill the mind,' but is not the mind necessary in order to understand what you are saying?" He explained that the mind-intellect *is* necessary. Any understanding in the beginning *has* to be at the intellectual level, but the intellect has to be keen enough to realize its own limitations.

The intellect must at some stage see that what it is trying to understand is beyond its comprehension, of a totally different dimension. At that stage the intellectual understanding begins to percolate into a deeper understanding. And when it goes deeper, something which the intellect understood suddenly opens up.

For instance, this morning a friend of mine said, "You said 'Thy Will be done,' and suddenly it struck me that it is not Thy Will *be* done but Thy Will is *being* done. Thy Will has always *been* done. And Thy Will will *always be* done." He said that understanding suddenly opened up a lot of wisdom which was not on the intellectual level. Such thoughts, such insights, suddenly come up, which leave no doubt that the understanding is percolating down to deeper levels.

ꘐꘐꘐ

In moments of nonacceptance, should part of you step outside, see this individual who is not accepting, and make a little adjustment to get back into the acceptance?

No. Again, who is asking the question? It is the individual, wanting to know what adjustments "I" should make to go from one state to another, what adjustments the "me" should make to get into the "I" state. No "me" can make any adjustments. Any adjustments that are needed will be made, will get made, will happen to be made, and the sooner the realization is that there is no "me" to make any adjustments, the quicker the adjustment can happen.

This is truly the core of it. It is the mind, the "me" wanting to know "How can I hasten the process? I'm impatient." Part of the acceptance, probably the final part of the acceptance, is, "What does it matter? To *whom* can it matter?"

All sense of veering off the path, of being more on the path, all that goes?

Yes, that's all in the mind, all in the "me." In fact, the astonishing thing is that the circle becomes complete. But before the circle becomes complete, the mind compares the position on the right with the position on the left and says, "What have I got? Nothing." You see what I mean by the circle? You start with the individual, the individual proceeds, seeking comes half way and the journey is full of pleasures, "I'm achieving, I'm on my way into space." Then gradually, when the understanding gets deeper, there is a letdown, "I don't know, I used to get along fine, and now I feel so... sort of flat." As it travels around the circle the mind compares its present position with the corresponding segment on its way up and says "I was going along nicely. Now I seem to be falling back off. What's happening? Am I veering off the course?"

What is happening is, you were never *acquiring* anything. It has been there always. If it had not been there always, it is useless. If something is achieved, then whatever is achieved is bound to go sometime. Only What-Is has been there for all of time, before time was.

Nobody is acquiring anything. All that is happening is, what was clouding that original state is gradually disappearing. That feeling of falling off or receding back is the "me" weakening.

So, when the "me" disappears completely, that is enlightenment?

So long as the body-mind mechanism is there, the "me" has to be there, purely as an operating center without any usurpation of subjectivity. The subjective center is recognized as the subjective center. The operative center in the body is there as long as the body-mind mechanism continues.

Then what changes?

Nothing, and yet everything is changed. From outside, nothing has changed. But from inside, everything has changed. All that has changed is the attitude, the perspective. Other than that nothing has changed.

◼◻◼

– THE ARISING SENSE OF FREEDOM –

Could you say more about freedom?

Freedom means the absence of fear. And the absence of fear means the absence of separation. When there is another, there is fear. When there is the conviction that we are all instruments through which Totality functions, the other is not there. All are seen as objects through which Totality functions. When there is no other, there is no fear, and when there is no fear, there is freedom.

And acceptance?

Acceptance brings about a tremendous sense of freedom. In L. A. last year I said, "That acceptance has to be a willing acceptance. That acceptance..." I was floundering for a word. And an elderly lady said, "The word you are looking for is probably a 'joyous' acceptance." And I said, "Thank you, Madam. That is precisely the word I was looking for." There has to be a joyous acceptance. Then that joyous acceptance brings about a tremendous sense of freedom. This morning Richard and I were talking, and this point came up. And what he told me was so appropriate, such a practical demonstration of what I've been saying, that I would like to ask Richard if he would say something about his own experience.

In respect to the joyousness of it?

Yes, and what it brings about.

Well, it is the sense of sitting in a constant flow of joy. Whatever comes seems like it's quickly seen and then it disperses. When Ramesh and I were talking this afternoon he asked me if I might say something. And my immediate response was, "Of course!" And then as I went away there was a residue of anxiety. What might it be like if I were to talk with people here?

Then there was just a quality of watching the anxiety. And in the watching there was a sense of joy. I was sharing with Ramesh what happens with me now when I find myself contracting, or out of that flow. First there's an abruptness that I feel, of the contracting taking place, which brings me back to watching it again. And then there's a sense of the witness coming in. And then whatever it is I'm watching becomes an object, begins to become more translucent. And then the feeling of not being separate comes back to me. And with that is the joyousness that pervades the whole experience.

Then there's the sense of just being caught in that, and the objects lose their strength. They don't have a pull anymore. And then it's just this quality of joy that you're speaking of.

(SECOND SPEAKER) This is not a question. I wanted to share a little bit of the joy this young man spoke of. Last night I couldn't come to the talks. My grandchild was having a birthday and we were in Sausalito. He was getting very restless in the restaurant. So I said, "Why don't I take him walking on the boardwalk?" It was nighttime. He saw the waves and the shimmering and he got excited.

He's fourteen months old, and is learning to walk. And each time someone came forward to us, they would respond to the child with love. And the love would keep coming and the child would respond back. For the first time, I had this feeling that the young man spoke of, that we're all one, we're all one Consciousness. It was one Consciousness responding to the other Consciousness, and it was all one Consciousness. Because the love came first through the child, it was easy for these people. They looked like people, but they were Consciousness responding to Itself. It was a wonderful experience.

Yes, quite. You see, we all have such moments. But we don't recognize them as such. And the mind doesn't like those moments. Because in those moments the mind is absent, and the mind doesn't like anything to happen in which it is not present. But these moments occur more frequently than we imagine. They have to, you see. They have to because such moments are the subtle connection between the objective expression and that Subjectivity that we are. So between the Subjectivity and its objective expression, the totality of manifestation, this subtle connection has to be there all the time. These moments happen all the time. And the gradual recognition of those moments, more frequent acceptance without chasing those moments, leads to this understanding.

We subscribe to a magazine for new parents. We have a three and a half year old girl. A mother in the magazine told this story: She had a young girl, just a few weeks old, and a small boy about three years old. One day, as she came into the room where the crib was, her three year old boy had crawled into the crib and was speaking to his little baby sister. He was saying, "Tell me about God, I seem to have forgotten."

Moments like these are the most precious ones.

❑❑❑

– RIGHT ATTITUDE THROUGH UNDERSTANDING –

I wonder if you would talk a little bit about attitudes. What I understand about attitudes from what Maharaj speaks about in I Am That[8] *is: If I have a concept and I look at it positively or negatively, or make a value judgment of the concept, that could be an attitude. But, I think what Maharaj is saying is that an attitude is to see everything as God's will and not the individual's. That becomes an attitude. Is this correct?*

Actually, I think what he meant was that that is *not* an attitude. That is an understanding which *leads* to the proper attitude, to the attitude of accepting the spontaneous action that takes place, because he understands that he is not the personal doer. So, in the acceptance of the fact that it is God's Will which has always worked, which is working now and which will continue to work, that understanding will produce the appropriate attitude towards life.

The moment you say, "What attitude should I develop?" the basis of it is still personal doership. Understanding that there really is no doer and continuing to act in life *as if* you are the doer, then the appropriate attitude of compassion

---

ibid.

gets developed. Then the appropriate attitude of tolerance where others are concerned gets developed, the appropriate attitude of one's self in life, doing what one thinks is right and proper, in other words, the attitude of having the highest standards of behavior for oneself and accepting the lower standards for others. "I must do the best I can with love and compassion, but the others may not have this understanding, therefore whatever actions take place are not *their* actions." With that attitude, tolerance will develop.

◻◻◻

– RIGHT ACTION THROUGH UNDERSTANDING –

Is every action of the jnani *"right action"?*

When there is true understanding, there cannot be any question of further conscious action as separate from the understanding. This can be clearly seen when one watches an expert at his craft, whether it be play, industry, sport, or any other activity. The expert is never seen to hesitate or wobble between the principles he has learned and the application of those principles. Only a beginner is seen to hesitate, because he has doubts about his understanding. An expert works smoothly, naturally, without thinking, because the principles of action have been absorbed in the very perfection of his understanding.

This is what Maharaj meant when he repeatedly asserted that, "Understanding is all." He would also say, "Once the understanding is true and perfect, you may do whatever you like." Whatever you like to do will not go outside the understanding. If a man is truly in love with his wife, giving him freedom to beat her is not going to induce him to beat her. The understanding can only produce what is contained in the understanding itself. If the understanding is not complete, then the question arises, "Maharaj, I have understood what you have just said perfectly, thoroughly. Now, tell me what do I do from tomorrow?!"

🔳🔳🔳

– CONCEPTS AS AIDS TO UNDERSTANDING –

There seems to be a slight difference between your teaching and Maharaj's. His teaching was Consciousness talking to Consciousness, but Supreme Reality was beyond that. Your teaching seems to be more into self-inquiry, witnessing. In I Am That[9] *he makes a distinction. He says that the quickest way is to focus the mind on the Supreme Reality, more than the witnessing.*

I did that for the first six months.

It's a concept.

What isn't?

The Supreme Reality is not a concept.

Oh, yes!

Really?

Yes, indeed! Before this Consciousness erupted into I Am there were no concepts. There was no need of a concept because there was nobody aware of anything. Anything that we say, in this sense of I Am, is a concept.

No awareness of anything?

That's right.

Well, isn't that the Supreme Reality he was talking about?

That is the Supreme Reality *I'm* talking about. Ultimately, there's no need to talk about it. You see, you can talk about the deep sleep state only in the waking state. In the deep sleep state there is no need, there is no one wanting to know

---

ibid.

what the deep sleep state is. For the first six months it was real torture for me. I listened. Maharaj would say, "Just be,"or "Be aware of this" or whatever. Repeatedly, I would say to myself, "To whom is he asking this? Who is to be aware of anything?" Although he repeatedly said, "I'm not an individual talking to an individual," this thought was real torture because that statement of his was not truly understood then. What he was saying is, "Any talking that happens is a concept. Any pointing is only a signpost." But the mind hangs onto the signpost and says, "I'm alive. I know. I understand."

When there was an understanding it became clear that Maharaj was not asking anybody either to do or not do anything. He was merely saying, "This is what is." He was not prescribing, he was describing, so that understanding would happen.

❏❏❏

Sir, I have a bit of puzzlement on one point. I could worship the lake behind us but it would create more dualism. Why did Ramana Maharshi worship a hill?

Because it was a concept which helped him.

Hmm. You mean, I could do the same thing?

Certainly!

❏❏❏

– STAGES OF UNDERSTANDING: MOUNTAINS AND RIVERS –

Is there a progression that is common to all seekers? I mean, does everyone go through the same stages?

The Buddhists have an excellent summary of not just how the enlightened see the world, but how the enlightened happened to come to see the way they do. The summary involves three stages of understanding. The first degree of understanding is the seeing by the involved individual. The second degree is when there is a certain amount of understanding. Finally, there is total understanding.

First, mountains and rivers are seen as mountains and rivers. An individual identified subject is seeing an object. This is total involvement. This is what the ordinary person does.

Second, mountains and rivers are no longer seen as mountains and rivers. Objects are seen as the mirrored objectivization of the subject. They are perceived as illusory objects in Consciousness and therefore unreal.

Finally, mountains and rivers are once more seen as mountains and rivers. That is, on being awakened, they are known as Consciousness itself, manifesting as mountains and rivers. Subject and objects are not seen as being separate.

In this summary, mountains and rivers refer to the world at large, including the totality of the human population. The involved individual will first see objects as an individual subject seeing objects. He considers himself a separate entity seeing other objects. Seeing other objects or events creates reactions in him, as an individual. So, the individual organism reacts to what is seen.

In the second stage, when there is understanding that all of this is a dream and unreal, the view changes and he begins to see that no event really matters. He sees them as unreal because, as the subject, he transcends the appearance. Appearance is something which comes about in Consciousness. When understanding arises at this level, there is so much enjoyment of the understanding that the individual concerned often has great difficulty keeping it to himself. He goes about telling the world, "All of this is unreal!" In trying to tell others that the world is unreal, he wants to change the world, change the perceptions of others. He doesn't realize that the change has to come from within. And so, wanting to change the world, he goes about creating problems for himself. These problems which this second stage brings about settle down only in the third stage.

In the third stage, objects are seen not by an individual, nor by an object seeing an object, nor a subject seeing an object. The true perceiver is realized as that which created the appearance and that which cognizes the appearance. They are both the same. At this stage, the ultimate realization is not only that the world is unreal, but that at the same time the world is real! The world is unreal in the sense that it is dependent on Consciousness for its existence. It has no independent existence of its own. The world owes its existence to being cognized in Consciousness. If every human being and every animal suddenly became unconscious, who's to say that there is a world? The world not only wouldn't appear, but wouldn't exist.

Could you elaborate on this idea of reality and unreality?

The analogy of the shadow is often used to explain "real" and "unreal." A shadow is unreal in the sense that it is dependent on the sun for its existence. Nonetheless, as a shadow, it is real enough. So it is both real and unreal at the same time. All manifestation is dependent on Consciousness for its existence. Consciousness is inherent in all objects, in all manifestation. Consciousness transcends the manifestation yet is immanent in it. Manifestation is contained within Consciousness.

In the second stage, before the final understanding arises, all sorts of concepts come into play. It is assumed that it is up to the individual to make efforts to join himself with God. At that level of subject and object, *nirvana* and *samsara* are treated as two. Therefore, they speak in terms of the sea of *samsara*, misery, which has to be crossed. The *jiva* has to cross it and it can do so only by doing *sadhana* of one kind or another. So the seeker goes through *sadhana*, the whole series. For years he practices. For years he watches what is happening, and finds himself in a state of pride and self conceit. Ultimately, when he settles down in contemplation, he throws aside everything. As the Sufis say, there is a sort of ceremony, a burning of all that he has learned and all that he thinks he has achieved.

So, in the third stage, it is realized that the world is both real and unreal. When that understanding arises, the knowledge settles down and in that organism where enlightenment has taken place there is no longer any active desire to tell the world about it, to change the world. In the third stage there is an acceptance of What-is, both the immanence and the transcendence. *Nirvana* and *samsara* are not two. *Samsara* is the objective expression of *nirvana*.

In the final understanding, the state of Beingness happens. There is no question of seeing anything. Everything is appearance and that appearance is being seen through the instrument of the organism, through the senses. But no individual ever sees. Though the individual says "I can see the mountains" it is only because consciousness is present that this can be said. The mountains are really seen by Consciousness, which is also the appearance! The Totality of manifestation is merely an appearance created in Consciousness by Consciousness. And this functioning of manifestation, what we call life and living, is also Consciousness. Consciousness plays and directs all of the roles of the billions of human beings. Every character is played by Consciousness.

The question, "Why does this *lila* exist?" is understood at the final stage. Therefore, at that stage, no problems arise. The seeker has no overwhelming desire to teach the world about what he has learned because the basic understanding is that he has not learned anything. The understanding has come by itself as a gift from God, a gift from Totality, Grace. All the words come later. When the enlightenment is accepted, there is no question of any "one" considering himself lucky. The individual considers himself lucky to be enlightened only when enlightenment hasn't truly happened.

ррр

– THE SCALE OF INVOLVEMENT AND REMEMBERING –

When I'm thinking, I am fully identified with my thoughts. There's not a witnesser. After that train of thought comes through, then I observe it as a memory and I judge it.

So when you understand this even intellectually, what happens is, at a certain point there will be the sudden realization that the mind has been getting involved. At that point it gets cut off. The involvement, otherwise, would have gone on. In most cases, without this understanding, even intellectual understanding, it's one involvement after another. Only in rare instances, when the mind is really tired, certain moments may arise when the mind is really vacant. Otherwise, from morning to evening, all that the human being does is conceptualize, create images. But when this understanding comes, at some stage of the involvement, suddenly it gets cut off.

◻◻◻

– SPIRITUAL EVOLUTION –

The use of the term "spiritual evolution" presupposes an involvement with time.

Indeed, of course. The entire process is in space-time phenomenality.

What is it that is involved with time, the body-mind mechanism?

Oh, no. What is involved in space-time is the identified Consciousness, Consciousness which has deliberately identified itself with an individual organism.

Why has this occurred?

So that this *lila*, this game, this cosmic dream can happen. This identification process is continuous. New creatures, new human beings are constantly being created, and in them identification happens. This identification goes on in a process of evolution. At some point the mind turns inwards and the process of disidentification begins. This process takes a lot of time and a lot of births. The whole game is identification, then the mind turning inwards and then the process of disidentification. Mind you, all this is a concept, but it could help to bring about the ultimate understanding.

So the word evolution is a concept only visible to the identified individual?

Indeed.

Why is a concept necessary at all?

Because the concept of the individual has arisen through this identification. The moment that this concept of the individual arises, the concept of God is necessary. Otherwise, if the impersonal is accepted, where is the question of an individual and God?

◘◘◘

Is turning within, a means of ignoring the ego?

No. Turning within can only *happen*, you see. Turning within *is* this process of spiritual evolution. Evolution goes on in everything. There is physical evolution, there is evolution in music, there is evolution in art, there is evolution in science, and there is spiritual evolution.

In this spiritual evolution, there is first identification which goes on through several thousands of body-mind organisms. I mean, it could be a hundred thousand or a million, that is not the point, but through a series of body-mind organisms. And in a certain body-mind organism the turning inwards will happen. A thought occurs or an event occurs or something occurs and, with this as an apparent cause, the mind turns inwards. And instead of the mind going outward, wanting more and more material objects, the mind turns inwards and wants to know its real nature, "Who am I? What am I doing here? What is the meaning of life?" Then the process of disidentification starts. The spiritual seeking in that evolution begins with the mind turning inwards and the individual beginning seeking. And that seeking, which is really the process of disidentification, continues through various processes in evolution. From one kind of seeking, you go to another kind of seeking and lots of frustrations, until finally there is that sudden understanding that no "individual" can ever be enlightened. Enlightenment, as an impersonal happening, can happen only through an object. For any event to happen an object is needed. So, when enlightenment is about to happen a body-mind organism is created in this evolution which is ready to receive that enlightenment. It has the characteristics, physical, mental, temperamental, which make that body-mind organism capable of receiving enlightenment. And that body-mind organism itself is a process of evolution.

The beginning of this understanding, in duration, is acceptance that enlightenment may not happen through this body-mind organism. It is a very difficult thing to accept for a seeker, for an individual seeker, but that is an important landmark in this process in duality. Then a "letting go" happens, and there is a tremendous sense of freedom. "If I cannot have enlightenment and if an object cannot be enlightened, what am I seeking?"

So then, this "letting go" happens and this identification with the body-mind organism, this "me," gets weaker. But certain quantum jumps happen in the process. And the ultimate quantum jump, just immediately prior to enlightenment, is this: there is no more seeking, no more caring whether enlightenment happens or not. When that acceptance arises, the "me" is practically gone. Because it is the "me" which is the seeker, not the body-mind organism. The body-mind organism, by itself, is only an inert object, necessary for enlightenment to happen.

The "me" is the "me" as long as there is the seeker, right?

That is correct. Yes. So when the seeking disappears, the "me" seeker also disappears.

So, is that the ultimate point, the evolution of this "me"?

Yes. The "me" gets evolved, but not *this* "me."

Yes, I mean collectively.

Yes. As I've said, a "me" called Albert Einstein was evolved for the theory of relativity. But for the theory of relativity only. For further evolution in science, other body-minds were created. Einstein was not ready to accept the subsequent development of the quantum theory. He was not able to accept Heisenberg's theory of uncertainty. Einstein said this theory of uncertainty meant "God is playing dice with the universe." He said that he cannot accept that "God is playing dice with the universe." Niels Bohr responded, "God is not playing dice with the universe. We *think* God is playing dice with the universe because we do not have all the information which God has!"

I thought Neils Bohr said, "Albert, do you presume to know what God is thinking?"

Yes, that could well be so.

Is there a plan or an ultimate goal, a final conclusion to all of this evolution?

There is no final goal. It is a continuous impersonal functioning of Totality. Scientists now call it a "self-generative" process. I prefer to think in terms of potential energy releasing itself. The question arises, "Why should energy activize itself? Why should there be this manifestation?" One answer is, "Why not?" Another approach is, "If you are thinking in terms of potential energy, it would not be potential if it didn't activize itself sometime. It would be dead."

◻◻◻

In reading I Am That[10] *and your books, it seems that you and Maharaj were both ordinary, dualistic men until enlightenment happened.*

Indeed! That is so! But, there is a difference. Maharaj said that the first time he listened to his *guru* say, "All of this is a dream, an impersonal happening and you are merely an instrument through which Totality functions; there is no 'you,' as an independent entity," he had accepted it. There was no questioning of it. That happens very rarely. In my case that kind of receptivity was not there.

Instantaneous?

Instantaneous in the case of Ramana Maharshi and in the case of Maharaj. I don't want to mislead you, there could be several instances not known, not in the public eye, where it also could have happened. The publicity has nothing to do with the actual happening. A certain organism, in a certain case of enlightenment, gets publicity for certain reasons. For certain others it could happen and go very easily. They know it. They understand it, but they are not concerned, because there is no longer any "they." They are not concerned about any fame or fortune or anything like that.

In my own case, the process was not as quick as Maharaj's. But it was smoother, it was simpler than in many other cases, I should imagine. I've had this intuitive feeling ever since I can remember that all of this is a dream and that therefore there is nothing that I can do to hasten my progress in life or in any way.

◘◘◘

– THE DISSOLUTION OF THE ME –

Experientially that intimate, close feeling that I have of "me," does that dissolve?

---

(10)   ibid.

It does dissolve, but who is to witness that dissolution? You see what I mean? It does dissolve, so what dissolves is the "me" itself. Who is to know that the "me" has dissolved? It is only the "me" that could experience it.

So the "me" will come and go, and then be gone?

Yes! And while the "me" comes and goes, the state of witnessing takes place. The "me" is the mind, so the mind cannot watch itself. If the mind watches its own operation, then there will always be comparing and judging: "This is good, this is bad, this is whatever." That is not witnessing. Witnessing is merely watching an event or a thought or an emotion as it arises, without any comparing, without any judging, merely witnessing. Witnessing is impersonal and is vertical, so it cuts off the horizontal involvement. As the "me" diminishes, the witnessing will happen more often and for longer periods. Suddenly it will occur that the reactions don't take place to an event or thought, that there is a sense of peace, a sense of well being, but no "one" to feel that sense of well being. It is not as if the "me" will suddenly say, "Oh, I have disappeared!" Who is to say it has disappeared?

But it does dissolve?

Yes, but not if you *want* it to dissolve.

❏❏❏

– THE DIVERSITY OF TEACHINGS –

In using concepts, as you do, to point to a state without concepts, I assume the concepts you use and the way in which you try to describe enlightenment expresses to a certain extent your life experience and your personal creativity. Would another realized person point to the same truth but with a different personal coloration?

Yes. The personal coloration is not only in the way in which I state things, but also in the way my statements are received, the reaction. The group draws what it needs. That's why you find, sometimes, different concepts coming out at different groups.

Maharaj once told me, "What I say has very little to do, in its outward form, with what my *guru* taught. He used different words, different analogies, different concepts." And he went a step further, saying, "What you teach will have practically nothing to do with what I have been saying. It will depend entirely on what your listeners need, according to their needs and requirements."

He had real contempt for people who wanted to copy the *guru*. Maharaj and his *guru* used to smoke, so twenty people would smoke!

◻◻◻

– GLIMPSES –

In your opinion, should we trust "free samples" as you called them yesterday, those glimpses that arise spontaneously?

Yes, Sir!

What is the basis for that trust?

The basis for that trust is that you do have the glimpses, that they exist. Others have them too, but don't recognize them as glimpses. In those moments their mind says, "You're wasting your time, get on with the job" and the glimpses are rejected. In some cases, glimpses are gratefully accepted. Even this acceptance of those glimpses is a matter of grace.

There's no way to win, is there?

Exactly! There is no way for "you" to win.

◻◻◻

– QUANTUM LEAPS –

In one lecture, you talked about shocks or jolts to the body-mind organism. It sounds as if some understanding took place, but it is not kept?

You see, the process goes on. The process is gradual, but the ultimate happening is always sudden. The usual example I give is, suppose you are climbing stairs. You don't know how many steps there are. You don't know if there are one hundred and fifty, three hundred, or three thousand, but you are compulsively climbing the staircase. Assume for our purpose, there are one hundred and twenty-nine stairs. Up through one hundred and twenty-eight, you don't know that the one hundred and twenty-ninth is the end. So the step from one hundred and twenty-eight to one hundred and twenty-nine, the final step, is always sudden. But up till one hundred and twenty-eight, there is a process.

There will be jolts or shocks on the way?

There may be. Those jolts or shocks are pointers on the way. That is because the mind thinks laterally, but the progress of the process is not necessarily even. More often than not, as in actual life, and as the subatomic physicist says, the process occurs in jumps, in quantum jumps. If the quantum jump is bigger than the previous one, then there can be a jolt. But jolts or shocks are not a necessary phenomenon.

You were talking about the seeker being miserable, but I don't feel miserable.

The seeker gets to be miserable when the seeking reaches a certain intensity. It need not reach a certain intensity, there can be a quantum jump. It may also be that the body-mind organism is born at the stage where all it needs is a push. There will not be any misery, any intensity. Think of enlightenment as a spiritual chart. In the spiritual chart, each body-mind is a dot on the chart. So long as the identification continues there is no question of seeking except for material wealth and happiness. So the person, until the mind turns inwards, is not concerned with spiritual seeking at all. Where each one of us is on this chart, we don't know. If you represent a certain dot, it doesn't mean you must live over a million lives. At any moment, anywhere, there can be a quantum jump. What brings about a quantum jump is not in your hands. It can only happen. So, if we don't know where our dot is on the chart, why bother? You cannot seek God. At the right time, right place, God will seek you.

🔲🔲🔲

— KARMA —

You said something earlier about the body-mind manifesting the results of actions. In other words, the thought comes through, which is Consciousness, and the body-mind takes an action. The consequences it doesn't know anything about. But the body-mind gets the consequences. It's all in phenomenality, none of it transcends phenomenality.

That is correct. None of it transcends that. But whatever actions take place are actions which happen through a body-mind organism as an object. Consciousness needs an object to produce certain actions. So it produces an object with certain characteristics that will produce precisely that action.

You have a certain computer program created for a certain purpose so the moment an input goes in you know what the output will be. Consciousness, knowing the computer it has created, sends an input by way of a thought and knows precisely what the action is going to be. And those actions together with the actions of billions of others will make up the totality of functioning at that moment.

And that is karma?

That is correct. *Karma* means action. *Karma* means causality. It has nothing to do with the individual doer, the individual entity because there *is* no individual entity as the doer.

Are you saying that the whole theory that people who do good works come back to a good rebirth and those who do bad things come back to a lower birth is false?

What you are saying is *karma* is based on people who do good deeds. What I am saying is good deeds can only happen, just as bad deeds also happen. Whose? Good deeds happen through particular body-mind mechanisms and bad deeds happen through certain body-mind organisms. Both good deeds and bad deeds together form the functioning of Totality at that moment. It is only the human being who says, "good deeds, bad deeds." All are deeds performed, in this life and living by Consciousness, through body-mind organisms according to their natural characteristics.

A psychopath has not chosen to be a psychopath. Who has created the psychopath? He is part of the creation of the Totality of manifestation. There is a lovely poem by Omar Khayam. He speaks of an imperfect pot saying, "People reject me because I am odd shaped. Did the hand of the potter then shake when he made me?" Did the psychopath choose to be a psychopath? Did the saint choose to be a saint?

It is past karma *from past lives.*

Past lives yes, but "whose" lives?

Of something that gets reborn.

So certain acts take place. Those acts have consequences. If those consequences are to be good, a body-mind organism is created with such characteristics that the good deeds will happen. If certain acts have to produce bad actions then Consciousness will create organisms with certain other characteristics, those characteristics may be termed a psychopath.

So there is no continuity in a personal sense?

Certainly there is continuity, but it is not on a personal basis. That is what I am saying. The whole process is impersonal. There is *karma* of course, which is causality, but there is no individual concerned with that *karma*. There is no individual "doer."

Ultimately, there is no individual. Ultimately that is the highest truth?

That is the truth, madam. Truth has no classifications. Truth is truth. No individual is guilty of anything. Certain acts happen through certain organisms and some get the Nobel Prize and some get punished, but there is no separate individual entity.

I want to ask about what you said earlier, about the sage accepting these acts and then they get voided.

No. Acceptance *happens* and it *gets* voided.

OK. In that moment, is that what it means to transcend karma?

The sage has no *karma*, precisely as the psychopath has no *karma. Karma* and the individual have been so interlinked, it's such an abused term. When you view the whole thing impersonally, there is no problem. You link the impersonal with the personal and you cannot stop creating problems.

Where does willpower fit in with your explanation of the alcoholic?

The alcoholic has tried a hundred times using his willpower and nothing has happened.

Why is it that a particular alcoholic, after many failures, finally succeeds?

That is my point. Same alcoholic, same willpower that tried ninety-nine times, and the hundredth time it succeeded.

Because he was ready?

The organism was ready to receive the Grace.

◘◘◘

– REINCARNATION –

Did you say that the disidentification would occur over several lifetimes?

Yes, indeed. But before you feel frustrated, the fact that you are here now, the fact that there are only certain organisms who are interested in this study, indicates that this stage of spiritual evolution has not happened suddenly in this organism. Obviously, for this evolution to take place in this organism, there have been many organisms' lives through which this process of evolution has been taking place.

I'm confused. Didn't we talk last night about the ego dying with the body? Then there is something besides the ego which goes from one body to the next?

Yes! But it's not the ego. It is Consciousness. It is Consciousness identifying itself with the separate ego each time a new organism is created.

But there's some similarity, or something carried over from one organism to the next?

Again, this is a concept. When the body dies, the bundle of thoughts, memories, impressions all go into the pool of Consciousness. For the subsequent functioning, certain actions or events must take place. For those events to take place, new organisms are needed. Organisms are created so that the deeds can happen. Deeds are not created to punish or reward an organism. It is an inert organism that suddenly becomes conscious when there is sentience.

Is the continuity of different functions which have to be performed by different organisms, cause and effect?

Exactly!

So any time someone is born, that's what's going on? Any time there's a new birth, Totality is manifesting a new mechanism through which to function?

Yes! That's it.

If there's rebirth that's what it is?

It *is* rebirth. There is *karma* and there is rebirth, but not rebirth of a particular entity. It's the letters "re" in the word rebirth that cause confusion. There are new births, new characters, new organisms, but not rebirth. Rebirth and *karma* linked together is what causes all the confusion.

The Absolute never was born and never dies?

Exactly. The functioning goes on.

This idea of there being a soul that chooses where it wants to be incarnated for the purpose of learning lessons seems rather silly.

It's bullshit! (laughter) First of all, "souls." You see, the mind wants to create a concept. The mind knows that the body must die, but the mind, the "me" wants to live forever, if not in this body—of course it cannot in this body—then in some other body. So the mind creates the concept of a soul moving from one body to another body, as if Consciousness has no business except to deal with "souls," punishing and rewarding them in each life.

I'd like to hear about what it means when you have a memory of yourself in a former life and you were a guru, *or a knight in armor, or a goat or...*

The point is memory. Yes, memory of a past life. Why not? There was a past life and the memory can go back to a past life. But why "your" past life, merely because you remember "a" past life?

So identifying with it is the mistake?

Yes! A past life, certainly. No reason why the memory shouldn't or couldn't go back, you see. But why "your" past life? Simply because you remember?

It's the mind?

Yes, it is the mind.

Yet, last night when you spoke of Ramana Maharshi, you said that he was so ready for that enlightenment that he must have had previous lives to prepare himself.

No. There *were* previous lives, there had to be previous lives through which the evolution towards this ultimate organism did take place. But not "his" lives.

The Tibetan Buddhists seem to believe in something like a soul. When they pick a new Lama...

Yes. You see, what they were originally thinking of is this spiritual evolution and they were thinking of another organism which had to come. Just as a highly developed mind can go back to a past life in memory, no reason why it cannot jump to a future. So there's no reason why he shouldn't project his mind to see another organism as a future Lama. But it is not one soul, not the *same* Lama taking on a new body-mind.

Now listen to Buddha talking about reincarnation. There is no statement which could be clearer. He said, "As there is no self there is no transmigration of self." Now, substitute "soul" for "self" and you will read, "As there is no soul there is no transmigration of soul. But there are deeds and continued effects of deeds. There are deeds being done, but no doer thereof. There is no entity that transmigrates, no self is transferred from one to another. But there is a voice uttered here and the echo of it comes back."

So about this reincarnation, which is supposed to be the very essence of Buddhism, here is Buddha saying that there is no "one" to reincarnate. But the monks and priests that have come later, they don't hear this. Just as many exegesists of the Christian religion do not hear Christ's original words.

I work with people remembering their past lives. And they not only remember past lives within bodies, but they also remember in between states in which they also had experiences that were not incarnate. So what's that? That's not a body-mind organism?

No. This is precisely what happens: certain actions take place and they have reactions. Call them ambitions not fulfilled, guilts about certain actions which have taken place. All of it goes into the pool of Consciousness from which it gets distributed to the new organisms that are created. That is how new organisms are created. Then through these new organisms future deeds can take place. Deeds are taking place, but there is no doer. And Buddha very clearly says this.

So the idea is that there are bundles of deeds, so to speak.

Yes. But you see, the same components of the bundle need not get transferred. That is what I am saying. All the bundles get brought together and then their components are distributed, but not in the same bundle, which would be the same as a "soul."

Yet some people in their present form remember being a bundle in between forms.

Yes. Some people.

They don't remember being distributed, in a sense. They remember being a bundle, but...

Exactly. Their memory will be associated with that bundle.

ᑕᑕᑕ

Is there an astral realm comparable to the physical realm where one might mistake oneself to be a separate entity again?

The astral plane could certainly be there as much as the physical plane, but all are in Consciousness. All there is, is Consciousness. And in that Consciousness how many planes there are is really a relative matter.

So could we say those planes are nonexistent?

Those planes are as existent as this plane we are in. A question like this was asked of Ramana Maharshi. The question was whether gods and goddesses in Hindu mythology were real or not. Ramana Maharshi's answer was that, "they are as real as you are." (laughter)

I'm a psychologist, and I've done a lot of past life work with people who have had very severe phobias for years. In trance, they will go back and relive an experience and that will clear up that phobia. Their concept and mine has always been that we've actually encountered an experience that they've had before. Is it more accurate to say that they are just going back to somebody else's experience?

Yes! That is quite likely.

And they have been given the memory of the experience?

Yes, and identified themselves with that memory.

◘◘◘

– GRACE –

In surrender, unconditional surrender, I don't understand how it can be unconditional when there's still a "me" that thinks its a "me."

Correct. That is not real surrender.

It is still conditional, no matter how real it may feel? It's just the play of Consciousness at that particular point?

Yes.

If Grace is supposed to happen, it's going to happen? It might happen with him or me even though we are both doing the same thing?

It may happen in one case, it may not happen in other cases. This matter of Grace is not necessarily only in the spiritual. A person told me that he used to be a very passionate hang glider pilot. One day something happened, he was flying along and all of a sudden he found himself falling straight to the ground, the earth rushing at him and at a certain point he said, "This is it." But it wasn't it. Suddenly he found himself looking at the sky. What had happened was, when he was within a few feet of the ground, the glider had broken through some power lines and they had slowed his descent. He was not electrocuted, he had not crashed, he was standing on his feet looking at the sky! He said then there was a sudden realization that this is a matter of Grace.

In a more practical way, we can say, "The destined end of that organism had not arrived." Nonetheless, from the individual's point of view, there was Grace. And that is true.

This same gentleman became habituated, addicted to alcohol. He told me he'd been addicted for nineteen years and then suddenly, totally unexpectedly one morning, the compulsion, the addiction, all desire to drink left him! He told me that that was the second time Grace had happened. The fact that he thought in terms of the word Grace itself means something. The third time Grace happened, he said, was when he found himself, unexpectedly at my very first public talk in 1987.

🔲🔲🔲

– SELF-INQUIRY –

Ramesh, if I forget about the concept of the "me"... (laughter) If I step back long enough, the moment seems to be going on independent of anything else, a very subtle gentle process, moments of humility going back and forth into it, out of it. Is the problem one of desire? If a man had a desire for a million dollar boat, as soon as his attention gets onto that boat the process of going back and forth stops. Are you saying that the desiring suddenly covers up this very gentle process that goes on all the time?

Yes.

A lot of quiet is needed to keep seeing that.

To try to continue this process of "quiet" is still the mind itself. What really happens is, this peace or quietude is always there until the mind intrudes. Understanding gradually reduces this intrusion of the mind. So it seems as if the state of quietude is on and off. It isn't so. The state of quietude is our real nature. Ramana Maharshi describes this as the natural state, the *sahaja* state.

Because of the intellect, we consider keeping ourselves personally involved to be the normal state. That is not normal. That is why Ramana Maharshi said thinking, in the sense of conceptualizing, is not man's real nature. The understanding is that the mind's nature is conceptual. Fighting the ego, the mind, is precisely what the ego wants. You cannot fight the mind. You cannot suppress the ego. Fighting, resisting, controlling it is an impossible action. What is really needed is a negative or feminine action. That is to yield, to see things as they are. It is the nature of the mind to flit about from topic to topic.

Instead of fighting it, find out who wants to know, who is doing it, who needs it. In the beginning it is necessary to ask the specific question, but the point of asking the question is not to seek an answer. Seeking an answer means the mind raising the query and the mind trying to find an answer, the mind trying to rationalize, the mind working within its own involvement.

The purpose of self-inquiry is to break this involvement. Who wants to know? It is a sort of mental slap with a fat stick. It means there is really no one other than the intellect creating problems. So it gets cut off. Ramana Maharshi makes it clear though, that this self-inquiry is not a meditation or *mantra*. This process is to go on all the time, though it does not mean stopping your work. You can't! You have to earn a living.

This process is sort of a negative process, understanding that there is no "one" to ask any questions, which is the same as witnessing. As soon as a thought arises, "I want a million dollar yacht," the mind starts getting involved in it. "How do I get it? Do I beg, borrow, steal? Can I earn enough?" All that is involvement. Even the first glimmer of understanding cuts off the involvement at some stage. As this understanding grows deeper, when the thought arises, it gets cut off quicker and quicker, nearer and nearer the starting point, until ultimately, when the understanding is truly complete, the arising of a thought and its getting cut off vertically without horizontal involvement is a spontaneous occurrence. That will take some time. In the meantime, the idea is to ask this question or merely to let the understanding vertically cut off this horizontal involvement at any time it happens, knowing you have no control over it.

The realization that you have no control is the start of the understanding. That understanding is the witnessing which vertically cuts off horizontal involvement. It is astonishing how quickly this understanding can establish itself and become a habit.

I'm still not quite sure I know what you mean by witnessing.

Witnessing is quite simple. Witnessing goes on all the time. For instance, if you look out your window onto the traffic, what is happening really is witnessing, until your attention is drawn to some event or person and you think, "That's interesting," or you say, "Oh, that's good or that's ugly." Then that continuous process of witnessing stops. Like in a movie, you suddenly stop at a particular frame. The process gets cut off by this involvement. So, the process of witnessing goes on all the time and gets cut off by the intrusion of the mind.

How does one resume witnessing after the involvement starts?

Knowing that the intrusion of the mind is a natural process, that it has to happen, that understanding itself will again bring about the witnessing.

It is the mind that says, "All right, now I shall witness. How do I go about it?" The main point about witnessing is the absence of the "me." Witnessing is vertical, in a totally different dimension. Therefore there can be no "me" witnessing. In witnessing there is no thought like "I should not have been involved," no comparisons with anything. The absence of comparing and judging is the criterion of true witnessing.

Thoughts, just witnessed, get cut off for the simple reason that there is no comparing, no judging, no decision making.

❑❑❑

Is there some instrument we can use in order to break this barrier between me and the real experience?

Who is to break what? That is the understanding. There is no "who" and there is no "what" to be broken. You see? In that understanding arises the ultimate understanding.

Ramesh, when we ask, "who?" that is a conditioned mind too, isn't it? That presupposes there is an answer.

Correct.

So the recognition that it's all coming from a conditioned mind can set you free.

Yes. And at a certain stage even that distinction becomes unbearable.

That there's an answer to the inquiry becomes unbearable?

Exactly. Therefore that inquiry gets dropped, although it may have begun with that. That's why I keep saying, "The seeking begins with the individual and ends with the annihilation of the individual."

The seeking begins with the individual asking "Who am I? What am I?" This "I," this "me" is very, very powerful. Then at the intermediate stage there is an understanding that there is no "me," but that I am That. But in that "I" there is still that shade of "me," the taint of "me." So the ultimate understanding is that there is neither me nor Thee, you see? All there is, is Consciousness projected as manifestation and Consciousness-at-rest when it is not projected. The individual seeker is irrelevant. Who is seeking what?

In regard to, "Who is questioning?" when I put this question to myself I keep coming to the point where I'm hitting myself up a high wall. I cannot go further, there is nothing behind this or beyond this question. As far as I look into it, I cannot come to an answer because there's nothing.

(laughing) That is precisely the point!

It is like a koan, you know, in Zen...

Exactly.

So why all this discussion about it? (laughter)

Why all these discussions? That is what I'm asking *you*. If you accept, as Maharaj did, that all there is, is Consciousness, who needs any discussions? But because that is not acceptable to the mind, to the intellect, to the "me," the "me" wants to have discussions.

We squeeze our minds. I've got a headache, confusion, only to find that there is nothing behind all of this! (laughter)

I wouldn't say there was nothing.

You wouldn't say it was "nothing"?

Not "nothing."

What's behind it, then?

Everything! (laughter) You see, nothing and everything. Actually nothingness of the noumenon is really the fullness of the plenum. Nothingness gives the impression of something negative, something dead. It is not so. The nothingness that is spoken of as the plenum is the potential energy. It is the potential which has activated itself in this manifestation. It is the unmanifest which has manifested itself. It is subjectivity which has objectified itself. It is potential energy which has activated itself. That's all that has happened. They are not two states. Repeatedly, the mystic will say they are not two states. All there is, is Consciousness, at rest or in movement.

And the rest and the movement are the same state?

They are indeed. That is why Ramana Maharshi repeat-edly said, and so do other masters, "Nothing has really happened. There is no creation. There is no destruction. There is no goal, no path. There is no free will. There is no destiny."

There is no action and no passivity.

Precisely. If this basic truth is accepted, that nothing has happened and there is no creation, no destruction, then all that can happen is witnessing of whatever takes place through each body-mind mechanism as an appearance in this totality of appearances. And we can only witness it without questioning it. You can only witness what is.

So who does the witnessing?

Consciousness. Consciousness has produced this play. Consciousness has written the script. Consciousness is play-ing all the characters. And Consciousness is witnessing the play. It's a one man show. (laughter) It's a play of Conscious-ness. You can remove the man and what remains is One, which is Unicity. So, all this is the play of the Unicity.

Ramana Maharshi told the story of a marriage party where there was one person there who was eating all the food, causing a nuisance. The people of the bride's party thought it must be a relative of the groom and the groom's party thought he was surely a relative of the bride's. Finally someone asked him, "Who are you? Who are you with?" Then he disappeared. He was found out.
So it seems the inquiry can reveal the thoughts that are hiding the reality. You said that reality is like an open secret and that the actions of our mind are what obscures it. Ramana Maharshi seems to be saying that by inquiry those are cleared up.

Self-inquiry is not a method. If it were, then it would be in duration. All Ramana Maharshi says is, in the beginning there may be meditation of some kind. And as a beginning meditation this is the best way. He also makes it repeatedly clear, it is not a method of meditation to be practiced at precise times in specific places. It just happens throughout your working, it happens all the time, because That which you are has been there all the time.

In the beginning, there has to be meditation or some kind of *sadhana* but he also makes it clear that there is a danger of the means becoming an end, what Jesus called "vain repetition." This vain repetition dulls the mind and whatever repetition is there, whether it is "Who Am I?" or some other *mantra*, it deadens the mind and becomes mechanistic. So, in the beginning, you ask yourself, "Who wants to know?" But the problem is that the human mind asks the question and expects an answer and when the answer is not there, it begins to get further involved. "I am not the body, I am not this I am not that," finally coming back to the question "Who am I?" All this is merely getting deeper into the mire.

So, what is the answer?

The answer is that there cannot be any answer.

Then what is the purpose of self-inquiry?

The purpose of self-inquiry is to stop the mind from proceeding with the question itself, which is precisely what is meant by witnessing. In the beginning you ask the questions, "To whom is this happening? Who is concerned? Who wants to know?" but very soon you will find that as these questions arise because of a thought or an event they get cut off. Then even the questions become unnecessary.

So, self-inquiry is a transitory thing?

Whichever path you go by, and they are all notional, leads to the process of disidentification. The most famous devotee or *bhakta* in Maharashtra was a saint called Tukaram. He wrote about five thousand spontaneous verses. In the beginning he tells his personal God, Vithoba, "Let those who want to see you in your impersonal form do it, but for me, life after life, please be in your form which I can adore and worship." And later on the same intense *bhakta* wrote verses which say,

"Vitobha, you are a cheat! You have misled me! You said you were a God and I was supposed to worship you. Now I find there is no difference! There is no difference! You have cheated me!" Then he goes further and says, "Devotion is only for the ignorant." (laughter)

Curiously, in the *Bhagavad Gita*, Lord Krishna says, "When the *bhakta* has reached a certain intensity, I give him knowledge. I make him ready to receive knowledge."

So ultimately it is the "me" which has to disappear, either by surrender or by acceptance, which basically mean the same thing.

◨◨◨

– THE ART OF LISTENING –

How do I witness?

The question is irrelevant. In the witnessing there is no "you" at all. That's the basic thing. Only in involvement is there a "you," not in witnessing.

But I would rather not be involved.

Exactly. You are seeking enlightenment. Therefore you say, "I am a seeker. I'm not supposed to get involved. I shouldn't have got involved." But that in itself is involvement.

What I hear you saying is, everything is a door and it's a question of whether or not you're available to that moment that's presented to you rather than getting focused on, "Should I do this or should I do that?"

Yes, the gate of compassion is wide open.

The fact that I'm here is because I'm supposed to be here. I couldn't possibly be anywhere else.

Nor could I! (laughter) The fact is you are here and listening. Some kind of listening is taking place. If the kind of listening taking place is total and basic, something more will come of it than if the listening is at the level of logic and reason.

I remember the dialogue in which Krishnamurti was having a talk with a Professor Bohm. One of the first things he said, just spontaneously, was "Yes, I am all alert, I am listening to you totally. Please go ahead." That is the kind of listening where your heart is open, your mind is open, the gate is wide open.

At the same time, listening is not supposed to be brainwashing. Therefore the Scripture says what you are listening to must be meditated upon. First is *shravana* or listening. Next is *manana*, meditating on it, weighing it, ringing the coin to see if the coin is genuine. Then if what you have heard appeals to your heart, only then accept it. And in accepting it, if there are some difficulties, then get them ironed out with your *guru*. Once the difficulties are ironed out, then the last stage is staying with it, *nididhyasana*. The quality of that listening will bring about the result.

When you leave these discussions, you don't take any of this with you? When you are finished tonight you are finished with it?

I'm finished with it.

And we should be too?

You should. That is very important. If you hold on to what has been said, then this listening which has been absorbed does not get a chance to transform itself into an understanding. That understanding has to be an intuitive, insightful understanding. And the listening can transform itself into this understanding only if the intellect doesn't intrude. But let me go a step further and say that if the intellect does intrude, that intrusion is also the part of the functioning of Totality. It takes time for the intuitive understanding to happen.

That sounds as if you are telling us, "When you leave here forget everything that's been said." How does this fit with the three stages of listening you just outlined?

That is a very good question. When this listening is transforming itself and becoming the understanding, in that process certain doubts will remain. It cannot be total understanding, because the listening itself has been subject to the intellect. The longer you let listening-understanding remain, the deeper it will go in.

What you have listened to, after it has transferred itself into a certain amount of understanding, that understanding has to be weighed by the intellect and there has to be deliberate meditation on what has been understood. Certain doubts may arise. The intellect has to meditate on those doubts and that is what I assume you are referring to. The traditional notional difference is, first is listening, second is meditation on what has been heard and understood. And when those doubts have been ironed out, then thirdly and finally is to settle in on that ultimate understanding.

On my way back home now, should I or should I not think about it?

If you do, you won't allow the listening any time to go deeper. But after some time, the next day or the day after, you must meditate on it. Otherwise, where is the difference between listening of this kind and brainwashing?

That's exactly it.

There should certainly not be any brainwashing.

The fact is that the thought comes in so quickly, the substance which is created by listening doesn't have a chance.

That is correct. That listening is not total. So, that is natural.

And we are bound to make mistakes, and that's okay too?

Yes, of course, of course. And that, I repeat again, is part of the functioning of Totality. Only in very rare cases does this listening go straight into the heart and become an understanding. By and large, this process has to happen; total listening, meditation on it and settling into that understanding.

❏❏❏

– MEDITATION –

The joy that arises from the state of meditation happening, that's an experience isn't it?

The joy happens later, when you think of that experience, or when you think that that state was good.

Is that involvement, that joy?

The happening of the joy is not. Thinking about it is.

What does it mean when you go into deep meditation and your "me" is gone and the I is there? What does it mean then when you can smell certain odors?

It simply means that the consciousness is present and the sentience is also there and perhaps someone is cooking. Consciousness is present because the sentience is working through the respective senses. But when the consciousness is temporarily absent, the "me" is not present. In that state when the "me" is not present Consciousness exists but the manifestation functioning is absent. In deep meditation, to that extent, it will be like deep sleep.

Chuang Tzu, one of the most impressive Taoist teachers has stated, "The knowledge of the ancients was perfect, so perfect that at first they did not know that there were things. This is the most perfect knowledge. Nothing can be added. Next, they knew that there were things, but did not yet make distinction between them. They did not make any comparison between them. Next, they made comparison but they did not yet pass judgments upon them. When they proceeded to pass judgments, the *Tao* was lost."

"The knowledge of the ancients was so perfect they did not know there were things." It is *that* knowledge we have when we sit quietly, when we close our eyes and sit quietly without any objective in it, without any motive. Quite often it happens by itself. And in those moments is the perfect knowledge Chuang Tzu is speaking about. What then happens is there is a sense of awareness but in that awareness no thing exists. And when no thing exists there is no question of comparing or passing any judgments. The only thing in that quietness is an open heart that is receptive to whatever that power that turned you into a seeker is prepared to send. It is only when the mind is quiet, when the mind does not conceptualize, when the mind does not create images and the heart is open and receptive, that something happens. That "something happening" is that the "me" becomes absent and then the "I," the Subjective Reality, comes in.

So, the only thing one can do is whenever the time happens to be there, to sit quietly without any motive, without any objective, without wanting anything. You don't have to sit at a particular time, you don't have to decide that you will sit for fifteen minutes or half an hour, or two and a half hours. You don't have to sit with your back straight and keep wondering every two minutes whether it is straight enough. You don't have to have any object in mind, which means you don't have any expectation at all. In these moments you don't find Reality, the Reality finds you. Just sit quietly for a moment.

Doesn't this meditation strengthen the ego?

Yes, when it is deliberately done, when there is a "me" doing it. When meditation *happens*, when it is not volitionally performed, then it is true meditation in which ego is absent. There is no "me" doing it. Where the ego is present there is a "me" expecting something to come out of that act. I am not against the practice of meditation. All I'm saying is that meditation has to be seen in perspective.

Often, the ego seems to resist meditation.

Yes indeed. True meditation means the annihilation of the ego. The ego doesn't want that. When meditation happens, promptly the mind says "Stop wasting time, do something useful."

There are techniques for stilling the mind, like meditation, but the still mind doesn't necessarily receive anything. It can be totally empty and never receive anything.

No. Are you saying that it is possible to *make* the mind empty? I would say that is incorrect. It is not possible to *make* the mind empty.

I experience stillness of the mind in meditation. Are you saying that that's not emptiness?

It *is* emptiness.

But nothing happens in the stillness.

How do you know that nothing is happening? The beginning of emptiness of the mind happens in every human being, at least in some moments, but those moments are neither recognized nor received. But when this emptiness of the mind is recognized and accepted, there will be more occasions when this emptiness persists. This emptiness of the mind can be achieved by certain techniques, *yoga* or meditation or whatever, but anything that you acquire is liable to be lost. Silence of the mind which is the result of a deep understanding, *that* meditation is a natural, spontaneous meditation which just happens.

When I first went to Maharaj, he asked me, "Do you meditate?" I said, "Yes. My earlier *guru* asked me to meditate at least for half an hour a day. Whenever it was possible, I did try to sit. Now that I've retired, I do meditate for half an hour."

Six months later Maharaj asked me, "How is your meditation getting along?" I said, "Maharaj, I haven't thought about it, but now since you asked me, I'm sorry but I do not sit in meditation as I used to." Then I did add, "I do know that meditation happens quite often when I am not thinking about it."

I thought Maharaj would shout at me but he said, "Excellent!" Then he explained that when there is a spiritual progress, the meditation ceases and not thinking about that deliberate meditation, not feeling guilty about it, not even being conscious of the cessation of that meditation, is a great step forward.

I can't imagine not wanting to meditate or not being able to meditate, because it's such a pleasant, peaceful thing for me. But at the same time I think there is a danger in that because it can become an addiction.

That's what I meant about the means becoming an end.

I started golf with a friend of mine many years ago. We both took lessons. He paid a lot of attention to the mechanics of it. So when we started playing golf he was not playing too well because he kept thinking of what the instructor told him to do. After a while he stopped playing but he kept practicing. He said he loved to practice. He'd get a basket of balls and he'd keep on hammering the balls. One day he said, "I'm progressing, they're going straighter and longer." So I said, "Why don't you come and play a round with us?" He said, "No thank you, I prefer to practice."

You are really at your best in any game when you are not thinking of the mechanics of the game. Spontaneity is all.

◻◻◻

I'd like to recite an incident. There is a game show host, Bob Barker, who's wife was being interviewed. She was asked what she liked to do and she said, "I like to vacuum my house. I really like my carpets." I thought that was the dumbest answer I could imagine.

This week, I was vacuuming my carpet and suddenly it was very special, beautiful and informative. The thought of how many hours it would have taken me to pick up all that dust, speck by speck and put it into the trash can, was very moving. I'm still high only from a vacuum cleaner.

Whoever would have thought that Mrs. Barker would be my teacher? It took this experience to appreciate what a master had told me years before.

You never know what sentence, what subject, can affect you or when. What happened in your case is what I call the happening of meditation. Meditation is a word people make a big fuss over. What is meditation? Some incident and the feeling of joy comes up, *that* is meditation when it happens. Not when you sit and wonder, is my back straight enough? That is not meditation. And therefore this meditation can happen anywhere, a gift from the universe.

◻◻◻

– WITNESSING –

Could you explain this "witnessing" thing again? I don't get it.

Yes. You see, in witnessing the three stages are: First, the ordinary man is fully involved. Second, the understanding begins to dawn and the state of involvement lowers itself into the state of witnessing. Lastly, the understanding is complete and the involvement gets replaced by witnessing. Witnessing takes place so long as there is something to witness. If there is nothing to witness, the state becomes a state of non-witnessing. Ramana Maharshi called this "the natural state." And when that natural state continues without disturbance for awhile it reaches a deeper state which can be given any name you like, but that is a deeper state.But the witnessing and non-witnessing, they go from one to the other like an automatic shifting of gears. There's no problem.

Ramesh. It seems witnessing is not really a goal that is far away, because in the truest aspect of witnessing, it's how it really is. There's really no emotion to it or no...nothing really. There's witnessing and that's simply it. So what you're saying isn't really like a goal that's far off, that someday you can attain it, but actually is how every moment really does happen.

Yes. And in fact that is why I said you have never really left home.

◘◘◘

How is uninvolved witnessing different from watching a movie?

There is no difference. But when you are watching a movie you are watching and reacting at the same time. Yesterday, we went to a movie that was rated X. Children were not allowed. Someone came in with an infant, gurgling away. The infant was seeing precisely what everybody else was seeing but was not reacting. The infant was witnessing because he was not involved. But when *you* watch a movie, you get involved with the characters and therefore it is not witnessing.

Just as we are involved with this character in what we call real life?

Exactly, yes. There's involvement because you say, "I am the doer, the experiencer." Then you get involved. But when there is the realization that whatever is happening is just happening through a body-mind organism, then witnessing happens.

◘◘◘

I find it really frustrating. I'm witnessing and then suddenly it's just gone. I want it to just keep happening all the time. Should I try something different? But I guess I'm asking the impossible.

Exactly. The moment you say "I witness," it is the mind merely watching its own mechanism. So, you go round and round and round and round, you see, like if your car is stuck in the sand, the more you accelerate, the deeper your wheel goes into the sand. So what is needed to get the tire out is an outside force. *This* witnessing is not of the mind. This witnessing is a totally different dimension, which does not compare, which does not judge, which does not use the word "should." There is no question of should or should not. The witnessing merely sees it. The anger arises, the anger is witnessed, but there is no "me" or a mind-intellect to say, "I should not have been angry." In other words, there is no association or identification with the independent, spontaneous movement which is termed "anger." So any thought or emotion or desire that arises, when it is witnessed without comparing and judging, gets cut off. Such witnessing is without an individual witnesser.

I feel that I am aware. I contemplate this awareness.

Exactly. Therefore the mind is not absent, the mind is always there. The mind does not want to be away from anything that is happening. It is the nature of the mind to want to be associated with everything that happens. That is why it is terribly afraid of being told that there is no "me" in control. The mind or the "me" or the intellect says, "If I'm not aware, if I'm not in charge, there will be total chaos." Was there chaos before you were born?

I don't know.

That's it! That is precisely it. So now why do you bother? You did not know before you were born and you will not know after you are dead. In between, why do you assume that the flow of phenomenality will suddenly stop if you are not there?

I am not worried about this.

You are concerned with yourself. A drop in the flow of Consciousness wants to be aware of itself as a drop and yet wants to be the flow. It cannot be done.

Ramesh, with reference to mindfulness. When I'm doing a task with complete absorption and there's no mental play of the mind as far as discursive thought, that is a positive state, the state to be in. When I'm just sitting, then it's easy for me to go into that same kind of state. But when I'm walking or driving a car, actions that don't require such a thorough absorption, all kinds of thoughts arise. Now my question is, I know the Zen master says, "When I walk, I walk and when I sit, I sit." But when walking or driving a car should the focus be on the walking or driving or should the focus be on witnessing the thoughts in the mind?

You see, witnessing the thoughts in the mind means that the thoughts do arise. And when the thoughts arise, if the witnessing goes on, then as the thought arises it gets cut off. Now, for instance, your digestive system and respiratory system are working and your thoughts arise and they can be witnessed. If there is no traffic on the highway, your driving becomes as automatic as your respiratory system. And as the thoughts arise, they will be witnessed or there will be involvement. Either the "you" gets involved in the thoughts or, if the "you" is not there and there is a certain amount of understanding, then there'll be witnessing.

So what did the Zen master mean when he said, "When I walk, I walk. When I sit, I sit." Does that not mean that his total attention is on the walking rather than on witnessing the thoughts?

That means that in the case of the master the arising of the thoughts will be rare and not arise as frequently as in the case of an ordinary person. But when they do arise, they'll be witnessed. And therefore walking can be a true meditation. I know because it happens to me. I walk about an hour and a quarter every morning and every evening. I don't go out on the road because there'd be distractions. I walk in my own apartment from one corner diagonally to the other corner. And during that walking, if there are no interruptions, it can happen without any thoughts. Or, if a rare thought arises, it gets cut off.

You're not thinking of walking. You're just walking.

That's quite so.

Ramesh, is witnessing also a thought? I mean, it occurs to me that to witness a thought or an emotion, it would have to take place afterwards in space-time, that there is the thought and then imme- diately after there is the witnessing. So is witnessing simultaneous with the thought or the feeling or the emotion?

Well, you see, the witnessing is really the understanding. *Understanding in action is witnessing.* And if the under- standing is deep and full, then the witnessing and the cutting off happens simultaneously and concurrently as the thought arises.

But even if that understanding is not complete, even if there is just a certain amount of understanding, I'll go to the extent of saying that even if the understanding is at an intellectual level, it is not that all is lost. As a thought arises, because the mind is used to being involved in it, there will be a certain amount of involvement, there will be a certain amount of horizontal involvement. But that involvement will get cut off at some stage, maybe a fairly late stage, but nonetheless a sudden realization will arise that there is in- volvement and then it will get cut off.

And as the understanding goes deeper the horizontal periods of involvement will become less and less, and less and less frequent, and less and less intense, until when the understanding is deep enough the process of the thought arising and its getting cut off vertically will be almost simul- taneous or concurrent.

So, there is a witnessing just for a second?

A split-second, then it gets cut off. Correct. In fact, wit- nessing means there is no involvement by the "me."

In witnessing there is neither a witnesser nor a thing being witnessed?

"A thing being witnessed?" Yes. A thought arises. That arising of that thought is witnessed and it gets cut off.

And afterwards, it is not even a thing.

That is correct.

But if you attempt to do that…

Any attempt to do that would be the mind watching its own process, which is *not* witnessing, but involvement.

Doesn't this occur naturally? If we got involved in a thought, eventually it gets cut off when we go into another thought?

Yes, but eventually. What ends then is the involvement. Then another thought arises, and there's further involvement. So, in this continuous conceptualizing, what is present throughout, is involvement.

There's no instant of witnessing between the two involvements?

One involvement and another one starts.

I was playing with this idea that a thought arises and nothing is done with it. So, is that the nothingness of Consciousness?

Yes, indeed.

It doesn't go into action?

Yes. Witnessing cuts it off. There is no further thought. Another thought may come. Then again the same thing happens. The only point is that when the thinking mind is not there the thoughts arising will be fewer.

When witnessing occurs, it is spontaneous?

Witnessing is spontaneous and in the present moment. Therefore any thought which arises gets cut off. It may come up again but again when it is witnessed it gets cut off. Each time it arises it gets cut off. As Ramana Maharshi said, "It is like an uninvited guest who, when ignored, gradually stops coming."

ㅁㅁㅁ

I just got to thinking about this word "advaita," the not-two. Doesn't it imply that if there is witnessing, then there is that which is being witnessed, so that I'm back into a duality again?

The thought arising and its getting cut off is a movement in Consciousness. Everything that happens in phenomenality is in duality. The thought arising is one movement. Its getting cut off is another movement. But they are so simultaneous and concurrent that they almost tend to become one. Nonetheless, it is all a movement in duality, a movement in Consciousness.

But if I think of myself, I am witnessing.

You are not. There is no "witness." Then it is the mind deceiving itself that witnessing is taking place, but witnessing is not taking place. The mind is merely observing its own operation and deceiving itself into thinking that there is witnessing.

Then I can sing, "I've got plenty of nothin."

The Nothing has plenty of nothing. The Emptiness has plenty of emptiness.

❏❏❏

Ramesh, Ramana Maharshi spoke of a method of self-inquiry. Now, would you call that a "description" of what to do?

No, it is a description of what happens. What he is saying is, that when the mind has turned inwards and the thoughts arise, "Who am I? Who wants to know?" this chattering mind stops.

In my process, as soon as a thought comes, before any judgment comes whether it is good or bad, I ask myself, "From where does it come to me? Who am I?" What would you call that?

Ramana Maharshi made it clear that it's *only* a process for a beginner. If you keep on doing it, then the means becomes an end.

❏❏❏

When you are aware of something and then you become aware of being aware of it, is that the introduction of the self? It seems to me that it's very close to witnessing. Is there a difference, and if so, can you explain?

Your question is based, wittingly or unwittingly, consciously or unconsciously, on the assumption that there is a witnesser, someone witnessing. But the fact of the matter is that in witnessing, there is no witness. So long as there is someone who says, "I understand," a trinity exists made up of the "me," the something to be known, and the process of knowing or understanding, all of which are in phenomenality.

In sudden, immediate understanding, or witnessing, there is no "me" to realize anything. You may say later on, after the fact, "I understood." But in the immediate understanding there is no "me" who realizes anything. In this witnessing there is no witnesser. It is an impersonal understanding. There is no feeling that, "I have understood."

I asked the question because I reflect on what I've read or heard about witnessing, and I have a sense, all of a sudden, that as things are going on around me there is a detachment and I become aware of that. Then I think, "Now who is it that is watching?" It is almost like I try to turn around in my mind to see who it is, but it's gone because it's like the eye being unable to see itself.

Yes. That is the whole point. So when this involvement is witnessed, that witnessing, the sudden witnessing, is not in phenomenality. The triad is not there, this triad of someone witnessing something isn't there. And that is why it gets cut off. It might arise again, or there may be an awareness later of this involvement being cut off because of that witnessing. But the witnessing cutting off this involvement is of an entirely different dimension and the criterion is very simple: in witnessing, there is no comparing, there is no judging, there is no rationalizing, there is no accumulation of anything.

◨◨◨

What cuts off the thought when witnessing occurs? Is it the action of the moment?

It is the witnessing of it. Witnessing means living in the present moment. Living in the present moment means not getting involved. The thinking mind is kept out, *gets* kept out.

Why is living in the present moment acting, as opposed to thinking?

Living in the present moment is vertical, whereas the thinking mind is horizontal in duration. Involvement is always in duration. Once a thought comes, two things can happen, neither of which are in your hands. If your understanding is deep enough, then that thought will get cut off, though it may come again. But if that understanding has not yet started, then your thinking mind will get you involved in that thought which spontaneously arose.

Krishnamurti said, "You cannot always control your attention but you can save yourself and become attentive again, and again bring your attention to the moment." Does not that represent some volition?

Krishnamurti says, "Get your mind back to the present moment, being attentive to the fact that you have slipped into involvement." Now, being attentive to the fact that you have slipped into involvement *is* witnessing. The moment of involvement is witnessed, and involvement gets cut off.

True understanding of the lack of volition would seem to automatically produce witnessing.

Yes sir! Correct! Precisely the point. No one can produce the basic understanding that "I have no volition."

Therefore no choice, just observation of everything that occurs. Seems as though it's totally spontaneous and immediately after that I experience...

The mind comes in, commenting on the witnessing.

◘◘◘

Some of us think witnessing is a method and you're saying witnessing is a result, a result of the understanding that there is no volition.

Yes and strictly, not even the result. Understanding is witnessing. Impersonal Consciousness becomes understanding. Understanding, in effect, in practice becomes witnessing. There is nothing other than Consciousness.

Does acceptance always automatically turn into witnessing?

Yes! Indeed.

◘◘◘

If we had a blackboard, you could put the observed over there, the observer over here and the observing in the middle, and draw a straight line through the observer and the observed and that would leave the observing.

Quite so, there's only the observing when there is no understander, no comprehender and nothing to be comprehended. Then what remains is understanding. When there is no perceiver there is only the functioning, the noumenal functioning of perceiving, which is what happens when you're listening to great music. At that moment, where is the perceiver, the listener? There is only music. And that is so in *every* experience.

So, the perceiver is a thought and the perceiving is not a thought?

Correct. Perceiving is the noumenal subject which goes on all the time.

So the witness is a thought, the witnessing is not a thought?

If there is a witnesser or witness or witnesses, it is not witnessing, it is thinking.

Doesn't the presence of witnessing stop the thought, stop the nonacceptance?

Right. You say, "I have only understood this partially." The witnessing of the confusion stops it there. The confusion is not hooked by the thinking mind into the horizontal involvement.

Same way that witnessing jealousy stops the jealousy?

At that moment, yes. It may come up again.

But then you just keep cutting it off.

No! (laughter) It *gets* cut off! It's very basic, so I have to repeat this. Take any experience that happens. In the present moment there is no experiencer.

It is only the experience. Later on, when the mind thinks about the experience, then there is the experiencer.

But in any experience, good, bad or indifferent, at any moment, there is only the experience.

But we can't choose or try to witness, it only happens based on the understanding that there is no choice?

Correct. In witnessing there is no individual witness and never any choice.

◻◻◻

Is witnessing the same as living the present moment?

Yes, but, living the present moment cannot be done by anyone, nor can witnessing be done by anyone. When witnessing goes on all the time, the organism lives the present moment which is the same as natural spontaneous, living, because there is no "me" living that life. It is merely witnessing the actions that take place through one's body-mind mechanism precisely as witnessing the actions taking place through any other body-mind.

There is the deepest possible understanding that the body-mind organism, whether this one or the other, had nothing to do with the functioning, that it is the pure Subject or Consciousness or God which functions through each individual organism.

No individual organism has any volition. When that conviction is firmly there, you just sit back and then there is witnessing and then there is silence. Even amid the din of the roaring world, then there is silence.

In the witness, it's really experience merging?

It *is* merging. We talk of this merging only so long as there is a feeling of a "me" and thou. Afterwards, you don't think of any merging. You think of merging so long as there is a "me" to merge with something else. When there is this deepest intuitive understanding that all there is, is Consciousness, what is to merge with what?

When the witness and the witnessed, the two objects come together, isn't that witnessing?

It happens that the observer and the object observed lose their separateness. Then there is witnessing.

ᗌᗌᗌ

Since the individual mind can't conceive of noumenon or ever know anything about the Absolute at all, why do we even talk about it? Then we go outside and try to conceptualize and manipulate these concepts and its all such a joke, an absurdity!

Yes! Absolutely! And when you *truly* realize that this is an absurdity, then you join in the dance. You take part in this absurdity. The body-mind organism continues to live in the world, but without any sense of personal doership. That is where the witnessing takes place, as this individual body-mind organism and all the others are recognized as merely instruments through which Totality functions.

ᗧᗧᗧ

Does witnessing occur during deep sleep?

No, because witnessing means witnessing an event. Thought is an event, thus witnessing means witnessing a thought or an event. In deep sleep there is no event to be witnessed. You can say that the deep sleep state is a sort of non-witnessing state, because there is nothing to witness. And because there is nothing to witness and there is no getting involved in it, the "me" is not there. So, what is absent in deep sleep is the identified consciousness. Consciousness, which is always present because Consciousness is all there is, *is* present in deep sleep. It is identified consciousness which is absent. The "me" is absent and therefore there is no conceptualizing in deep sleep. When conceptualizing starts, the dreaming happens.

Some spiritual leaders say that they witness twenty-four hours a day.

What they mean is that the "me" is no longer there. There is total disidentification with the "me," which is the same as identification with the whole. "They witness twenty-four hours a day," means that Consciousness is always present, impersonal Consciousness is always present.

Is witnessing by impersonal Consciousness?

Yes! Witnessing is always by the impersonal Consciousness!

ᗧᗧᗧ

Is the witnessing that I do the same kind of witnessing that occurs for the spiritual master?

Here, again, you're thinking of the spiritual master as an individual entity. The individual entity does not witness. So, when the master says that there is witnessing all the time, or that the Consciousness is always present, he refers not to the "me" but to the "I" which is the impersonal Consciousness. There is no personal entity at all. In fact that is what enlightenment means, the absence of the sense of "me," as the doer.

Last night after the talk Marsha said, "Tell me, Ramesh, do you see all things, all human beings as the same?" I said, "Certainly not. The difference in things and human objects I see precisely as you do. In fact, if there is any difference, the difference would be this: there is a sense of marvel at the tremendous diversity in this objective expression. That is there, together with the deepest possible understanding that behind all of this diverse objective expression there is the Subjective Reality."

The example I usually give at this point is: suppose you have ten photographs taken of yourself in ten different costumes and you spread them out. No one else will know. To them, they are ten different people. But *you* know that they are the expressions of the same you. You know because there is knowing. When enlightenment happens, it is this knowledge that all these objective expressions, billions and billions of objects, including human beings, are merely different objective expressions of the same Subjectivity.

There's this knowingness. Is there a knower of that?

No, there is just the knowingness. Just as, in that understanding, there is no individual comprehender, just as, in this witnessing, there can be no individual witness. This impersonal attitude, this impersonal perspective, is so very important.

The impersonal "I" is just knowingness.

That is correct. In fact the moment you use "I," this "me" slips in. The best thing is not to think in terms of "I," because the "me" slips in.

In witnessing, is there name and form of the perception? If you're just perceiving, does the name and form still exist?

Oh yes, indeed.

But there is no sense that "I am perceiving this?"

That is correct. Comparing and judging doesn't take place.

ロロロ

When there is true witnessing, that's close to enlightenment isn't it? There's no sense of self.

Correct, no sense of self. There's another thing. I use the words, "Consciousness, understanding and witnessing," but they are not three different states. The understanding translates itself into acceptance. The understanding becomes witnessing when there is something to be witnessed. The understanding becomes non-witnessing when there is nothing to witness.

Is that state the absence of absence?

No. That is the absence of the presence. That absence of the absence is only a conceptual state prior to this manifestation. Because the mind says "There must be something prior to this," then, at that level of deep understanding you say, "Yes there is, but not in the way you think. That state is not the presence or existence that the mind wants, but the absence of the absence of the sense of presence." At the deepest level, when the mind has reached the understanding but has this final block, then, for that final block to be removed, this double negative is used as a concept.

ロロロ

I still can't quite get it. If the person is witnessing the thought rather than acting, that witnessing process is also cause and effect, it is Grace. He has been given the causes and conditions to be able to witness rather than to react. In that moment there is, in a sage, no karma *being created.*

Karma is being created every second, but it is not anybody's *karma*. *Karma,* as such, is created. In fact, that *karma* is the very basis of the continuity of life. The basis of witnessing is understanding, and the understanding begins to take place only when there is Grace.

And then there is no reaction at that moment?

Right.

So, if there is witnessing taking place there is liberation in that moment, there is freedom in that moment?

There is freedom in that moment, yes. There is freedom because a thought is not taken delivery of. There is freedom in that moment, but it is the understanding itself which functions as witnessing. There is no "me" to witness.

◻◻◻

In the scheme of all of this play, in the last twenty-five years, I have had the occasion to find a guru and to be at the feet of the guru. My question is, if the guru says "Don't call me a guru," but functions as a guru, is he the guru?

Yes. So don't call him a *guru.* (laughter) Where is the problem?

No problem.

No problem! (laughter) This is what happens. The mind creates a problem and wants a solution. In most cases, problems don't need solutions, they need *dissolution.* Problems need to be dissolved, not solved, because there is no solution. The only way the problems get dissolved is, as soon as they arise, they are merely witnessed. They are not "taken delivery of," as Maharaj used to say. When the mind gets involved, then the problem becomes a problem. Otherwise it is just a thought. And if that thought is merely witnessed, it disappears.

◻◻◻

It would appear to me that the witness itself is an aspect of the Consciousness, awake unto itself.

Quite right. Therefore I am saying that it is Consciousness which becomes the understanding in the process of disidentification. And in the process of disidentification, when there is something to witness, the understanding in action becomes the witnessing. Consciousness, understanding, witnessing are only notionally different. It is the same Consciousness in the process of disidentifying itself from the individual that becomes the understanding, which in turn becomes the witnessing. But basically, it is the same Consciousness.

In the witnessing there's no difference. The phenomenon is not separated out from the noumenon in which it arises?

In other words, it is the Subject witnessing its own objective expression as the functioning of phenomenon.

Which means no separation, right?

That is correct. No separation.

Which to me is where the joy comes. Because when there is no separation, there is just this quality, which is joy or love.

You see, even when there is no separation, the separation, phenomenally, still has to exist. When you are in the sun, there is you and your shadow. As a substance and a shadow there is a separation. But the shadow has no independent existence. Therefore, there is no separation. That is why the question, "Is the manifestation real?" can only be answered with the paradox, "It is both real, and unreal." It is real to the extent that it can be seen, perceived. Therefore it is real. But it is only an appearance against the background of Consciousness. Without Consciousness, there is no appearance of manifestation. Therefore, the manifestation is unreal.

◘◘◘

– WITNESSING PAIN –

You said there must be identification of a kind with the body-mind until it is dead. What could you say, in that respect, about suffering and pain, particularly physical pain?

Physical pain is a factor which depends a lot on the natural ability of each individual organism to bear pain. I've always believed that my ability to bear pain is less than average. Many years ago, long before I was actively interested in this subject, I had an appendix operation and the surgeon was talking with me while operating. He said, "Now the pain isn't there because I've given you an anesthetic. Maybe half an hour, maybe an hour from now the pain will start. The nurse has been instructed to give you further anesthetic." I knew the nurse could reduce the pain, so when the pain started I said to myself, "Let me see what the pain is like." So when the nurse came she said, "Is there pain?" I said, "Yes, the pain has started, but it's still bearable. I would like to experience it and, if I find I need you, then I'll send for you." And this pain continued, continued to climb up. I could witness it, all the time, until it leveled off into a plateau.

Once the pain had leveled off, I could accept it as part of my body. And the result was that throughout the day I didn't send for the nurse. And later in the day she came and said, "I will give you the injection so you will be able to sleep better." So that was all right. The experiment was over. I could bear it by merely witnessing it. First witnessing the pain as something detached from me, later on I could accept it as part of my being, part of the body. I even had the thought that if that pain had been with me from birth, I would not have recognized it as pain, I would have accepted it as part of my beingness. So, being one with the pain at a certain stage and earlier merely witnessing it, helped enormously.

Who is this "you" when you speak about your accepting the pain? Who is this "I" that is accepting?

The pain was accepted as part of the body. And the thought occurred that if that pain had been with me since birth I could not have recognized it as pain but as part of the body. So there was really no "I" accepting the pain. There was just the acceptance of the pain, something like being blind since birth.

And then the "I" came later?

The "I" came later. "I" came later with the thought that if this pain had been with me for a long time it would have been accepted as part of the body, like an arm or a leg.

So, there is no acceptee, no accepter, there is just accepting?

There is acceptance. And the acceptance or the understanding that I am talking about is an understanding or an acceptance where there is no comprehender or no accepter. Therefore, such acceptance can only happen, can only come about. You cannot achieve that understanding, you cannot achieve that acceptance.

I take it that suffering must be accepted when it occurs.

Indeed yes! And because it is not accepted, the question is often asked, "Why me?" But if you had won a lottery, a million dollars, you wouldn't ask, "Why me?" (laughter)
So the only answer really to, "why me?" is, "why not me?" The basic understanding has to be that no "me" is special. The human being is merely part of the totality of manifestation. So when that acceptance gradually expands, then life becomes easier. Suffering becomes more easily bearable than when you look at suffering as something to be rejected, something to be ended.

◻◻◻

– ACCEPTANCE AND SURRENDER –

Regarding the word "individual," the very root of the word means undivided.

Correct. You see, what is indivisible is Consciousness.

Yes.

And in the understanding of that, the individual, as we understand the word, gets demolished, gets annihilated.

Because we see it with the ego and so on.

Yes.

That is the way we interpret life. As a person, as a life, as a person with a life, as a living entity.

From the point of view of knowledge or *jnana*, that there is no "one" who has any volition or choice in anything in this phenomenal world, is acceptance. From the point of view of devotion, the word would be surrender. But basically, it means acceptance that there is no such thing as an individual entity with independence of choice and action. "Thy Will" be done. Then the mind becomes quiet.

It's so simple, but it's so difficult.

Famous last words!

 🔲🔲🔲

The organization of a physical organism is far more complex than that of any political or commercial corporation, and yet it works with a minimum of conscious control. The circuits of brain and nerve are more subtle than any computer system, and yet we hardly know how we use them. When history began, we put on clothes, picked up tools, and learned how to speak and think.

In the words of a writer called Lancelot White, "Thought is born of failure. When action satisfies, there is no residue to hold the attention. To think is to confess a lack of adjustment which we must stop to consider. Only when the human organism fails to achieve an adequate response to its situation is there material for processes of thought." Only when one thinks that he is not happy, only when one thinks that the what-is is not acceptable, does the thought arise, "What should I do to make the what-is more acceptable?" Then the whole train of misery begins. To be anxious is to wear oneself out, and to seek power and to use force is to overstrain one's system. One is best preserved by floating along without stress, which is the same as Jesus' doctrine of not being anxious for the morrow, and of earning one's bread by the sweat of one's brow.

This theme runs throughout the spiritual literature of the world: "You will get it if you do not want it" and "To him that hath, shall be given." To those who feel that they have not, this is an exasperating paradox. If deep down inside you want most desperately to survive and be in control of things, you cannot genuinely take the attitude of not worrying about it. And trying to stop worry means making an effort to control. You must allow yourself the freedom to worry, to let the mind think whatever it wants to think.

So, we come back to the old formula of witnessing. You cannot deliberately stop worrying. If you try to stop worrying, you get more involved in it. So what is the answer? It is simple: when worry comes up, let it come up. As worry comes up, if it is witnessed, you are not taken deeper into further involvement. Because we believe that worry causes tension, we feel that we must not worry. But you cannot not worry. The only way the worry will stop is through the proper understanding that change is the very basis of life, that we cannot continuously have something we like. We've got to be prepared to accept things in life which may not be acceptable. That is the *only* understanding which will ultimately reduce and perhaps remove worry. But you cannot deliberately stop worrying.

Trying to control the mind, or trying to control the senses, means there is an individual wanting control for his own reasons. There is still the individual wanting something and therefore acting with a certain purpose.

So, with enlightenment all desire ceases?

It is not that desires do not arise. Desires arise, the senses are drawn towards their objects, but there is no involvement by a "me." On the spiritual path the person is told, "If you are to unite with Shiva, you must control yourself, you must control the senses." So, he's trying to control the senses and becomes neurotic. When understanding at least begins, then it is accepted that the senses get attracted to their objects. So there is no hindrance. The senses and their objects getting together is merely witnessed.

A sincere seeker asked Ramana Maharshi, "I'm carried away by the sight of the breasts of a young woman neighbor. I fear I will commit adultery. What can I do?"

Ramana Maharshi replied, "It is your senses and body which tempt you and which you confuse with your real self. First, know who is tempted and who is there to tempt. But even if adultery does take place, do not think about it afterwards because you are, yourself, always pure. You are not the sinner."

What this means is that it is not the *act* which is the sin. Your thinking about it and attaching the sin to your self is the trouble. So the sinning is really not in the act itself, but in assuming the guilt. Remember, this was addressed to a seeker who was deeply concerned about his committing a sin. It does not apply to the person who is not a seeker, who, if he were to commit a sin, would then say, "Look, Ramana Maharshi says that I'm not the sinner, anything goes."

Could a jnani *commit adultery?*

It would not be the "*jnani*" committing adultery. An act takes place and will have its consequences. If adultery does take place, then the point, which is not relevant here, is that that act of adultery could lead to certain consequences which that organism will have to bear, because the action has happened through that particular organism. Understanding will prevent him from taking personal guilt for it and he will also be ready for the body-mind organism to accept the consequences, such as they are.

They tell about a saint named Kamile who lived in a hut. A neighbor girl became pregnant by her lover. When she was pressed, she said, "Kamile is the father." When the child was born, the girl's parents brought the child to Kamile and said, "It's your child, so *you* bring him up." He said, "So be it," and he brought up the child. Later on, the girl repented. The girl and her parents came back and said, "Look we're very sorry, we made a mistake, the child is ours, please let us have him back." He said, "So be it."

An act will have consequences, but the consequences may not relate to the person through whom the act happened. For example, a man driving a car throws a lighted cigarette out the window. A forest fire starts with disastrous consequences but this man is two hundred miles away. So the consequences of that act may not involve him at all. They may involve a lot of other, what we call, innocent people. All of it is part of this functioning of Totality. The point here is that assuming personal guilt means assuming personal doership and in spontaneous, virtuous living the question of credit or guilt just simply doesn't arise. All of it is merely witnessed. The fact of the matter is that the human being, as such, cannot exist as an independent entity. He's only an infinitesimal part of the totality of manifestation.

What man desperately wants is security for the future. He cannot be happy even if he has everything his heart desires. He has a future to look forward to and his experience of the past tells him that change is the very essence of life and that security has never had anything resembling permanency. The result is that even against his better judgment he cannot help chasing the will-o'-the-wisp which he has named "security." The real tragedy of this situation is that he is afraid to enjoy himself. There is fear of being happy because he knows he cannot hang on to it.

But, when there is true understanding, there is an un-qualified joyous acceptance of the fact that life and living is not a stagnant pool, but running water which you cannot store in a bucket. When there is an understanding of the present moment as the marvelous eternal moment, unre-lated to time, then there is an uninhibited enjoyment of what the present moment has provided.

ロロロ

Is the process of meditating, of going through all those steps, important to some body-minds and totally unnecessary for others?

Precisely so, and this is the danger I told you about. When you reach a certain stage, the tendency is to say to someone still meditating, "You damn fool, what do you think you are doing? All that is a waste," which is wrong. When the understanding is really deep, he doesn't bother to tell any-body. He thinks, "Fine, that's the way his evolution is pro-ceeding. Then, let it proceed." So he accepts it as part of the What-Is. All this trying, in one way or another, is accepted. Whatever is happening in the What-Is, is accepted. It is never resisted or challenged.

You called those rare moments of spontaneous mediation, "free samples."

Yes! They *are* free samples, free samples from Someone who is not trying to sell you anything.

ロロロ

Stephen Hawkings, when asked if there was intelligent life in outer space, said, "It's possible, though it may have destroyed itself already. Let's hope to prove this theory wrong." You say, "If we should blow ourselves up, that too is in the scheme of things. So, why worry about it?" But I feel obligated to worry and I use the worry as a tool to try to pry me into doing what little I can to prevent that from happening. I am using the worry.

As I said before, you cannot deliberately not worry. If a certain fear keeps coming up, that's what we call worry. That worry could be an apparent cause for some action to take place through this organism which would be part of the functioning of Totality. So let it! What this understanding will bring about is that it is not *your* action.

When one begins to feel a growing sense of disidentification, is that like a sense of defeat?

Not defeat. There is a sense of acceptance, a sense of tremendous freedom. Can you imagine? You think you have this burden and all this responsibility. Then you begin to understand that the same actions will continue to happen, based on reactions of this body-mind organism. The same actions will continue. Whatever you may do to fight what is supposed to happen, they will still happen. When you understand this deeply, you have a sense of tremendous freedom. "Whatever is going to happen, is going to happen, why should I worry? All I can do is whatever I have been doing." You continue to act with a sense of responsibility, with a sense of compassion—if that is your nature—but knowing that you have no control over the consequences of your actions. The basic point to understand and accept is that whatever you do, the consequences are not in your hands.

What about talking about this kind of stuff all the time? Like with friends, talking about how you view yourself and how you want to act? Is that just perpetuating...

It is just conceptualizing.

So, it really doesn't serve any purpose?

It's really a waste of energy. Understanding that, will make you naturally talk a little less.

Sir, the other day I was talking about how all my life I've felt bad about what I thought I was missing, that I wasn't brave on a roller coaster and all that. It's occurred to me that my role in life is to be a sissy, just as Arjuna was supposed to be a warrior.

That is correct.

And so, theoretically, I shouldn't feel bad about not being brave?

Not theoretically. Anything *but* theoretically. There has to be such an intuitive conviction...

That it's all right to be a sissy?

That it's all right to be what you are! "Sissy" is a labeling by the split-mind.

I'm always wanting to be something other than what I am.

That is precisely the point. You see?

◻◻◻

It's been said that God became men in order to enjoy himself. Is Consciousness arising in one entity called "me," talking to Consciousness in this entity called Ramesh?

Indeed. That is so.

Having a conversation so they might enjoy it.

Yes, all there is, is Consciousness. And this process of seeking is really the personal consciousness, the personal identified consciousness, seeking its impersonality as part of this life, as part of this game, as part of this *lila*.

Concerning all that you've talked about, if I'm doing it all wrong, that's still the way it's supposed to be?

At that time! But you happen to be listening to this teaching. Some power has brought you here and you are listening to the teaching. And if that listening turns itself into some kind of an understanding, then that understanding will change your perception.

But what if I'm understanding it wrong?

Then, that...

That happening is what is supposed to be?

That is correct. That is precisely what I am saying. In other words, if there has to be a misunderstanding, that misunderstanding will happen. No way could you have avoided that misunderstanding at the time.

Although the working mind may spontaneously do what is "right," those of us who are still identified do suffer if we do something "wrong" at times. Having suffered so in the past, we are on guard to act correctly and avoid further pain.

Yes, but even the wrong-doing which results in suffering is part of the functioning of Totality, part of God's will.

Many years ago when I was watching a movie, they showed a count who had a family motto. And that family motto was, "This too shall pass." It made a tremendous impression on me. I was probably fifteen or sixteen. "This too shall pass." Accepting this will bring about a double-sided effect. When something is bad you will know this too will change, so there's no need to go into the depths of despair. When something is good, you won't have to go into the peaks of ecstasy. This too will pass. You will be able to accept life as it comes.

The very basis of life, living and the whole entire universe, is continuous, constant change. The human being seeking security in a world which is continuously changing is bound to be frustrated.

Is it true that surrendering truly means that we're not giving up anything at all except the belief that we are in charge?

Precisely. The word "surrender" is a most misunderstood word. The surrender is merely the surrender of volition, surrender of personal doership. But it's interpreted by the average person to mean giving up all his material possessions. True surrender is purely and only the giving up of the idea that one has volition, accepting His Will in everything that happens.

Volition is an illusion, anyhow.

Precisely. So the understanding is that there cannot be any volition, that God cannot let two billion people have volition and still run this universe with any kind of precision!

❑❑❑

Reading Maharaj sometimes, something I read is so absolutely clear... there is something that knows. And this understanding brings freedom. But I can never bring it back and its very frustrating. My question is, how do I not get so frustrated because I can't bring that back? Where did all that clarity go? Those moments, I can't bring them back! And now I don't know anything, I'm in darkness, in stupidity. Which was real? I don't know which was real.

I do understand the intensity of your problem. In phenomenality, both are real. The acceptance of this fact that in phenomenality there cannot be any unchanging conditions, that these ups and downs, elation and depression, are part of the functioning of the Totality through the body-mind organism, will gradually bring about the witnessing of such ups and downs. The frustration will gradually disappear.

But, I also feel that these other moments bring a knowledge, and I can't take that back with me. It's as if I'm going back to another place, and I have to leave whatever was there, there.

It is the mind that wants those experiences of considerable peace. The paradox is that so long as the mind seeks such moments, you are farther away from what is happening. So the ultimate word is acceptance, which is the same as surrender. Whatever is happening is part of the functioning of Totality. If it includes the frustration, then that frustration has to be accepted. Whereas, instead of accepting, the mind says "How can I get rid of it?"

Doesn't that have to be accepted to? The instance of protesting?

Yes, indeed!

Before you can accept, you also have to allow the stage of non-acceptance.

Yes. All of it. That's is the misery of the seeker I am talking about.

But I don't want this frustration and that's why I can't get rid of it.

That acceptance of that frustration means the beginning of the understanding.

Which is why you are always going back to what-is.

Precisely. That also has to happen.

That's where the jnana *and the* bhakti *meet, the devotional aspect of the knowledge. Faith enough to accept that it will happen again.*

In *jnana,* knowledge, the word is "acceptance" acceptance of what-is. In devotion, the word is "surrender," surrender to His Will.

Acceptance and surrender are the same?

Exactly! Ultimately, there is no difference between the paths. In both cases the ultimate condition immediately preceding the happening of enlightenment is the deepest conviction that there cannot be any real "me," that the "me" is an illusion. No "me" can persuade God to accept him. The "me" has to surrender and then God happens.

There's a problem talking about acceptance, as there's no "one" to accept or not accept.

Correct. That is why I keep saying, "acceptance without an accepter, acceptance, as such, understanding without a comprehender." A sudden flash of understanding and there it is. In that spontaneity there is no comprehender and comprehended. All there is, is acceptance. There can only be witnessing because there *is* nothing else.

To me, if I accept that whatever is, is all there is, then what I'm doing is just living my life from moment to moment and this whole thing is unnecessary.

Yes, as e.e. cummings said, "If you can just be, be. If not, cheer up and go about other people's business, doing and undoing unto them until you drop."

Just continue what I've been doing up to now, without worry?

Absolutely. There is no need to change. In fact, the more you think there is need to change or alter your life, the more of an obstruction there is.

It's one thing to have complete understanding and accept. But with partial understanding, how can I accept? Can I accept the imperfections?

Yes. The only point is there's no question of "one" accepting wholly or partially. The partial acceptance or the whole acceptance can only happen and that is part of the destiny of the organism.

So, is there any point in trying to change results?

Here again, if you are trying to change results, you cannot stop that trying unless this deep down understanding happens that you cannot control the results. Therefore, why try to change results?

When you say, "There's nothing that you can do," do you mean volitionally? Because there's still action that's going to take place and there is room for social action if you are so predisposed.

Yes! That predisposition is part of the functioning of Totality. Not everybody is predisposed towards that. Social action will take place through those organisms which have those characteristics which produce that action.

It seems the way you are talking, everything is a process. There's no entity, there's nothing, everything is witnessing.

Everything is an *impersonal* process. I'll tell you a story about this.

On a day when there weren't any talks, our hostess in Tiburon was out working in the garden with her gloves on. Then suddenly she had a thought and came in and said, "Ramesh, I just have one question. Tell me, if I am able to accept that the whole thing is an impersonal process, then I need not be concerned with anything else, right? Not self-inquiry, not devotion, not anything else?" I said, "Correct! That is beautiful. You are not concerned because of one very simple thing: if that impersonal process is accepted, there is no 'you' to be concerned with anything."

She was delighted, so she went back to her gardening. You see, the moment that this is accepted, everything else is understood to be conceptual and not necessary, absolutely unnecessary. But that impersonal functioning is not easy to accept so long as the individual still thinks in terms of separate entities.

Isn't that the same thing as just acknowledging that "I have never truly done anything, anyhow?"

Yes !!

It's not saying, "I'm going to surrender."

Absolutely correct! "You" cannot surrender! The surrender can only happen with the understanding itself, that only His Will can prevail. It goes really deep down, you see. The fact of the matter is, it is His Will which has always prevailed. It is His Will which is now prevailing and it is His Will which will prevail in future. That is a fact. The longer it takes one to accept that fact, the longer will one suffer. Now, I happen to have the patience to explain this. Maharaj didn't. (laughter) When somebody said, "Maharaj, I cannot accept," he said, "Oh, you can't? Alright, then suffer!!" (laughter)

🐾🐾🐾

In the disidentification from the idea that it's only an idea, what gives up? It feels like emotion that is continually wanting an objective something, wanting an understanding.

The "me," the identified consciousness, *is* the wanting, *is* the thinking, *is* the desiring.

It's giving up the idea that there is a giver-upper at all, that there is somebody to do it?

Correct. Consciousness, which has identified itself with a particular body-mind organism as a "me" for some reason, is suddenly transformed and that identification drops off. Saying "identification drops off" simply means the sense of personal doership drops off.

Can you say how surrender relates to that absence of personal doership?

Curiously, the word "surrender" is the absolute, ultimate word for enlightenment happening, and yet in our life it's a most despicable word. In life, when you use the word "surrender" there is someone who surrenders. And that one who surrenders is shamed. But in the surrender we've been discussing there is no "me" to surrender. Surrender happens. The word "surrender" is used where there is a duality between "me" and God. When this surrender happens, this "will" which I think of as mine drops off, and there is total acceptance that all that prevails is His Will.

I am reminded of a story I read somewhere. A man found himself in the unenviable position of hanging by his fingers on the side of a cliff. After a few moments he shouted, "Is there anyone up there? I need help!" He heard a voice that said, "Yes. I'm here." The man shouted again, "Who are you?" The voice replied, "I am God. I'll help you. Do exactly as I say." The man was relieved and said, "OK, I'll do whatever you say." God said, "Just let go, you'll be safe." After a pause the man shouted, "Is there anyone *else* up there?" (laughter)

At some stage in life, we reach a point where we have to really have some trust. I think trust includes certain facts. One is that it is impossible for the human intellect to understand the working of the universe. The second is that however much we think and believe that we're living our own lives, the fact of the matter is that our lives are being lived. If we just look back on our own lives and the lives of those who are near to us, we cannot but come to the conclusion that the most important events which have led to further important events were unplanned, accidental. You'd say, "If that hadn't happened I would not be in this position," good or bad.

With these two facts, a certain amount of trust gets developed. Other than these two principles, I doubt if we can have any others to guide our lives. Life can be really and truly simple if we don't fight it. Our lives become difficult simply because we fight life. Not fighting life means accepting what-is. Accepting doesn't mean not taking any available evasive action, such as taking aspirin for a headache. Accepting life means dealing with it as it comes along, without thinking of the past or projecting into the future. If we accept life from day to day, from moment to moment, I think we'll find that life can be amazingly simple.

What more can you say?

That's precisely the point. What more can *anyone* say? Anything more that is said is just building a conceptual structure which can only be a hindrance.

❑❑❑

My friends and I have read your books and we keep trying to be in the I Am. If I was at a table with these guys, drinking coffee, I could have said almost everything you just said and so could the people I'm with, but I'm still a schmo. *I'm still miserable and I don't know what the hell's going on!*

Yes.

So, how come you got it, and I don't get it?

It's a very valid question.

I don't care about karma *or anything. I just want to get out of this.*

You see, until this joke is realized as a joke, it can be a most tragic joke.

Oh yeah, it's pretty unpleasant. I can't be in the I Am when I want to be.

The acceptance of this fact *is* being in the I Am, just accepting that there is *nothing* this organism can do to achieve enlightenment. Can you imagine the sense of freedom that arises from this one acceptance? The one acceptance that enlightenment may not happen in this body-mind organism? Just that acceptance means a tremendous sense of freedom!

Sometimes when you talk about acceptance, it sounds to me like you mean something volitional, which I know you must not mean.

Acceptance is what happens when the understanding takes place.

Then I can't do anything about it?

No.

When you were talking yesterday about the original state that little children are in up to three years or so...

Yes!

That, then, is not the enlightened state, it is a state prior to the need for enlightenment?

Yes. Young children often intuitively accept what-is. Now, I often relate in this case the instance of my granddaughter. In Los Angeles, for several months, we had a very lovely person who used to prepare the food. And while she was cooking, she was listening to the talks. I had repeated this story at least three or four times. So, one time when I got onto this point I thought I would skip the story. But this lovely person pokes her head out from the kitchen and says, "Tell them about your granddaughter!" (laughter)

My granddaughter, Aksheta, was about four, and an extremely restless child. At the end of the day, her mother used to be thoroughly fagged out. So one evening Gita, the mother, said, "Aksheta, look, you've absolutely worn me out. Now I'll give you a bath. Then after that you go to your room, stay there quietly for five minutes and pray to God that He'll make you a better girl." So, Aksheta readily agreed and when she went to her room she came out after probably two minutes. So her Mother asked, "Did you pray to God?"

"She said, "Yes Mother, I really prayed, because I really don't want to tire you, so I really prayed hard."

"What did you pray for?"

She said, "I did just what you asked. I prayed that He make me a better girl so that I don't bother my mother so much. I really prayed." So her mother was pleased.

But the next day, Aksheta being Aksheta, she did all the same things again. So at the end of another long day, the mother said, "Aksheta, I thought you had prayed last night?"

She said, "Mother, I did pray. I prayed very hard. So if He has not made me a better girl it means either He can do nothing about it or He wants me to be as I am." (laughter)

◻◻◻

– WHO IS SEEKING WHAT? –

Aren't you going to tell the story about the Sufi?

I wasn't going to, but now that you ask, it's this:

The royal court was assembled awaiting the arrival of the king, when a raggedly dressed Sufi *fakir* strolled in and sat in the seat reserved for the king. The chief minister was aghast. He said, "Who do you think you are, coming in here like this? Do you imagine yourself a minister?"

"A minister?" asked the Sufi. "No, I am more than that."

"Well you can't be the Chief Minister. I am the Chief Minister. Are you the King?"

"Not the King," said the Sufi. "I am more than that."

"Are you the Emperor?"

"No, I am more than that"

"The Prophet?"

"No, I am more than that."

"Do you think you are God?"

" No, I am not God, I am more than that."

" But more than God there's nothing!!"

" Yes, that is correct," said the Sufi. "I am that Nothing."

That which is nothing is the source, is the everything that is manifest. The unmanifest has become the manifest. The noumenon has become the phenomenal manifestation. The absolute has become the relative. The potential energy has become the activated energy. On the empty stage has come this play. On the empty canvas has come this painting. The source of everything is that Nothing.

Because of our perception, we think what is real is that which is perceptible to our senses, whereas the real is that which is *not* perceptible to the senses. So metaphysically we are back to the question, "Who is seeking what?" The who, as we have seen, is nothing but emptiness, so there cannot be a real who, there cannot be a solid who, there cannot be a solid individual entity which is the seeker. We have also seen that *what* is being sought is also nothing. The "what" that is being sought is not something which can be seen by the eye, which can be heard by the ear, which can be smelled by the nose, which can be tasted by the tongue or touched by the fingers. So, that something which is being sought is not some *thing* at all. Let us see how wise people have described this something that is being sought:

The Master Yung ToAh Shi calls it the Great Gate of Compassion. He says, "It is only when you hunt for it that you lose it. You cannot take hold of it, but then you cannot get rid of it and while you cannot do either it goes on its own way. You remain silent, and it speaks, you speak and it is dumb. The Great Gate of Compassion is wide open, with no obstacles before it."

Another master said, "What is great *nirvana*? Great *nirvana* is not to commit oneself to the *karma* of birth and death. What is the *karma* of birth and death? To wish for great *nirvana* is the *karma* of birth and death."

So, the very idea of seeking one's true nature, the very idea of wanting enlightenment is itself the biggest obstruction.

We are all seekers. If we just think back and ask ourselves, "What made us seekers? Did we choose to be seekers? Did we suddenly one day decide, 'Starting tomorrow, I will seek my true nature?' How did it happen?"

You didn't choose to be a seeker. What brought about the beginning of this seeking is some thought from outside. A thought which impelled you and compelled you to find out your true nature.

ㅁㅁㅁ

– WHO IS RESPONSIBLE? –

It's impossible for me to give up responsibility and let go. What keeps coming back to me is that I am responsible for the health of my body and if I let go of that responsibility my body will deteriorate. And it probably would.

Yes! Therefore, you will not let go. You will continue to take care of the body. But if you don't, and let the body deteriorate, that also was supposed to happen. The same teaching, the same readings, could have different effects on different people.

Yes, I do worry about the results.

That is what this understanding will bring about. You continue with your normal practice without worrying about it. If you are meditating, continue. If you are not meditating, you need not deliberately bring in meditation. A vegetarian? You continue to be a vegetarian. A non-vegetarian, continue your diet. No one need bring about any deliberate changes. If changes are necessary they will happen. And if something changes, you do something new or you cease doing something, there's no need to feel any guilt. It's part of the functioning of Totality.

If I murder someone and I don't get caught, I'm sure that I would always have a fear that I'm not going to get away with it. I don't have to feel guilty, but there's something about murdering someone that...

You don't feel guilty if you understand that what has happened is not *your* doing, but is part of the functioning of Totality. If you committed a crime and at the time you knew it was *your* crime, how can you not feel guilty? See? But if there is this understanding and something happens whereby somebody gets hurt through this organism, you accept that and also the consequences. Then there is no need to feel the guilt. If the "me" is there, the guilt is there, of course.

◻◻◻

– INDIVIDUAL NATURES AND SPIRITUAL PATHS –

What is the best spiritual path?

We should keep in mind Ramana Maharshi's statement of the final truth, "There is no creation, no destruction, no path, no goal..."

The question really is misconceived because it assumes that there *is* a path, that there *is* a goal, that there is a best path which would suit everybody and which anybody could choose. This is a basic misconception. No human being has natural characteristics quite like any other. The individual human body, as I pointed out the other day, is really nothing but an individual pattern of dynamic energy. That is all an individual is, energy vibrating and pulsating at an incredible speed in a particular pattern. And that pattern has characteristics which are peculiar to that particular body-mind organism. The Hindu Scriptures refer to this as *dharma*. *Dharma* has been misconstrued through the ages and has assumed different kinds of meanings. *Dharma* literally means "the original nature." So, the *dharma* of a rose is to smell like a rose. The *dharma* of an individual organism is to react to an outside event, including a thought, in a particular way. And that way is based on the natural characteristics with which that individual organism has been conceived and created.

My only suggestion is, if you are directed from one path to another, that there is really no reason for you to think that you are being disloyal to the earlier path, let alone to the earlier *guru*. Forget the *guru*, you are not being disloyal even to that original path. So my suggestion is, go with the flow, go where this universal Consciousness leads you without any feeling of guilt or disloyalty. That feeling of guilt or disloyalty is one of the worst feelings one can imagine.

There's a very fine quotation from the Arabian sage, Monoimus. He says: "Learn whence is sorrow and joy, and love and hate, and the waking though one would not, and sleeping though one would not, and falling in love though one would not, and, if thou shouldst closely investigate all these things, thou wilt find God in thyself one and many, just as the atom, thus finding in thyself a way out of thyself."

Yesterday you talked about the intersection of bhakti yoga *and* jnana. *Could you talk a little more about that?*

Yes. There really is no distinction between *bhakti* and *jnana*. Each person gets directed by that power which turned him into a seeker to move in a particular direction.

There's a very good story about *bhakti* and *jnana*. There was a saint named Namdev who offered some food to his God, Vithoba. The legend is that Vithoba actually ate it. Consequently, Namdev acquired a certain fame as a true *bhakta* whose offering of food had actually been accepted by God.

On one occasion, Namdev sat with several saints in a tent. One of these was a *jnani* called Gora Kumbhar. Kumbhar means potter. Someone said, affectionately, "Gora, you are a potter and so know whether a pot is properly baked or not. Take your stick, tap everybody's head, and tell us who is unripe, not completely fired." When he came to Namdev and tapped his head, he said, "This one is unripe. This one is not properly baked."

Namdev was very angry. He went to Vithoba the next day and said, "This is bad. This is unfair! Gora Kumbhar has said that I am not ripe. What of my *bhakti* you accepted?"

Then Vithoba told Namdev, "Look, now you are traversing in an area over which I have no control. This is beyond me, beyond God. There is nothing I can do." But finally Vithoba said, "I'll tell you what to do. Go to a particular Shiva temple. There you will find a man who lives there. Go to him and see what happens."

Namdev went into this temple and found the man lying there, totally absorbed in his own state, with his feet on the *Shivalingam*. Namdev was horrified. "What are you doing?" he exclaimed. "You have placed your feet on the sacred *Shivalingam*." The man replied, "Have I? I wasn't aware. I am so sick and debilitated, I don't even have the strength to lift my feet. Would you please lift them and place them where there is no *Shivalingam*"? So Namdev lifted his feet and wherever he put the man's feet, a *Shivalingam* appeared under them. In frustration Namdev finally placed them on his own head, whereupon he suddenly experienced total understanding. So that was the lesson and the message which Vithoba wanted him to have.

Is the path of knowledge the hardest?

Jnana, the path of knowledge, is the hardest for those who are drawn by nature to *bhakti* or *karma* yoga, just as the path of action, *karma yoga*, will be very difficult for the one following the path of knowledge. My own experience and the experience of others is that *bhakti* and knowledge often come together. That is, the path of knowledge doesn't exclude *bhakti*. The man of knowledge can sit, listen to *bajans*, and become so absorbed that tears flow from his eyes. Obviously, the body-mind organism is responding to something which is not the preserve of only the devotee. And when the devotee, in the extreme case, loses his identity as an entity devoted to a separate God, his identity merges into the love and devotion.

❏❏❏

– LONGING FOR THE SOURCE –

When we're very tired, we long for deep sleep. Is that similar to our longing for the state prior to Consciousness?

Yes. This longing is basic. There has to be a solution of continuity between noumenon and phenomenon, between *nirvana* and *samsara*, between the unmanifest and the manifest. They are never separate. There has to be a continuation, and the searching, the longing for the source, is the continuator. The search for the source is innate. It is not by the individual. It is impersonal.

❏❏❏

– THE DESIRE FOR ENLIGHTENMENT –

When the mind is moving it's in the process of becoming, but as I understand it we have to become what we already are. If that's the case, as you're witnessing your thoughts can't there be a thought there, or some kind of presence or filter that says, "As long as thinking is there, the object of this thought will never be realized." Does that happen, that one thought will trigger another thought and rather than get involved you have an awareness that this thinking is what's preventing you, that the process of becoming is preventing you from being what you actually are?

That is correct. The wish to change what-is into something else is the obstruction, and the accepting of what-is happens when the understanding goes deeper. You cannot hasten that process.

From the point of view of the individual, who still thinks in terms of improvement and its final culmination in enlightenment, I've always felt that the most encouraging statement is that of Ramana Maharshi: "Your head is already in the tiger's mouth. There is no escape." So why be in a hurry for the tiger to snap his mouth shut? Until then, enjoy yourself.

I know that my head is in the tiger's mouth. I've been neither here nor there for years.

You are worried that the tiger might snap?

I want to be snapped! And probably this prevents me from being snapped.

Yes, this wanting is precisely what prevents it. But even the knowledge that you are already on the way may not prevent you from being impatient!

🔲🔲🔲

– THE DILEMMA THAT CREATES GOD –

When one says, "Not my will, but Thine," there is no "my" will to start with, to do Thy Will.

Right. When does a person really begin to think of God? Only when he finds that his own efforts do not succeed in giving him what he wants. So, when a person finds that his own efforts are fruitless, then he turns to a power, he *creates* a power, conceives a power, which will give him what he himself cannot get. He creates a concept, worships it, prays to it and begs it to give him what he wants. Having created a concept of God, he wants that concept to be some superior entity, but still an entity. And, when even that entity fails to give him what he is seeking, then frustration and misery arises.

At some point, when his own conception of God as a conceived entity does not give him what he wants, then he has to realize that his mistake lies in his asking and not in his not getting. The mistake lies in his wanting, his desiring something. He desires and wants something because he considers himself an entity.

The understanding is that he will only get what he wants if, in the functioning of the impersonal Totality, his individual will tallies with the will of God.

◻◻◻

– INTENSITY AND EARNESTNESS –

Ramesh, I'm a little bit confused about your use of "intensity" with regard to effort without the "me." I always associate intensity with a purpose.

Precisely! That is the point. The intensity you refer to is not "per se." Intensity need not be with a purpose.

Can it be per se?

Oh yes, indeed!

Then it's my mind getting in the way.

Yes! The mind saying, "I want it badly! I want something badly." That something may be the latest model of a particular car. That intensity of purpose for the "me" could be anything.

Well, you advocate continuing the intensity.

Yes.

I'm just trying to clarify it for myself.

Yes.

Could it be intensity with what I do in my everyday life, without thinking of a purpose? Like when I sit in meditation or when I greet a friend, I might use more intensity?

You see, this is the point. "You" will *use* more intensity! (laughter) That is not intensity, per se.

Let's use the case of love between a man and a woman, for example. The intensity of love from the personal point of view could lead to hatred or even murder because the mind says, "I must have him," or "I must have her, or no one else will." Intensity yes, but intensity for the purpose of a "me."

But the intensity of love, per se, in this particular instance could be that the love for the other is such that if he or she wants someone else, let him or her have them. That kind of intensity is one in which there is no personal purpose. The love, even as physical love, is of such intensity that it results in the ultimate sacrifice. Where the seeking, the spiritual seeking is concerned, the ultimate sacrifice is the "me." You see?

In all of the powerful symbols of religious transcendence, the ultimate sacrifice is the "me."

Quite so. It has to be!

So there is a sacrifice involved. (laughter)

❏❏❏

– HEALING THE SPLIT BEING: FROM DUALISM TO DUALITY –

I've been a therapist for many years. I've noticed, in recent years that I wasn't doing anything anymore. People would come to me and there would be some initial complaint of some sort, but in a very short time whatever strategies that I had learned just weren't present anymore. It was almost as if there was something working through me, or through us, as a medium, and that all I was doing was being there. At first, that was very confounding because my therapist ego was watching this other dance going on. Then things become peaceful.

At the very first talks I gave in LA, almost forty percent of the visitors were psychotherapists. One of them continued right through. At a certain stage I asked her if there had been any changes. She said precisely what you just said, that there was a confusion of the ego seeing things happen and not liking being kept out.

She said, "I wanted to know what was really happening. These experiences with my clients opened up an insight as to what was and I accepted that what was happening through me was beyond a personal me." I asked if that understanding produced any change in her relationships with her clients and she said, "Indeed. They suddenly began to realize that there is no separation between the therapist and themselves. They feel a kind of oneness, a kind of harmony, a kind of spontaneity and the result of that has been that when the ego has healed to a certain extent, the client himself begins to think in terms of healing the split at a higher level!"

ΠΠΠ

– SPIRITUAL PRACTICES –

Is it necessary to meditate in order to get into the natural state?

No. In fact, in that case, it will not be the natural state. It *cannot* be the natural state.

It's all very amusing. I think I'm doing a lot of things I don't need to do. But it's all necessary because that's what's happening, right?

Indeed, that is so. Anything that happens in the present moment is necessary. So, if someone is doing meditation, I just say continue with your meditation. If you're doing *yoga*, continue with the *yoga*. The only thing is, if some change happens,not to have a feeling of guilt. Therefore, don't try to make any changes. Continue with your life and if some changes do take place, accept them without a sense of guilt.

◘◘◘

I would have preferred to speak privately to you, but regarding mantra repetition, some wonderful changes have taken place. No real dramatic experiences.

Which is a good thing. Otherwise you'd be holding on to them.

As a child, swimming in very cold water, I was always startled by the cold, each time expecting to be used to it. It was startling, like waking up. The first time I investigated repeating "I Am," it was that same startling experience. Now a natural shifting is occurring. Should that be pursued? (laughter)

Accept it, without the should or should not questions.

Is there any value at all in these so called spiritual practices and disciplinary methods?

The human mind is more than ready to be told to do something. You'd be surprised how many people are of the firm belief that not only will various spiritual practices lead to enlightenment, but the very practice of those methods *is* enlightenment. It is sheer idolatry and superstition.

But to treat all spiritual practices as idolatry and superstition is to keep your mind closed, isn't it?

By all means keep an open mind. If you find yourself in a position where you are doing some practice, try it and see.

In my own case, before I went to Nisargadatta Maharaj, I had a *guru* for twenty years. He was a traditional *guru* who gave traditional initiations. At that time, my need for the *guru* was so intense that when I went to him during a short initiation ceremony, during that process I was so overwhelmed I couldn't stop the tears. A built-up emotion, a built-up need to find a *guru* was expressing itself in this way.

Very soon I realized that what he was teaching me, in all sincerity, was not what I really wanted.

If someone came to Maharaj and said, "My wife is ill" or "My son's out of a job," Maharaj would say, "I'm very sorry, I can't help you." Whereas my earlier *guru* would consider it part of his function not only to take charge of your spiritual life, but also to help you—most genuinely and sincerely— in your material needs.

Maharaj's teaching was totally impersonal, universal. But this earlier *guru* was first a Hindu and then a non-dualist, an Advaitin. He would say, "You do this *puja*, you do that disciplinary practice, go visit this temple." He was not a fraud. He was genuine. But his belief ended with the one firm conviction that what his *guru* had told him was the ultimate, that his individual *guru*, dead many years, still guided his actions.

Very soon it was clear to me that this was not what I had been after since the age of twelve. But it is not the nature of this organism to break off with anyone violently, so the relationship continued for twenty years. A curious fact about this relationship was that it was astrologically predicted back in 1950. Not by an astrologer who read horoscopes but through one of the South Indian predictions called *nadi*. There was a foot long dried bark or leaf, so elastic it wouldn't break. On it was carved, in small letters, the prediction that I would first have a *guru* for twenty years and that nothing much would come of it, but that after I retired I would meet my true *guru* and then the progress would be quite rapid.

After I retired, I read an article about Nisargadatta Maharaj written by Jean Dunn in *The Mountain Path*. When I climbed up the steps to Maharaj's loft for the first time, Nisargadatta's first words to me were, "You have come at last, have you? Come and sit down."

So, if someone has the gift of healing, why not? The gift of astrology, the gift of psychotherapy, why not?

I did not *waste* the twenty years before I met Nisargadatta. Everything is preparation for the next scene. So, if some mysterious power directs you to some practice, I suggest not to shun it or not to give it up. Accept it, try it. If later, these spiritual practices drop off, let them. And if they do, my only suggestion is, don't feel guilty about it. It is a happening, over which you have no control.

Chuang-Tzu said, "The master came when it was time for him to come, the master left in the ordinary flow of events." When there is even an inkling of this understanding, even at the intellectual level, you begin to have a sense of freedom, or, more precisely, the sense of freedom replaces the sense of frustration.

The sense of frustration is the volition, which the "me" is very reluctant to give up. When there is really a conviction that I am only an instrument, like the billions of human beings through which God or Totality functions, how can there not be a tremendous sense of freedom?

I was reading in some books where they encourage you to be more conscious and to observe yourself and your thoughts, and also what goes on around you. I find when I do that, it makes me do effort, and I find it frustrating.

When this is realized, your thinking and effort may become automatically less.

I thought we had to be more conscious, to be a more perfect extension of Consciousness.

This is all rubbish! The amount of rubbish that exists is tremendous! But the existence of that "tremendous rubbish" is also part of the functioning of Totality, so that enlightenment can happen only in a limited number of cases. For enlightenment to happen in a limited number of cases, this rubbish has to go on.

It keeps the seeker searching.

Yes. It keeps the search almost unending because the seeking and the search are part of the functioning of Totality. It is not the individual who is seeking.

So there is no practice of meditation, yet one finds oneself meditating?

That is real meditation. But at a certain point, as I say, if meditation is necessary in this organism, for the spiritual progress, then that organism will have to meditate. That organism will be directed to a place where meditation of one kind or another is mandatory and he will meditate. For twenty years I had to go to an earlier *guru* who told me that you must meditate for at least half an hour every day. Those twenty years of regular meditation must have had some effect to get this organism ready to receive instruction from Maharaj.

What about japa?

It is one of the spiritual practices that may be necessary in particular cases. But spiritual practices are not an absolute necessity.

You don't have to do a lot.

You don't have to do a lot. In fact, honestly, what I am teaching is really the lazy path to enlightenment. (laughter) Just accept what-is! What can be lazier than that?

❑❑❑

– PRAYER –

Where does prayer come in?

Now, that depends on what you mean by prayer.

Supplicating yourself before a personal God.

Yes, but usually with a certain object. I'm not saying that you pray only for yourself. It may be you are praying for someone else. Why should we assume that prayer is anything different from other forms of energy? That intensity of desire, the intensity of wanting to do something is a kind of energy. To what extent that energy works, to what extent this energy produces results, one can't know. So you pray for something, it happens, and you say, "My prayers have been answered." On the other hand, in many cases the prayers are not answered.

You remember the ones that are answered.

And there's absolutely no reason why you shouldn't.

◘◘◘

– SPIRITUAL EXPERIENCES –

I have a question that has been bothering me for a very long time. I used to be a Zen monk. For ten years I would sit every day and just disappear. I would hear a bell and become the sound of the bell. I would look at a tree and the distance between me and the tree would disappear. I would become the tree. There was immediate presence. Identity was everywhere but there were no specific objects. But I would always come back from that as the same person. This happened over and over again, for ten years, and I wondered, what is the value of this since it did not change me in ordinary consciousness?

What is that state I was going through and how does it relate to the personality and to what you are saying?

What it relates to is that the mind makes an effort. This did not come naturally, did it?

No. It was very hard.

It is very, very hard. Some "one" made very hard effort. And those efforts resulted in a certain state of mind.

Absolutely.

Make any physical experiment or a chemical experiment. It is very clear, and this is the same in *yoga*. Do step one, step two, step three, step four, step five. Ultimately, if all the earlier steps are done, a specific final result must come. But it is all still in phenomenality.

That is why Maharaj used to say, you may go into *samadhi* for ten minutes, you may go into *samadhi* for ten days, you may go into *samadhi* for ten years, you may go into *samadhi* for one hundred years, but you must come back where you left. Therefore it has no value.

I agree. (laughter)

You agree from experience, not from an intellectual level.

Absolutely. And I then had to struggle to become an ordinary person again, letting go the samadhi *and the specialness of that.*

Quite so. But when this kind of state happens by itself, when there is no "me" making hard effort, then that kind of state arises only from one thing. As Maharaj repeatedly said, "Understanding is all."

Understanding at the beginning has to be at the intellectual level, necessarily so. That is why both Ramana Maharshi and Maharaj used to say, "To be a *jnana yogi*, to seek knowledge, you have to have a very keen intellect, an intellect keen enough and honest enough to come to the conclusion that what it is really seeking is beyond its comprehension."

This seeking is not a matter of comprehension, it is a matter of intuitive apprehension. But it has to be arrived at through the intellect.

❑❑❑

One day, I was reading a book by Sai Baba. I've never met him, never talked to him. A little while later I smelled an odor which I did not know. A few pages later I read that he had produced sacred ashes, and I recognized that odor of the sacred ashes because a few months before this I had smelled some. But I didn't know that those things had a connection. What does it mean?

It simply means that anything can happen in Consciousness. You see, the intellect insists that everything be explainable.

Does it means you are on the same level of consciousness, the same vibration as that person?

You could put it like that if you want some sort of explanation.

It means like tuning in a radio station?

A hundred years ago, if you talked about a radio, everyone would have thought that you were crazy. In another hundred years from now everybody may know everybody else's thoughts. Who knows? In Consciousness, anything is possible. You can call it a miracle if you like, if that satisfies you.

No, I don't seem to think it was a miracle. I think it is like the same level of vibration that you are tuning in and that you will hear, know, or feel or understand the other vibrations.

Yes, in other words you are talking about the mechanics of it.

I suppose.

And I am talking about the nature of the phenomena. The mechanics, we do not understand now. In a few years science will probably give out an explanation about the mechanics of it.

Thank you. If we can lose our involvement in the mechanics, then every moment becomes a miracle.

Yes. That is precisely what Ramana Maharshi meant when he said, "Thinking is not man's real nature." Thinking means conceptualizing, going away from what-is.

◘◘◘

I had an experience in Maine. I was sitting on a rock, watching the ocean and tide. I had the feeling of a sense of movement that was beyond the human scale. I'm still looking for some kind of connection to that power or whatever that was. I haven't been able to connect that experience with what you are talking about. What was I doing?

You were doing nothing and precisely because of that this experience happened. After the experience, you didn't let the experience alone. You wanted more of it. "How did it happen? Why? Why to me?" All the "why"s push the experience further and further out.

In the spiritual chart, if the dot representing you had been further evolved, then the experience would have ended merely in a sense of wonder. You'd get up and walk away. The experience could then come more often, constantly. But it was not the time, so the mind starts asking questions. You went after the experience, so the experience goes farther away. This is quite normal. You want to tell twenty people about this wonderful experience, but it is a pitfall nonetheless.

◘◘◘

– JUST BE –

Ramesh, you've said that Maharaj kept repeating to you, "Just be." What did he mean?

There again the question of language comes in and for six months it was absolute hell for me. Just this, "Whom is Maharaj asking to just be? I can accept that there is no 'me,' so who is Maharaj asking to just be?" Until it suddenly dawned one morning, Maharaj was not asking *anybody* to "just be." No "one" can be in the beingness. Beingness is all there is. It is all Consciousness.

But that had to come through understanding, an impersonal understanding without an individual comprehender trying to understand something.

So in I Am That[11], *it must be a problem of language, then, when Maharaj says, "Be still and be quiet." He's not talking about the body.*

This is exactly what I meant just now. There's no "me" to understand or do anything. But, no master can continuously speak in the passive tense. There wouldn't be any spontaneity. The words just come out any way they wish.

Maharaj was sometimes asked to explain some discrepancy or contradiction between what he was saying and what was in *I Am That*. Maharaj would say, "Look, I did not write *I Am That*, Maurice Frydman did. There are bound to be some apparent discrepancies and contradictions—just imagine the various stages the book went through before it was finally printed. First, I Know; the knowledge I have is an intuitive conviction which I express only because people come to me with questions. What I say is limited by the extent of my vocabulary in Marathi, which is further limited because of my lack of education. What I have said must then be understood by Maurice whose knowledge of Marathi would be necessarily restricted. Thereafter, Maurice has to put whatever he has understood into English. Then it has to be edited before the final manuscript is published. Is it not more than likely that there would be considerable distance between what I Know and what appears in *I Am That?*"

□□□

– RAMESH'S SADHANA –

Your first guru, was he interested in Advaita?

He was interested in Advaita, but basically Hindu Advaita, which is Vedanta. My tremendous inclination has always been toward *Tao* and Lao Tzu, which has nothing to do with Hinduism. Curiously, Maharaj had never heard of Lao Tzu or the *Tao*, but his teaching was extremely parallel.

---

ibid.

Aside from Lao Tzu, another person who interested me in my early reading a great deal was Wei Wu Wei. He's abstruse, not easily understood. In one of his prefaces he says he's deliberately trying to be abstruse, that anyone who needs a deeper explanation is not ready for the book. Someone presented me with a copy of one of his books in 1965. I went through it cursorily and I knew then that it was a real treasure, but I couldn't appreciate it at the time. So again, like the astrological reading, I just kept it aside.

When I started going to Maharaj, I suddenly remembered the book and it was astonishing. Maharaj would give talks in the morning. What I would read in the book in the evening, next morning Maharaj would talk about. It was fantastic! Wei Wu Wei was not Chinese, you know. He was an Irish aristocrat, a millionaire. He had a chateau in the south of France. He was an authority on wines, a huge man, six foot three inches, and very heavy.

Was Wei Wu Wei fully realized?

I don't really know.

Did you meet any other jnanis? *They say that only a* jnani *can recognize a* jnani.

No *jnani* came in search of me. And I didn't go in search of any other *jnani*.

Is it true what they say, that only a jnani *can recognize a* jnani?

Probably so. After a little talk, it would be clear.

Ramesh, are you familiar with the Ashtavakra Gita?

Yes. In fact I have translated it. (laughter)

As a matter of fact, that's right! (laughing) I've read your translation! (more laughter) I don't know what brought that to my mind.

❐❐❐

I would like to express my gratitude for your being here.

Absolutely no need, I assure you.

And for your tremendous patience.

As I said, this organism has been blessed with a certain amount of patience, though certainly not as much as Ramana Maharshi. Maharaj however, was not patient.

I'm glad I've come to you rather than to Maharaj, he probably would have thrown me out!

❐❐❐

– LEVELS OF TEACHING –

In one of Maharaj's books he talks about Westerners, saying they were warriors from Rama in their past lives. Were you there when he said that?

He used to say that quite often.

What did he mean by that?

That refers to the mythology of the *Ramayana* in which Lord Rama was helped by an army of monkeys. When Rama won the war, it is said that he gave a boon to the brave monkeys that in their next life they would enjoy both the manifest world and enlightenment.

That was evidence of his sense of humor. There was no real significance to it. What Maharaj really meant when he referred to that story was that among the Indians who came to see him, there were few who were really interested in his teaching. Most were interested in seeing what Maharaj could do to help someone's illness or help someone's son get a job, that kind of thing. In many cases he would say that they would not find anything there. He said all he talked about was Consciousness, so if they were only interested in routine meditation or other kinds of practices he could not help them. There were very few people who were interested in the perennial philosophy, in Advaita, although the *word* was familiar to them.

But the Westerners who came were very deeply interested, you see. I think he was referring to this point. Were you there in Maharaj's time?

No, I was reading a book. I think it was Jean Dunn who edited it.

The significance is not the reference to mythology, but to the fact that Maharaj was most impressed by the sincerity and the intensity of the Westerners. He would say that they have come five thousand, ten thousand miles, at a great deal of expense, so they were really interested in the subject.

Also, when you read *I Am That*,[12] or any of the books, you may get the impression that there was always a vast crowd present at Maharaj's. It was actually an extremely small group. The average number of people was around eight or ten. On weekends, there might have been twenty.

I am not saying that all of the Indians who came were not interested. Many *were* interested. But Maharaj found them not as open to the teaching as the average Westerner. The average Westerner was not burdened with the same cultural conditioning. Their conditioning was of a different kind. The Indian was conditioned by the routine practices. For instance, it was quite normal for someone to point out apparent contradictions between such and such Scriptures and ask Maharaj how he would reconcile the difference. Maharaj would invariably say, "Look, I am on the border of being illiterate, so if you ask me these things I'm not able to answer." He would direct the questioner elsewhere, saying, "Here is this lady who has an M. A. in Sanskrit and a doctorate in Indian philosophy. You discuss it with her."

He repeatedly said, "I am not concerned with any Scriptures. I am not concerned with any books. I am only concerned with the fact that you are present, I am present, there is a world outside and we are able to see each other and talk

––––––––––––––––––––
(12) ibid.

to each other. Therefore, there must be something because of which we are able to communicate. There must be something because of which our senses work. I am concerned with that principle and that principle is Consciousness."

He would say at least twenty times during his talks, "All there is, is Consciousness."

❑❑❑

– FOR SOME, SILENCE IS NOT ENOUGH –

In all the sessions that we've been together, my perception is that a lot of the questioning that's been going on is intellectually centered. Everyone is crying, "Ramesh! Ramesh! Ramesh! Ramesh!" And gracefully, you've been responding to everyone. My question is, "What is silence?"

Silence is what I needed with Maharaj. If I were alone with him, that's what he would give me. Silence is the most powerful medium for transmission of this knowledge, for this knowledge to arrive intuitively. Silence is the most potent medium, but in many cases it is not enough.

In the spiritual evolution a certain amount of guidance is necessary, and for those who needed this guidance Maharaj would use various concepts. Incidentally, silence doesn't mean not talking. Silence is silence of the mind. Silence is absence of questions, absence of thinking, true meditation. That is the most potent medium for this understanding to take place. When the inquiring mind, intellectually creating problems, gradually comes to the understanding that the more problems it creates the more veils it creates between the Self and the understanding, then there is silence. Again, that silence can only arise at the right time, at the right place. You cannot bring about that silence. And when that silence comes, no word at all becomes necessary. Indeed, any word becomes unbearable! When the understanding dawns, even the great phrase "That thou art" becomes unbearable. Because the "thou" comes in only so long as the understanding is not there. Therefore, all these books have been written for the "thou," who is not at the place in his spiritual evolution where he can grasp it without words.

The words are necessary until it suddenly dawns that all these words are a waste of time. It is only after understanding that this is realized as a vast joke. You laugh at this joke only when there is that understanding. Until then, the joke can be a most tragic one.

❏❏❏

– THE MIDDLE WAY –

In the culture of India, versus our culture, would it be easier to slide into a non-dualistic understanding? We're so materialistic here in the West.

You see, this process is going on. Our young men in India who are the best in their academic career, come here to the West and seek material wealth. And those in India who are below the level of poverty, they are more materialistic than any person in the West!

Now the young people in the West, who have everything, have been given all the material things, they are going to India to seek this teaching.

In the *Bhagavad Gita*, Lord Krishna mentions that the chances of something happening are greater in the case of ordinary people in ordinary circumstances than when they are too rich and successful or too poor and downtrodden in poverty.

❏❏❏

– FALSE TEACHERS –

Why are there so many false spiritual teachers?

Regarding sincere and insincere teachers, let me tell you what William Law said: "Would you know whence it is that so many false spirits have appeared in the world who have deceived themselves and others with false fires and false lights, laying claim to information, illumination and openings of the Divine Life, particularly to do wonders with their extraordinary calls from God? They may sincerely believe God is giving it to them. They have turned to God without turning from themselves. They would be alive to God before they are dead to their own nature. Religion in the hands of self, or corrupt nature, serves only to discover vices of a worse kind than in nature left to itself. Hence are all the disorderly passions of religious men, which burn in a worse flame than passions only employed about worldly matters. Pride, self-exaltation, hatred and persecution under cloak of religious zeal will sanctify actions which nature left to itself would be ashamed to own."

Pretty strong words, written two hundred and fifty years ago. I would have asked William Law, "Who produced these false teachers? Who makes them do what they do? Is it some power other than that which produced saintly people? Are not even these wild spirits part of the functioning of Totality?"

◘◘◘

– IS A LIVING GURU NECESSARY? –

Regarding the process of the act of Grace occurring, many have said that it's not absolutely necessary, but that usually you need a teacher in order for enlightenment to occur. Is that so?

Yes, that is so. But the point is, the coming together of certain disciples and a certain *guru* is part of the functioning of Totality. The disciple and the *guru* are only polarically separate. The *guru*/disciple together form one relationship and the forming of that relationship is part of the functioning of Totality.

And that won't happen unless the guru *and the disciple are at a particular place, at a particular time, when it is time for that relationship.*

Correct.

In your book Pointers[13] *you say there are signposts or pointers, or indicators that the seeker is making progress along a path.*

Yes, on your way to the one hundred and twenty-ninth step, when you are near the end, you do get indications. Also, at that level the "me" is very much there. So, the "me" may say, "Ah, I am progressing," and then the "me" gets stronger! Finally, the pointers are realized as mere pointers and no particular significance is attached to them.

The importance of seeking a guru *is something I think about a lot. What's the need of a teacher? The concept for me is that I should be able to figure it all out for myself, on my own.*

Ramana Maharshi did not have an individual human being as a teacher. Not in his life. Earlier there may have been one. His organism was highly evolved enough so that he didn't have to do any *sadhana* as such. Whatever he did just happened. But earlier in the spiritual evolution that culminated in the body-mind organism called Ramana there may have been organisms that had gone through teachers.

For him, the hill Arunachala was his *guru*. From the very beginning he said Arunachala did something to him. It aroused a feeling. He didn't know what it was. So when he left home he went to the railway station with the money that was given to him to pay his school fees, put the money down and asked for a ticket to wherever that amount of money would take him. And that ticket took him to Tiruvannamalai, the site of Arunachala.

So each body-mind organism through which Consciousness is journeying, will toward the end meet the kind of *guru* and do the kind of *sadhana* which is supposed to happen through that organism at the time. That is why the questions, "Will I need a guru? Which is the best path?" are really misconceived. There is no best path or worst path. There is

---

(13) ibid.

just the path to which each individual organism gets directed.

◘◘◘

– LIVING IN THE WORLD –

I've been reading Experiencing the Teaching[14] *and have read other books you've written. I've also attended several of your seminars. I've noticed something about my interactions with others, and I wonder if it might somehow be linked to the effect this teaching is having on me. I'm having trouble relating to the average person out on the street. I find that there's no contact between us. The interaction seems almost nonsensical. This sounds as if I'm setting myself up to be superior to other people, and I don't want that at all. Could you shed some light on what I'm doing?*

You will always be more comfortable in the company of those who share your deepest interests. It's even more so in the case of addicts. If you were deeply addicted to alcohol, the only time you wouldn't be lonely would be in the company of fellow alcoholics. Outside the company of that group, you would be lonely. Maharaj called Advaita, nonduality, an addiction. He once asked me, "How long have you been addicted to this vice?"

I replied, "Ever since I can remember."

◘◘◘

– PLEASURE –

Why is it a good thing to have Bajan?

Does it give you pleasure?

Yes.

---

ibid.

I assure you that there is no reason why you should avoid pleasure, no reason at all. When pleasure comes your way, accept it wholeheartedly. When it does not come your way, don't hanker after it!

ooo

– SEX –

Is having sex really a hindrance to realization?

I would say sex would be a hindrance only if it is thought of in terms of guilt. That's my interpretation. Guilt is always in the mind, not in the body.

A teacher I had in the past stressed discipline in curbing the sexual drive. But I think the sex drive is natural and suppressing it is unnatural.

I would say the same thing. If an act happens, accept it as part of the functioning of Totality, as God's will. Then there is no guilt. If you say, "That's my act, I shouldn't have done it. Let God forgive me!" All that is in the mind, based on guilt.

That's true, because Consciousness is doing it.

It all depends on your conviction. If a sex act happens, why should you consider everything else as God's will and not the sex act? Why should you take that responsibility and guilt as your own and leave God with all other actions? Mind you, actively pursuing sex and the sex act *happening* are two entirely different phenomena.

Are you suggesting that sex should only arise out of love?

In adolescence, sex generally transcends love. Love is immaterial, irrelevant. Later on, in adulthood, sex needs love. Without love, sex loses its meaning. Still later on, love may or may not lead to sex. And ultimately, love transcends sex. That's how the process goes. After a certain stage, the love transcends sex and love remains love, as part of the universal Love.

◨◨◨

– CHILDREN: ENLIGHTENMENT PLUS IGNORANCE–

I have a small daughter. Is there nothing I can do to foster her becoming a seeker or to enhance her understanding?

On the contrary, if you try too much she will resist.

She's going to do what she has to do?

Quite so. All you can do is be there if she shows some curiosity, if she asks for information. How old is she?

One.

Then at this stage you won't have to tell her anything. She knows. She knows, but she doesn't know that she knows until the circle becomes complete. That's why you find children saying the oddest things. Children have an intuitive understanding of their impersonality which is reflected when the child begins to talk. They speak of themselves in the third person, saying things like, "Jane wants a piece of candy." They do not say, "I want a piece of candy."

The child sees itself as a part of Totality. Later on after the conditioning starts and gets intensified, the child says "I want something" then this identification is complete. Until then, there is an intuitive feeling of the impersonality.

Does that mean then that the child is enlightened?

The child is enlightened but it doesn't know it. In the case of the child, there is enlightenment plus ignorance. And the ignorance proceeds until a time, if it is to happen in that body-mind mechanism, when the mind turns inwards. Then when the process is complete there is enlightenment plus knowledge.

So, the process has to be gone through and the circle is then complete. Originally, it is enlightenment plus ignorance. Later on, it is enlightenment plus the intuitive knowledge.

❑❑❑

– CHILDLIKE UNDERSTANDING –

When you talk to us you use concepts that require comprehension. How could we talk about the nature of God to our children that are four and five? How could we explain it to them? We would need simpler concepts to explain...

No, you don't have to explain. The children can tell *you* what God is. Children don't need to be told anything about God.

A German lady attended the seminars in India. She and her husband both work. They have a governess, Karen, looking after the children. The governess told the mother when she came home one day what the almost four year old Philip had said that afternoon.

The boy had said, "We are all dreaming and we'll wake up when we are dead."

That evening, the mother checked up. "What did you tell Karen today? Something about a dream?"

"Oh yes," said Philip, "I told Karen that we are all dreaming and we will wake up when we are dead."

The Mother asked Philip, "Who told you that?"

She said Philip looked at her as if she were crazy. The child didn't understand the question! When the mother continued to look at him, obviously expecting an answer, the child consoled the mother by saying, "Who told me that? God told me that."

Do all children have the same comprehension?

Oh, no.

Then how could we explain to a child who does not necessarily understand the way I could understand? I can't just talk to him the way you talk to us. How could we explain in an easy manner?

Why do you think you have to explain anything about God to a child?

Because children always ask, "Why? Why? Why?" I can't just tell them, "Why not? Why not? Why not?"

You will be really astonished how easily the child will accept your answer "Why not?" Try it! All the child cannot understand, basically, is being misled. The child asks, "Who made me?" Even if you said, "God made you," promptly the child will ask, "Who made God?"

That's it! I've always had that question. Since I was born I've always asked myself "How was God born?

So, the only answer left is to explain to that child that God is what made us, and God made this universe and we cannot know who made God.

That's a mystery.

That is a mystery which we cannot know because we are not as clever as God! And again, you will be surprised how quickly the child will accept it.

Does that mean that a child who is not conditioned by people could accept the reality, the truth easier than adults with concepts and everything?

That is correct.

How can we perfect our educational system so that the children aren't conditioned?

You can't! If you did, the world would come to an end. Every child would be perfect and would grow into a perfect human specimen. By perfect I don't mean saintly. If you see some children playing, they can do some horrible acts.

A friend of mine was telling me about two young boys aged five or six. Do you know what they were doing? They were collecting all the ants into a heap. One was collecting, the other was lighting a match and setting fire to them. And yet we speak of the innocence of the child and that is correct. The innocence of the child is in not ascribing any guilt to itself. The child has no concept of guilt and that is innocence.

Wouldn't the child have a feeling that what he was doing, at some level, was wrong?

Oh yes, when he is subsequently conditioned. When the child is conditioned with the principle of right and wrong. But as one *Tao* master said, "The right and wrong are a disease of the mind."

What do I do if I come out and find my child is burning ants?

You tell the child whatever comes to your mind. But whatever you tell your child, the conditioning has begun. The imbibing of this feeling of guilt has started. The "disease of the mind" choosing between right and wrong has started. And it *must*. It is part of life.

❏❏❏

8

CHOICE AND VOLITION

– INTRODUCTION –

If you haven't already noticed it, the human being is a funny animal. Any other animal would certainly think so if it noticed just three things.

One, for thousands of years every sage and prophet has been saying over and over that the only happiness for human beings lies in love and universal brotherhood. But nobody seems to be paying attention to them. They're all seeking a new and different answer.

The human being doesn't want to know the truth. All he wants is to have more information about what he thinks he already knows, so he goes about hopping from *ashram* to *ashram*, from *guru* to *guru*, reading one book after another and seeking. He tries one kind of *sadhana* and then another kind of *sadhana*, all the time ignoring that the basic truth has been repeatedly told him over thousands of years.

The second thing is that the human being has such enormous intelligence, unbelievable intelligence, he has been able to send a man to the moon, and yet he has not been able to control his own social behavior and conduct. The human being is absolutely unique in what he has achieved in his technological advances and the human animal is also unique in the way it has not been able to manage its social and political life.

Lastly, the world is on the brink of disaster, where it has been for many years now with one crisis after another. Yet the human being who certainly has the intelligence, and who is supposed to have free will, has been unable to combine these elements to make the world a better place.

Nobody likes being told that he has no free will, that he is merely a puppet being manipulated by an intelligence of an order to which human intelligence simply cannot be compared. He resents it! He likes to be told, he likes to believe, the future is in his own hands, that he can make of his future what he will.

Yet, there are so many intelligent people who are leaders in their respective fields that are interested in astrology. If they really believe in their own free will, why are they interested in astrology?

If you think along those lines, the only reasonable conclusion is that the human being has been acting in this fashion because he has no control over his thoughts and emotions. He has remarkable intelligence, but he has no control over his thoughts and emotions. What he considers *his* actions are truly only *reactions* of the individual organism to an outside thought or event. The organism reacts according to its natural characteristics, physical, intellectual and temperamental.

❏❏❏

– THE IMPERSONAL ARISING OF THOUGHTS –

Something occurred to me while you were talking. Even though we think we have choices, we really don't have choices.

That is correct. You think you have choice but how much choice do you really have?

You are going to buy a dress. Fashion tells you this is the dress that you should buy. But a year ago you wouldn't have bought it. So fashion and the magazines and the media tell you what kind of a dress you should buy, and you buy it and say that it was your choice.

If I come to a fork in the road and have to choose path A or path B, I will still get to the same place because that is where I am supposed to go.

The whole point is, you say you choose path A or path B. What do you really do when you choose A or B? What happens when you say, "I'm going to go along path B?" It is really a thought which comes to you, isn't it?

But it is coming through me?

Oh yes, indeed! The thought comes in your brain from outside. That is the point.

The whole process is: A thought comes, gets vocalized and then gets actualized into action. So, the basis of any action has to be a thought, which gets vocalized through the conditioning already there.

At different times, in the same circumstances, the thought may be to do something else. They are both your choices, but sometimes you choose path A and sometimes you choose path B, because at that time the thought comes to make that choice.

Is that why you can never predict what you will do in a certain situation?

Precisely. The process is thought, word, action. You can not will a thought.

Is that what you meant before when you said you cannot make a mistake?

Yes! Whatever is to happen will happen.

◘◘◘

– EFFORT –

It sounds as though you're saying that there is nothing you can do by self effort to gain enlightenment. Is that true?

Absolutely.

Does one just wait around for evolution to take place or does one engage in spiritual practice?

This is precisely what I mean when I say, "The problem is from the individual's point of view. Look at it from the point of view of Totality, then what happens?"

It means that you think in terms of possessing Consciousness. "It is 'my' Consciousness. I am conscious. I am capable of doing whatever I want to do." Truly, it is Consciousness which possesses *you*. It is Consciousness that possesses this body-mind mechanism and the billions of others and produces through each such acts as it wants to produce. And in order to produce those acts, each body-mind mechanism has been conceived with particular specific characteristics. Each is born to particular parents, which is nature, and is effected by a particular environment with particular conditions, which is nurture.

Neither nature nor nurture is in the hands of the individual, nor is that event called "death." Yet, between those two points of birth and death this illusory "me" has the audacity to say, "I control my life. I'm the master of my destiny!"

◘◘◘

– PRIDE OR SHAME IN ACCOMPLISHMENTS –

Sir, at one point somebody asked Sri Ramana, "In the case of India's gaining independence from England, would the individuals involved be entitled to be elated?" And his answer was, "Theoretically, no. But, in as much as we're still thinking we're individuals it would be perfectly understandable that everyone would be pleased in what had transpired."

Oh yes. But he's talking at the level of the phenomenal individual. In other words, if I've understood you correctly, what was meant was that until enlightenment happens it is natural that an individual should pride himself in his achievements.

Or feel bad about his failures.

Yes, precisely. Or feel bad about his failures. So at the phenomenal level, that is normal.

❐❐❐

– TO ACT OR NOT TO ACT –

Here in the United States it seems like people are really obsessed with psychological self-improvement. From what you've been say-ing though, it would seem that that just perpetuates the ego.

It does perpetuate the ego, yes.

Yet, to purposefully not do something is just the same as doing.

Yes, you see, the point is that to do something positively is a positive act of volition. Deliberately not doing some-thing, as you said, is also volition. It's a negative aspect of volition. But doing something deliberately and not doing something deliberately are both volition in which the "me" is concerned.

Better to just say, "Let me wait and see what happens." Then whatever happens will be a spontaneous action.

Would you say that is non-action?

You can call it non-action if you like, but basically it will be a spontaneous action. When it happens, it will be a spontaneous action in which you will not have exercised positive volition *or* negative volition.

With everything being the will of God, how would it matter if one was involved in a self-help group or in therapy? I mean, if everything is the will of God how can anything be negative or positive?

You're quite right. They cannot. And therefore...

I mean, observing our thoughts, if that is His Will, then that is what will occur.

That is correct. That is absolutely correct. There is nothing you can do about it. Except that this listening may lead to some understanding, which may then lead to this witnessing. But that will not be you doing anything.

❏❏❏

– HITLER'S DECISION NOT TO INVADE ENGLAND –

Will you share with us about Hitler facing England and making the decision, during the last war?

Yes. Whatever decision we think we are making is actually made *for* us, because the decision is the end result of a thought and we have no control over the arising of the thought.

You are referring to an incident which I mentioned in one of the books, *Explorations Into The Eternal*,[15] I think. I said that the most important decision which Hitler probably had to make was when he stood on the edge of the European continent looking at the cliffs of Dover. Although all his generals said, "Give us the order and we will bring England to its knees in less than a week," Hitler made the "wrong" decision. He turned his force eastward and the result was good from the viewpoint of the rest of the world, but bad from the point of view of Hitler himself.

He made that decision with considerable thought, but the thoughts on which that decision was based were not "his" thoughts. Because Hitler had to lose, because Hitler was

---

[15] Ramesh S. Balsekar, *Explorations Into The Eternal* (Bombay: Chetana, 1987)

supposed to make a "wrong" decision, that particular thought came into his brain at that moment.

I'll give you another example. You have a decision to make. You are the president and you have six vice presidents, but the buck stops at your desk. So you get all six vice-presidents together, you explain the situation and you ask them, "What do you recommend?"

Three say yes and three say no. What do you do as president?

You have to make the big choice. So, you can turn your back and toss a coin or you can wait for inspiration. Ultimately, when you do make a choice, what is that choice? A thought comes that says, "do it," or "don't do it." So your choice, ultimately, is what that thought from outside tells you to do.

A free, guiltless kind of choice. Is that what you're saying?

Yes. But what happens is this: the mind tells you it is *your* choice. So if the choice happens to be good you say, "I am a brilliant president and I deserve to be made the chairman." But if the choice happens to be bad you say, "I'm loaded with six useless vice presidents." (laughter)

חחח

– PLANNING –

Is there any use for planning?

Certainly! Certainly there's use in planning. In fact, planning can be a very well paid job. (laughter)

Other than to be paid for.

If we have to go to the airport to catch a plane at a particular time, we then have to plan. But that planning is part of the doing.

No one can sit without doing anything. So, the doing takes place and planning becomes part of the doing. When the thinking mind is not present, when the "me" is not present, then there is no worry and anxiety about what is to happen. Where the "me" is present there is anxiety and worry about whether that plan is going to succeed or not.

Planning is certainly necessary. You cannot do without it.

So you make the plan but you don't try to control the outcome.

It's not that you don't try to control it. You understand that you *cannot* control it.

Can I say that I appear to be planning but that I am not the planner?

Quite so. Yes, sir. That is precisely it.

❏❏❏

– PREDESTINATION –

Would you say that free will is illusory? I mean that choice itself is an illusion, it doesn't exist, that all is destiny?

Yes. Quite.

How does that differ from what we term predestination?

It *is* predestination. But this predestination is subject to the fact that it is part of the natural law. And also subject to the original truth, which is that, as Ramana Maharshi said, "There is no creation, no destruction, no path, no goal, no freedom, no predestination. Nothing has happened."

Subject to that then, we can have all these concepts of spiritual evolution, scientific evolution, evolution in arts and sciences, all in phenomenality, all in space-time. Everything must be subject to this basic truth that nothing has happened. If that is accepted, nothing else need be used as a concept.

It's one thing to understand, and it's another thing to live it on a daily basis.

Oh, indeed. That is why the answer is simple. Even at an intellectual level you say, "All right, that is so. So what do I do? Do I make any change in life?" No! You continue doing precisely what you have been doing. There's nothing else you *can* do. That is the point. There is nothing else you can do. And what is more, it really doesn't matter. To *whom* can it matter?

🔲🔲🔲

– ACTING ACCORDING TO ONE'S NATURE –

If you know that things just happen through Consciousness, there really isn't any reason for taking credit for anything and also there isn't any reason to be upset about anything. Because it's basically just happening, right?

Absolutely. That is why I said there is a tremendous sense not of frustration, but of freedom. If this is all just happening and there is nothing I can do, why should I worry about it? Why not just sit back, let things happen and just witness them?

And enjoy the show.

Enjoy the show, precisely.

Could you also use that analysis as a philosophy to abandon your social responsibilities? If I kill someone, do I just say, "I'm not responsible?"

In other words, what you are saying is, you are not killing someone only because you are afraid you will be arrested and executed. Is that so?

Say I just don't act in a socially responsible manner. I just go about my life and I don't care about anyone else and I just...

What I am asking is, suppose God tells you, "Alright, you can do whatever you like and you will not be punished either

in this world or the next." Will you take a machine gun and
go out and kill other people?

Of course not.

What I am really saying is that you cannot do anything
which is against your normal nature, which is a term for the
characteristics in your organism. Every organism is created
with certain characteristics and that organism is born to a
particular set of parents. Your characteristics are fixed, your
parents are fixed, your environment is fixed. Therefore your
conditioning also is fixed. So your nature is fixed and your
nurture is fixed.

So with this kind of constriction, how much real choice
do you have? Being limited by inherent characteristics and
limited by conditioning in the environment, you will per-
force be compelled to do certain acts and not other acts.

That's why I say that even if you are told you are not going
to be punished, you will not go out and do something
horrible. It's not possible. On the other hand, someone who
is naturally inclined to perform horrible acts, a pathological
case, doesn't need a teaching like this to make him do
something horrible. He will do it anyway. That organism has
been created in order for certain horrible things to happen.
And those horrible things are all part of the functioning of
Totality.

Is it not the same Consciousness, the same God which has
created the saint and the sinner?

It's not, "The devil made me do it." It's, "God made me do it."

Yes. Indeed.

ⁿⁿⁿ

*During World War II, Krishnamurti used to travel and give
talks such as you do, and he took a lot of heat because he didn't spend
time talking about Hitler. But his explanation for that was very
similar to what you are saying tonight: that the individual has got*

*to find himself and find out where he's coming from before the world
can be changed for the better.*

That is correct. You see now, you mention Krishnamurti.
Let me tell you what happened when the same incident
presented itself to Krishnamurti and to someone else. I read
in Krishnamurti's book that he once had the television on
and he saw baby seals being clubbed to death for their furs.
Krishnamurti said it was horrible, he couldn't bear to see it.
So what did Krishnamurti do? He switched off the TV,
because that is precisely what was to happen through the
body-mind organism named Krishnamurti. And there the
reaction stopped. But the actress Brigitte Bardot saw the
same scene and it moved her so much she couldn't sleep
nights. She started a movement which grew and grew inter-
nationally until the practice was officially stopped. So does
it mean that Krishnamurti doesn't care and Brigitte Bardot
does care?

You see, the reaction is different in different body-minds.
Different body-minds have been created for different things
to happen. What is happening is just the functioning of
Totality. *And we have no choice in the matter.*

That's it.

And that's it?

That is it. (laughter)

🔲🔲🔲

*If we continue to understand that our natures are our natures,
and watch that more and more, doesn't that, in itself, reduce the
influence of the "me" in our life so that something else can express
itself?*

Yes. Quite so.

So, life isn't empty even though it doesn't have a goal?

That is correct. To think of a goal is a mistake. Life goes on. Life is continuous.

Life is fun! (laughter)

Yes. Quite so. Life can be quite beautiful if you don't fight it.

If life is doing all this, it must be enjoying itself, and it must be for itself.

That is why in Hindu philosophy, the whole manifestation and its functioning is considered a *lila*. *Lila* is a game or a dance. It's just a happening.

If there was a dance going on here and some extra-terrestrial being came and saw people dancing, he'd probably ask, "What is the meaning of this?" He'd wonder, "What are they doing? What is the meaning and purpose of this?" It would be difficult to explain that it's just a dance, with people enjoying it and all they're doing is enjoying the dance.

ㅁㅁㅁ

– ACCEPTING THE WILL OF THE TOTALITY –

In the process of making choices, which I'm faced with everyday, how do I know what is His Will?

You don't! And you cannot! Therefore, all you can do is to cheer up and go about other people's business, doing and undoing unto them like you have been doing so far. (laughter) And trust Him to do whatever is necessary.

Your organism has been created with certain characteristics, in other words, your organism has been programmed to act in a certain way. It cannot *not* act in the way it's programmed. So you just continue to work, continue to behave...

In other words, the choices occur spontaneously by my nature.

Yes! And if a change is taking place, perhaps because of what you have read, or what you have heard, or because some thought comes from outside, okay! Let it take place.

I have pictures of cheerful rapists and murderers and you're saying that's proper.

It is not a question of proper or improper. Every act will have its own consequences.

Then would it be proper to have a cheerful murderer? You see what I'm saying?

So the cheerful murderer goes about cheerfully murdering people. That is what is happening, but you have nothing to do with it!

That's what I was afraid you were going to say.

But you have nothing to do with it except, if possible, to stay away from his path.

◻◻◻

– LIVING "AS IF" THERE WERE CHOICE –

Did you ever have a kundalini *awakening experience?*

No, I know nothing about *kundalini* except as a word. I've had no experience of it at all.

The whole idea of manifestation being an illusion can be kind of a trap, can't it?

Yes. Therefore you must act in life *as if* you are the doer, knowing that you are *not* the doer. The human being lives on fictions. For example, the human being knows that the sun is stationary and that it is the earth that is in movement but nonetheless in his daily life he accepts the fiction that the sun rises and sets.

So the understanding is that all this is an illusion and that you do not have any free will, but in life you must act as if you have free will.

I was surprised to read that Ramakrishna said, "You must know that you as an individual are not the doer, but in life you must function as if you are the doer."

I'm not sure why you were surprised.

I was surprised because Ramakrishna was a *bhakta*. Mind you, Ramakrishna didn't use the English language, so whoever translated it used the words "as if." These are the same words the German philosopher Hans Vaihinger used in his *Philosophy of "As If."*[16] "Man has no choice but to live by fictions. He must act *as if* there is a god to reward virtuous conduct and punish the iniquitous conduct; *as if* the illusory world of the senses was reality; *as if* he had a free will which made him responsible for his actions; *as if* humanity was not under sentence of death. It is only by virtue of these fictions that the individual can keep his sanity." So the meaning of *as if*, is very clear. He says you have to act. In fact, you cannot *not* act. The body-mind organism must react to an event. You must make decisions and you must make them as if they are your own decisions.

The confusion that arises as we discuss these things is that they sound like prescriptions for the way I should lead my life.

They're not prescriptions! They're just *descriptions* of the way it is when awakening occurs.

Not being awakened, there are a thousand different ways to lead my life and a thousand different ideas about nearly everything. How do I chose among them?

Yes, for the ordinary person it is a very valid question: "I understand that I am not the doer, but how do I lead my normal life?"

---

[16] Hans Vaihinger, *Philosophy of "As If"*, trans. C.K. Ogden (Telegraph Books, 1924)

That question has to be answered. The answer is, "Let your intellectual understanding be that you are not the doer and continue to function as if you are the doer." Over the course of time, this intellectual understanding that you are not the doer will go deeper and all actions that happen will be recognized as spontaneous actions, not "your" actions.

Many people on the spiritual path are in therapy. They describe a certain moment when there is a shift, a breakthrough. Before that moment there is a feeling that they are a victim and that someone is to blame for them being a victim, in very subtle ways. They are hurt, so their parents somehow are wrong. Then the shift occurs and after that moment they accept responsibility for whatever hurt has occurred. Now, at that very moment when that shift takes place, many people describe it is as if they are making a choice. It is as if they are saying, "I no longer will be either a blamer or a victim, I will no longer be an accuser, I will no longer keep a heart full of resentment. I will make a different way of life, as if I am totally responsible for everything that happens to me and no one is to blame, and I will just take what comes my way."

Yes. You see, all this is the mind deceiving itself. Self hypnosis is still the mind. It is still the ego and the mind trying to be better.

When this "me" itself disappears, when the understanding is of a different nature, then there will be no "me" wanting to do anything. Then whatever happens will happen by itself with the "me" not there.

Now of those two types, the victim and the one who is taking responsibility, would you say that the second is a little better off than the first?

No. If anything, he is worse because he has a sense of pride about having achieved something.

🔲🔲🔲

At the stage when people are not enlightened and have not yet accepted that life is an impersonal functioning, they have the illusion of choice. Is there any guide or suggestions that you could make to help people make every day choices?

Understand that it is only the *mind* which creates a big problem. It says "now I am a seeker, I have read books, I know all this is a dream, I know I have no volition, so, from tomorrow, what do I *do*?"

The meaningful point is that having read, having listened, if that listening and understanding has any value at all, it will bring about, by itself such changes as are necessary. Especially if you don't try to interfere. So the answer is, just don't try to do anything out of the ordinary. Don't try to amend your way of life. Don't try to alter your way of life. Don't deliberately add anything. Don't deliberately subtract anything. Just carry on as you have been doing.

What could be simpler than that?

❏❏❏

When enlightenment occurs and Consciousness-in-manifestation becomes aware of Consciousness-at-rest, does that not transform the expression of manifestation that one is experiencing? I'm thinking in relation to our trying to uplift the world, make it a better place, more love, less war, all of that. If each individual expression of Consciousness becomes aware of its counterpart in Potentiality, then will not the whole series transform into something that feels different?

If that were to happen then this *lila* would end. The show would end and the curtain would fall. Do you see? The play would be over.

But when looking around, as one does, aware that the eyes in which you're looking are yours, we can have a play and play together with that knowledge, and yet also express total individuality and diversity, which is such a joy.

You mean "we" could achieve that? If "we" could have done it, why haven't we done it?

Lack of awareness. The belief that one is separate and that one is incomplete.

Lack of understanding... yes, I agree. Lack of understanding that he has no volition and therefore wanting to change everything instead of accepting that this is What-Is.

I'm not saying that, even having accepted that, the world would not be in this state. The world is in the state it is in because that is precisely the way it is supposed to be. Please understand, I'm not being a pessimist. What I'm saying is, if the world is *not* to blow itself up, what is to prevent two or twenty or two hundred of the most influential people in the world from getting a thought from outside which could change the situation overnight? What is to prevent this from happening? Nothing.

So, is it appropriate to conceive a more desirable world without rejecting and criticizing what is now?

To conceive, yes. I mean you conceive an ideal, you conceive a state of perfection. So if conceiving that state of ideal perfection makes you feel happy, go ahead.

◘◘◘

9

WHAT IS TO BE DONE

– GENERAL DISCUSSION –

In the instant that I realize I've been lost in thinking about the future, in the thinking mind, is there anything in particular to do?

Nothing. Absolutely nothing.

The next moment will take care of itself? I may forget about it and think about the future again?

That is correct. What I am saying is, there *has* been listening with a certain amount of receptiveness. Otherwise even this question would not arise. So this receptive listening will turn to understanding and that understanding will be the witnessing, which is necessary to avoid the involvement. It is the "me," the thinking mind, which in spite of understanding, asks the question, "So what do I do now?" The answer is, "Do nothing."

That means, effectively, ignoring the thinking mind. The only way this thinking mind shrinks is when it is ignored. There is no other way it will end.

In Vipassana, *one method of returning to the present is to focus on some body sensation. This sounds similar to what you've been saying.*

No, that kind of "doing" is still the mind watching the mind, a mental process. Self-inquiry does not mean that every time a thought occurs one should methodically begin to think, "To whom has the thought occurred? I am not the body" and so forth. All of that is in time and duration, isn't it?

Anything that happens in time and duration is involvement. So, instead of getting involved in a mental process, it is simpler and more effective to remain in a position of joyous acceptance. A thought has come, it is witnessed, and it gets cut off. The witnessing does not need any mental processes.

What's the best way to understand that one is not the doer?

The best way to understand that you are not the doer is to realize that you are not a solid body. You are merely an emptiness in which the energy vibrates according to a particular individual pattern. So, you are not an individual being, let alone an individual doer. You're not even an individual entity! You are nothing. You are merely a pattern of vibrating energy. Truly understanding that, with conviction, will help tremendously.

But one can understand that in one moment and then, during the rest of the day find that he is again assuming doership.

Oh, yes! But it must come. Let it come!

But the understanding gets compartmentalized...

On the contrary, it *doesn't* remain in a compartment. It gets down right to the root of existence, to the base of existence. You don't have to repeat again and again, "I am, I am alive." There is no need to say, "I am a man." The knowledge is there. If those thoughts occur, it's a temporary clouding of the awareness. To what extent that clouding will happen is not in your hands. There is no technique which the "me" can employ to make these thoughts go away.

So, one moment of purely understanding that one is not the doer is more important than smaller understandings.

Absolutely correct. How long it takes is beside the point.

Many times in I Am That,[17] *Maharaj would admonish people to cling to the sense of I Am.*

That answer was given to the person who needed to *do* something. For this man of action, the *karma* yogi, to be told just to understand would be extremely difficult.

It was difficult for me to understand who Maharaj was addressing when he said, "Remain in the I Am." Obviously he was addressing it to someone. It was a troublesome question which bothered me deeply for six months. That was your question, too.

Yes, but I hope it doesn't last six months.

You can be thankful if it doesn't last six years! But it is a basic question. The question would pester me every morning and for the rest of the day. Finally, there was this sudden understanding that those suggestions, "Just be" or "Remain in the I Am" were not addressed to a "me." If I accepted the basic truth that the "me" is merely an appearance in Consciousness, there was nothing further to be done.

This acceptance does not come quickly in all cases. Until it comes, during the process of this acceptance becoming firm, Maharaj is addressing that "me" who needs a certain

---

(17) ibid.

amount of guidance. He wasn't addressing the suggestions to anybody who didn't need them. The basic facts he had already made clear, that there is no such object as a human being with independence as a separate entity, with independence of choice and decision, with volition. A mere appearance cannot have any volition.

In Maharaj's own case, he was by intuition and nature inclined towards devotion, that is, *bhakti*. He used to go to a temple every evening and sing *bajans*. He said, "I had a very good voice, so I delighted myself in this singing and it made me very happy. I was not interested in any knowledge, nor in repeating God's name. This is what I liked to do and I did it."

One day, a friend of his who used to go to a certain *guru* insisted that Maharaj accompany him. So Maharaj did. The traditional way was to take a garland of flowers. "Even this token garland of flowers was purchased by my friend," Maharaj said. This *guru's* basic essential message was that there is no such thing as an individual entity, it was merely an appearance in Consciousness. Maharaj said, "I accepted it, perhaps because I was an unlettered person. The intellect was not developed to a keenness where it wanted to know the whys and wherefores of everything. Whatever the reason, I could accept and that was the end of the matter."

Maharaj continued to go to the *bajans* and at the same time this understanding took root in his heart. Gradually his going to the temple ceased, but without him making an effort to stop.

ㅁㅁㅁ

Maharaj, about staying in the I Am, was asked, "What did you do?" He said, "I went to my guru who told me to stay in the I Am. I did, and in three years realization happened." Later on, he amplifies it a little by saying that in those three years he stayed in the I Am more and more. Was it that the witnessing kept occurring and he simply was aware of it more and more often, until he didn't leave the state anymore?

Correct. That's why I say you cannot keep talking in the passive tense. All Maharaj can do is repeat that there is no "one" to remain anywhere. The remaining in the I Am *happens*. It has to be understood in the passive tense.

I have felt quite inadequate and guilty, ignorant, because of the feeling that I should be able to sustain the I AM awareness. I know that is silly. So one has to let go of the reaction too? It is all part of the same delusion?

Yes, and the delusion will last as long as it is supposed to last.

I have been thinking that there is something I can do about it, but there isn't.

No. One thing I *can* tell you is that there is not a thing you can do about it, because the "you" has to disappear. The "you" will not make "you" disappear.

It can't. I have tried really hard. (laughter)

It can't! You see the ego will not commit *hara-kiri*. And the joke is that it is the ego, the "me," that wants enlightenment and enlightenment cannot come until the "me" is demolished. That is the paradox.

ꗃꗃꗃ

– TRYING TO CHANGE –

We have a natural love of our "selves." How can that love for myself be used as a door to the Greater?

My friend, who is to use it and why should he use it? That is my whole point. Why should you use this love for yourself to transform anything? If anything is to be transformed, it will get transformed, and it will get transformed in spite of you, not because of your efforts.

So sadhana is useless?

If there is *sadhana* to take place, it will take place. If there is no *sadhana* to take place, *sadhana* will not take place.

So, if a person likes to meditate...

Then he will do it!

Okay, that's what my question is. I'm interested in doing, so I'm asking you if you have any methods to suggest.

No, my way is extraordinarily simple. If you want to do your work, do it. If you want to sit in meditation, do it. If you want to achieve something, do it. I say "do it" for one reason only, because I am using active tense to your question.

In fact, what I'm saying is that there is no way you could avoid doing it. There is no way in which you can prevent what is happening from happening, or cause something which is not happening to happen. That is one absolute fact.

ᗡᗡᗡ

– PRACTICES AND TECHNIQUES –

I was always told that if I didn't try hard I'd end up slothful, so I'm afraid to abandon my practice.

When you're afraid like this, it usually means that you've been told, if you don't sit for so many hours of meditation something terrible is going to happen or that you are going to go ten steps backwards. When that fear arises, if it is merely witnessed it will die down. I'm not saying it will disappear forever, but as it arises each time, if it is merely witnessed and there is no involvement in it such as "I should do something or this involvement will continue," it will get cut off. The fear, if it is witnessed as it arises, will be cut down vertically and no horizontal involvement in duration will happen.

I was told about a *Vipassana* teacher who fell and broke her leg. Someone then asked her, "Were you not being mindful?!" (laughter)

◘◘◘

Aren't there certain things you can do with your body-mind to make it more receptive, such as meditations, pranayamas, *certain diets, or whatever it is that makes you more open?*

Yes. But, even that is not in your hands. Believing that meditation can help and then practicing the meditation are things that you think you are doing, but that meditation that is happening, is happening through a body-mind organism, which has been created for those acts to take place. You can't get away from this basic point: you will be able to do only that which you are allowed to do!

You can sure try though.

Oh, yes, you can try, if you are allowed to try, by God, or Totality or whatever you call it.

Maharaj talked about focusing on the I Am. When I do that, soon I become an object.

Again it's the "me" thinking, "I'm making a personal effort." This continues until there is the realization, "There's nothing I can do. If it is to happen, it will happen." This is surrender.

◘◘◘

When I hear everything you are talking about, I can't disagree with it, but it always comes down to how one gets to there from here? I guess it happens by Grace. I have spent seventeen years of my life involved in spiritual practices of one kind or another. At first, I was with a teacher who said if you do this and you do this you will get to Cosmic Consciousness. Then I was with another teacher for many years who basically said that it is already the case, and it does happen by Grace and it happens by the grace of putting your attention and devotion on a spiritual master. And then there were a whole bunch of devotional practices, observances, meditations, diets and so forth and so on. This whole bunch of things that you get to do to get from here to there. So I did all that for seventeen years, and here I am. (laughter)

Yes, you haven't come anywhere. (laughter) You see, the point is, there has to be a total change of viewpoint. You have been thinking in terms of you as a seeker seeking something. What I am asking is, "Who is it that is seeking what?"

I knew you were going to say that: "Who is it that is seeking what?" But I still get to this same point even after I hear that there is no individual who gets enlightened or that enlightenment happens as an incident. So what do I do? What do I do to get there? (laughter)

That is a very correct question. The answer is extremely simple. The answer is, you continue to do what you have been doing. There is nothing else you can do.

You mean all the same things I have been doing?

Whatever you are doing now!

But I don't want to do them anymore. (laughter) The reason I don't want to do them is because I feel I have reached the limit of their usefulness to me. They don't seem to be bringing about what I had started them for.

Good, then don't do them!

It is in despair.

No! That is the point, it is *not* out of despair. It is out of the acceptance of His Will. Basically you come again and again to the point, His Will or your will?

It is *your* will you have been following for seventeen years, doing something, trying to change. Give a chance to

His Will. Give one little chance to His Will and see what happens. I think you will be surprised.

◻◻◻

Ramesh, is there any practice in your teaching which could give one a feel for this Totality of which you are speaking?

You see, that is precisely the core of the problem. The "me" wanting the feel of the "I." How is it possible? The other way around, yes!

Now, it *can* happen, but you cannot make it happen. That is the core of my teaching. That is why in *I Am That,*[18] you will find lots of contradictions. To one person Maharaj would say, "you must meditate" and to someone else he would say, "your whole trouble is that you meditate."

Meditation in the beginning can be a purifying process. But the danger is that the individual who practices it, the meditator, likes the practice so much that the means becomes the end. In Los Angeles last year there was someone who was talking of meditation, and he came up with the fact that he meditates 14 hours a day. He meditated 14 hours a day!

So Maharaj's point was that the pleasant effect of that meditation can lead to the meditation being an end in itself.

Shall I meditate?

How long have you been meditating?

I don't know.

The real answer to that is that meditation will fall off when it needs to fall off. In the conceptual spiritual chart, if a dot representing an individual is placed at a particular point which requires meditation, meditation will take place. Whether it is misconstrued as an end in itself or not it will continue. And if and when that dot is wiped out, and another dot is created in the future, that dot, further along, will find

---

(18) ibid.

that there is no need for it to meditate. Meditation will have taken place earlier.

Therefore, whatever is taking place at any particular time, the question of right or wrong, correct or incorrect, improving or not, is truly irrelevant. You cannot help doing precisely what you are doing. You cannot help being here now listening to what is being said. And nobody knows what effect that listening will produce. The question is truly one of acceptance.

It also means accepting a great paradox, doesn't it?

Of course.

❏❏❏

– TRYING TO "HOLD ON" TO UNDERSTANDING –

If there's a concern with the function of the mind or any aspect of reality whatsoever, isn't that the loss of the bliss in a sense, the loss of the ananda?

Yes. Though what is not really understood is that "being" includes the doing. Therefore there is often the complaint that when one is involved in doing something, one is not aware of being. The desire is to be able to stop doing whatever is our normal doing so that we can be in the "being."

Total misconception! When there is total involvement in the doing, it *is* in the being! There is being for the simple reason that the mind is not there then, creating images. When the mind is not creating images, the doing will be taking the full attention. And when the attention is not being dispersed on the periphery, the total attention is on the doing. The mind is absent. Therefore, that doing is the being.

So, the problem really is just the thought, "I'm missing something."

Exactly! Exactly.

Which is never true.

You see, it is the mind saying, "I don't like this doing. I like something else." So wanting to change what-is *is* the mind, and *is* the problem.

❏❏❏

At a time like this, when we're all together and giving our full attention, what you're saying about Totality, and that there's nothing we have to do, seems quite clear. But tomorrow morning it'll be a real struggle to recapture. What do you suggest we do?

You see, the mind says, "Those were great moments, I want more of them." The mind wants to grasp and hang on to what you've heard.

When people come to Bombay to see me, we have a talk and after a couple of hours they leave. When they're about to go they sometimes say, "Have you any last words for me?" I say, "Yes, don't think about what you've heard."

So you start every day fresh?

Yes. Indeed. Whatever you have heard, if you let it alone you give it a chance to go deeper. But if the mind grasps it, it will *lose* the grasp, you see?

❏❏❏

– RIGHT AND WRONG –

When the sense of personal doership and responsibility starts receding, what principle guides us to do what is correct and appropriate in situations?

The working mind will spontaneously do what is right as far as a job is concerned, if the thinking mind doesn't interfere. But right and wrong will be concerned only with the job that the working mind is doing at the time. The working mind will not be concerned with the *concept* of right and wrong.

You can find a lot of people who are, in a sense, amoral. They are not concerned with morality. They may say they are

WHAT IS TO BE DONE

atheists. Those people who are bound by a moral code of some kind are often surprised and perplexed when they find that these people, not concerned with morality, are such good people. They are amazed. They assume that because amoral people are not self-consciously aware of ethics they will be concentrating on doing everything wrong, which is not so. They're surprised when they find that these people are really good people, that by and large what they are doing happens to be right, and not evil.

What you're talking about is a pair of opposites.

Yes, indeed!

So, they are the same...

They are interrelated. That is the point.

It explains why in psychology it's understood that mistakes are always for learning. If we're doing everything wrong, we'll find out that we are doing it wrong and won't have to do that again.

That is right. And more often than not that will be noticed subconsciously, not consciously. Now, I'll read a passage from a Taoist sage on this right and wrong. He chides Confucius, who was a big moralist, for his moralizing.

He says, "All this talk of goodness and beauty, its perpetual pin pricks unnerve and irritate the hearer. You had best study how it is that heaven and earth maintain their eternal course, that the sun and moon maintain their eternal light, the stars their individual ranks, the birds their flocks, the trees and shrubs their station. It is not through being self-consciously aware of what is to be done. They just do it, because it is natural. This too you should learn: to guide your steps by inward power, to follow the course that the way of nature sets. And soon you will no longer need to go around laboriously advertising goodness and beauty. The swan does not need a daily bath in order to remain white."

It is precisely as you said, this concept of interrelated opposites and the human mind not accepting them as interrelated opposites, but wanting to choose.

It seems to me that what's right and wrong will vary from one person to another, and also involves judgment.

Yes. That is precisely right. And you cannot, in this life, always uphold altogether what society and law says. And when you don't, you will likely suffer. Indeed, one organism was crucified for saying something which was not acceptable to the law and society of the time. But nonetheless what was said, was said.

❏❏❏

– MISUNDERSTANDINGS STEMMING FROM THE USE OF WORDS –

In I Am That[19], Maharaj says all the time, "There's nothing you can do, but you have to be quiet and return to the Source and dwell in the I Am." But I can't do that either.

No. As I told you, for six months the same problem almost drove me crazy! Your point really is that Maharaj is asking you to do something which you cannot do.

He says that's the only thing you can do. And I say, "Well, I can't do that either, so I'm really screwed."

So therefore I had to come to understand that Maharaj was not asking "anybody" to do anything.

Often he was asked, "What is the condition precedent to enlightenment, or at least to the process starting?" He would say, "Earnestness." Then while talking, he would use that phrase, "You have to be earnest." You see?

So you will say, "How do I become earnest?"

---

(19) ibid.

But what he meant really was that the process starts only when there is earnestness. One has to use words.

A visitor to Ramana Maharshi mentioned that he sometimes had a state of consciousness where everything was very passive. He heard sounds, he smelled smells, but there was no reaction to it. So he asked Ramana Maharshi, "Is that a good state to be in? Or is it the mind deceiving itself?" And Ramana Maharshi said, "That is precisely the state of mind, or the state of consciousness, to be *aimed* at." Now, you see? He had to use the words, "To be aimed at," but he did not mean, to be aimed at *by* anybody.

And he added, "But because this state happens only occasionally, you have a doubt. And you have expressed it. But you will have no doubt when this state happens more frequently."

So the words have to be used, yet those words can cause months of anguish. I can vouch for that from personal experience.

So what did you do, or not do?

Just waited in anguish until the understanding came that Maharaj was not asking anybody to do anything. And then, "Of course!" But that had to happen in this organism. The understanding had to come that what Maharaj was saying was a description, not a prescription.

❑❑❑

I suppose that if you're a real seeker, you're going to be seeking. You're going to be seeking this everywhere. You're going to notice books, and you're going to read.

That is correct.

And you're being dragged along by this seeking.

All of it is part of the functioning of Totality. And "dragged along" is quite accurate. (laughter) It is precise and accurate, because that is what is happening.

So, we should just pour another beer and enjoy it. (laughter)

You couldn't have put it better! (laughter) If you are not supposed to have that beer, something will happen and you won't get that glass of beer.

About this matter of acting "as if." As long as I think I'm an individual, believing I have control and choice in my life, this concept of "as if" is a little hazy.

You see, there is nothing else you can do. So, what do you do? You go on doing exactly what you have been doing. Whatever happens will happen in any case. If any change is needed, as I've said, it will happen. If no change happens, it means that no change is necessary in the functioning of Totality at that moment. So you do carry on "as if" you had the choice, and "as if" you had control over your life.

10

THE GURU/DISCIPLE RELATIONSHIP

– INTRODUCTION –

Howdid the guru/disciple relationship
first arise?

All organized religions have initially been based on the
perennial philosophy that there is a ground of all being and
nonbeing, something that is not a thing out of which everything has come. But when the original teachings began to be
conceptualized, interpreted and propounded by the unenlightened, based upon their limited understandings of the
original truth, a tremendous gap arose. The gap arose between man and God.

The gap arose because in the process of interpreting the
original truth, both the individual and God were conceptualized and addressed as entities. This created a sort of spiri-

tual hierarchy with God as the highest entity, a divine entity but nonetheless an entity, to whom all prayers or worship had to be addressed so that the individual might get what he or she desired.

When this separation arose between man and God, the gap had to be filled. The gap was filled by many intermediaries who placed themselves between man and God and the concept that no individual could reach God, without the intercession of these intermediaries was encouraged.

As interpretations of the original truth varied, eventually there grew up sects and sub-sects, each with a religious head who became the *guru*. This religious head had tremendous power over the members of the group, extending far beyond the power of the law. The law applied only to mundane matters, but the assumed power of the religious heads extended beyond this world. Thus arose the inequities, faults, and terrible happenings that have occurred in the name of religion.

The question arises, "Why is it that now and then we find such terrible false spirits arising, creating religious havoc?" William Law provides the answer, saying it is because, "These men have turned to God without first turning from themselves."

Various sects promise superhuman and even supernatural powers, and people get attracted to these things. And it must be said that these powers can indeed be achieved with certain disciplines practiced in a determined way, precisely as results are obtained from any determined pursuit of a physical or a mental discipline. It is not that these supernatural powers, or *siddhis* as they are called in India, cannot be acquired. The question is, "Why? What is it that the seeker really wants?"

When I was in Los Angeles in 1987, someone said that he wanted to be able to walk on water and was doing *hatha yoga* to that end. He asked if I could help him to achieve his goal. I had to tell him, "That kind of power, I'm afraid, I am not able to give. I don't have that power myself. I wouldn't care for it even if someone could give me the power. I would say, 'No thank you, I'm quite willing to use a boat.'"

◘◘◘

Where does the true guru *come into this spiritual picture?*

The true *guru* comes in this way: throughout spiritual history, certain spontaneous occurrences have occurred in every corner of the world in which an intuitive insight has produced a person of radical, transcendent vision. This vision has transformed reality into a totally new dimension in which what was previously perceived as real is seen as unreal and what was apparently unreal is experienced as the real.

It is important to note that these few people, in these very rare instances, realized that what had happened to them was not due to any effort on their part, but was a spontaneous happening, a gift from heaven, or Totality.

In some of these cases, they were deeply inclined to share this tremendous secret with others. But they soon realized that doing so would bring them into trouble with the religious heads in the area and perhaps even with the law of the land. So they went about their lives casually, as if nothing had happened, and nobody really knew. Relatives and friends might have sensed that something had happened. Something had made them more kindly, more compassionate than they had been.

The change was not phenomenal, but purely internal, a change in perspective. What they had previously seen as real, those occurrences and phenomenon which are apparent to the senses, were no longer seen as real. The unmanifest, which is not perceptible to the senses, was experienced as real. They continued to live their normal existence but were surprised to find that some people who were on the threshold of this transcendental knowledge were, through mysterious events and circumstances, directed to their doors. Most were, of course, open and willing to impart the teaching to those who had come to them. Thus arose the real relationship

between the *guru* and the disciple. This was not a relationship in which there was a flaunting of a teaching which was,
if I may say, "sold," but rather an extraordinarily quiet
relationship where there was a realization that people on the
threshold of this knowledge were somehow directed to the
doors of the *guru*. The imparting of this knowledge was on
a very small, very quiet, scale. Such disciples, who themselves became enlightened, experienced that the reality
within them and the reality within the masters was identical.
It could not have been any different. It was the same reality
which the master had seen earlier which the disciples experienced. In spite of that understanding there was such a
tremendous love for the *guru*, so much gratitude for this
knowledge which had been imparted, that many disciples,
even after enlightenment, have written some beautiful
verses, paying homage to their *guru*.

This kind of love for the *guru* is essential for the Eastern
disciple. But before coming to the West I had the impression
that it required a certain softness which probably did not
exist in the West. Therefore, in 1987, just a few weeks after I
arrived in the West and started talking, I was surprised and
I must say considerably confused when someone handed me
a closed envelope, saying, "This is for you."

Later, when I opened it, I found that it contained a very
short poem which moved me extraordinarily.[20] I'll never
forget it, it mirrored tremendous love for the *guru*.

It confused me all the more because I had never set myself
up as a *guru*. It was purely a *coincidence* that Henry Denison
got me over to America. Then, here was an American giving
me a letter, the core of which was, "Here I am, a grown man
with a wife, two children and a reasonably prosperous business. I don't understand this tremendous, overpowering
love for a man who I've never seen until a couple of weeks
ago."

He was astonished to find such tremendous love and
compassion arising in him. At that moment I even thought

---

[20]   See Editor's Notes for text of poem.

that perhaps there was some feeling which had been exaggerated, but that proved not to be the case.

So, the true *guru* comes into the picture as I have just described. When a certain group of people are mysteriously directed to their own *guru*, they may be predominately *bhakti* or they may be more inclined to knowledge, or most likely a combination of both. The real *guru* and the real disciple are part of an impersonal happening, part of a spontaneous happening in phenomenality, a part of the functioning of Totality.

The *guru's* grace manifests itself in the form of spiritual instruction. The word in sanskrit is *upadesha*. This word has often been misinterpreted. *Upadesha* is supposed to take place in various ways: looking into the disciples eyes, whispering in his ear, all kinds of things. The literal and real meaning of the word *upadesha* is restoration or being restored to the real nature. It suggests a healing of the split-mind of the individual—which has been split into subject and object, me and the other—into its original wholeness and holiness of the primal state of pure being.

How does one recognize a true guru?

Ramana Maharshi's answer was clear, specific and powerful. He said, "He who instructs an ardent seeker to do this or that is not a true master. The seeker is already afflicted by his activities and seeks peace, rest and quiet. What the seeker needs is the cessation of his activity. If a teacher tells him to do something in addition to, or even in lieu of his activities, it cannot help the seeker. Activity means creation of images in the mind, conceptualization. Activity, as personal effort, means the destruction of one's inherent state of happiness, *satchitananda*, through strengthening of the ego. If activity is advocated by a teacher or advisor, he is not a master but a destroyer. In such circumstances, either the creator, Brahma, or death, Yama, may be said to have come in the guise of a master. Such a person is not a true master. He cannot liberate the aspirant. He can only strengthen the fetters of his bondage."

These are strong words. But their strength and power come not from Ramana Maharshi's own point of view. He couldn't care less. The strength of the words comes only from his compassion for the seeker. In other words, there can truly be no doing by anyone, but merely a seeing in perspective, only a reorientation of mind, a transformation that is spontaneously brought about.

But what can be done about the pseudo-gurus and the thousands of people who are influenced by them?

The fact is that thousands of people *do* go to them and this situation is itself part of the impersonal functioning of Totality, of What-Is. The question of a remedy is irrelevant. Whatever exists in the manifestation of Consciousness has to be accepted as a fact.

There is an evolution which proceeds from the sinner to the saint, from the disciple, who has not yet fully understood, to the disciple who ultimately gets the realization. This impersonal evolution is all that is taking place and the final enlightenment is not the transformation of any individual, but the transformation of attitude, viewpoint, the transformation of the identified consciousness into its impersonality.

The understanding dawns that there cannot be an individual to attain any enlightenment. Therefore, all one can do is go about one's business and let whatever happens happen. This is against all "usual" advice, I know, but there it is.

ロロロ

– DARSHAN –

I mentioned to you once that I felt it was important to spend time in your presence, so that whatever you have will rub off on me. You laughed. Even if I were to spend more time with you, enlightenment may not happen, right?

That is why I laughed. Even if you kept me embraced for years, even then the thing may not happen. There is no question of enlightenment rubbing off.

But, just being in your proximity...

It is said that the proximity of the *guru* does bring about some kind of helpful change.

How?

I don't know.

Tantric teachers talk about transmission of energy, shakti. With a jnani, is there a transmission of any kind?

If this transmission is supposed to happen at a particular moment, it can be in any one of several ways. The basic and ultimate fact is that nothing can happen as long as there is a "me" wanting and expecting a transmission from another. That much I can say.

❐❐❐

– LISTENING –

You indicated that silence was the best way of teaching. I am curious about that. Is it better to be silent in the presence of someone who is awakened, as opposed to being silent by yourself, and if so why?

Is the basis of your question, is the *guru* necessary?

That is in there somewhere, but there seems to be a quality of silence that happens when I am in the presence of a realized being.

The quality of silence, or the silence itself, is the ultimate point when enlightenment happens. You see the presence of enlightenment means the total absence of the "me." Unless the phenomenal "me" has totally disappeared, the noumenal cannot come in. The total annihilation of the "me" is silence and silence is enlightenment.

Can you imbibe that quality from a teacher, soak it in so to speak?

You can, provided, as I said, the listening is total. And then the listening leads to the acceptance that nothing may happen, the acceptance that nothing that the mind considers worthwhile need necessarily happen in a particular body-mind mechanism.

The acceptance of that creates a receptivity, creates an understanding, a total acceptance of His Will. The total acceptance of His Will leads to the automatic rejection of "my" will. The rejection of "my" will means the absence of the "me."

This is really thinking horizontally, one leading to the other, but when the understanding happens, it is all one thing. Vertically it is just one thing. Horizontally one thing leads to the next. So, vertically this sudden acceptance of His Will, total surrender, and the silence, is all one. That is why enlightenment is always sudden, silent, vertical.

❑❑❑

– WHEN THE DISCIPLE BECOMES ENLIGHTENED –

What becomes of one's relationship with one's teacher or guru when the disciple himself ceases to identify with the body-mind mechanism?

There is no difference at all between the disciple and the *guru*. They're both in the same state. In India, the relationship continues to a certain extent because of tradition. But I've heard and read that in China, when enlightenment happens in the disciple, the *guru* looks into his eyes, sees the situation and they both start laughing. They embrace, they laugh, sometimes they roll on the ground. Both have realized the absurdity of all the efforts that had been made to reach or to achieve something that is already there.

In India, I must say, I haven't yet seen that sort of thing. The formality remains.

You haven't seen them roll on the ground?

The formality persists.

◻◻◻

When Maharaj died, his body had ceased to be the focal point of his identity a long time earlier, had it not?

The identity as an individual being, as a separate entity, that was already gone a long time.

Right. So they say that after the great death, the little death is not a great consideration.

Quite so.

◻◻◻

– LETTING GO OF THE GURU –

Would you say something about the split between yourself and Maharaj?

There was no split. The split was in my mind.

There was the concept that you separated yourself from Maharaj. Did you experience any integration, like a dissolving of that concept, a falling away of the separation?

Yes. Not just the separation between "me" and Maharaj but between this "me" and everything else.

Were those two things exactly the same? Like Maharaj wasn't anymore? The concept didn't have any more power than the rest of the objective world? Because the guru can be a very strong identity if you have identified as the disciple.

I know what you mean. What I would like to say is that I have always felt that the concept of the *guru* can be the final obstruction. It remains for a very long time. There is not enough you can do for the *guru*. When the relationship starts with the Divine, whatever you do is not enough. The concept of the *guru* as something separate from you is the final obstruction which has to go.

It is from this point of view that Zarathrushtra gave his disciples the ultimate message, "Now forget whatever has been said. Forget everything I have said except this: Beware of Zarathrushtra!"

∎∎∎

– MAHARAJ –

How and when did people start going to Nisargadatta?

A man by the name of Maurice Frydman who for thirty or forty years was associated with Krishnamurti, and also for many years associated with Ramana Maharshi, somehow found himself in Nisargadatta's presence.

Mr. Frydman told a friend of mine, "Don't make the mistake of discounting Nisargadatta, the mistake which I made. Don't be taken in by his simple appearance and his homey way of speaking. Don't be taken in. I made the mistake, but fortunately that mistake got corrected."

People from the West began coming only after *I Am That*[21] was published.

Did Maurice Frydman finally accept Nisargadatta as his guru? Did he make that transition from Krishnamurti?

He might have, but I don't think he made any particular declaration.

Did Nisargadatta speak in a dialect?

He spoke in Marathi. Curiously, his normal way of speaking was most pedestrian, but the words that came out about the teaching were unimaginably profound. He used to say that he didn't know how the words came out, as he was on the borderline of being illiterate. He also said that many of his colleagues didn't like it because he was not parroting what his *guru* had said.

---

[21] ibid.

Would you tell us a bit about how you came to meet Nisargadatta the first time?

Yes! I thought nobody would ask that! (laughter) What happened was Jean Dunn, who has edited books of Nisargadatta's talks, wrote an article about Maharaj and the book *I Am That*[22] in the October 1978 issue of *The Mountain Path*, the official journal of the Ramana Maharshi *ashram*, of which I have been a founder subscriber for twenty-five years. In that article there were a number of quotations from the book. So I got the two volumes immediately. I read them over the weekend and went to Maharaj on Monday morning. When I first climbed up the steps to his small, attic room, there was no one else there except Maharaj and his personal attendant. As I climbed up the stairs and stood before him, his first words were, "You've come at last, have you? Come and sit down."

Thinking he'd addressed those words to someone else behind me I looked back, but there was no one. What was most impressive to me was that I had the distinct feeling that he was not aware that he had spoken those words. So those first words were a tremendous inspiration to me. That's how I went to Nisargadatta.

Did Maharaj ever say that you were his successor or words like this?

Maharaj was not concerned with a successor. All he said was, "Seven or eight books will come." Maharaj also said, "Many people don't like what I'm saying," meaning the other disciples of his *guru*. "They expect me to say precisely what my *guru* said. But I'm not parroting what my *guru* said. Whatever comes out of me is needed at that moment."

His *guru* was of a traditional lineage. One thing about Maharaj was that he never paid undue attention to lineage. I had a feeling that he thought too much was made of the lineage and not enough of the core of the teaching. He went

ibid.

a step further with me. He said, "When you talk, you will not be parroting my words." At that moment, there was no question of my talking at all!

So, he sort of predicted it.

The prediction *happened*, Madam. He was not concerned with predictions.

◘◘◘

– MAHARAJ TELLS RAMESH TO TALK –

How is it that you started giving talks?

When I went to Maharaj, one of the first things I decided was that if he asked a question he would get a straight answer without the intellect interfering and wondering if the answer would please him or not. So whenever a question was put, he got a straight, spontaneous answer.

Maharaj had realized that on a particular day something had happened with me. So from that day forward there was a certain change in our relationship. The formality disappeared and I could take certain liberties with him which I could not have dared take earlier.

My sister is a very traditional religionist, and when she found that people were coming to see me and we were talking on this subject, she was greatly distressed because, according to her, to talk on such matters without an authorization from the *guru*, was a sacrilege. So I had to explain to her that I *did* have Maharaj's specific authorization to talk.

This authorization came in a peculiar way. When I started translating, there was a certain need. Maharaj's favorite word was "need." Every event happens in order to satisfy a need, so my being at Maharaj's feet satisfied a need in two ways; from Maharaj's point of view and from my point of view.

My point of view was obvious. I had wanted to go to Ramana Maharshi almost thirty years before I went to Maharaj. I had made several attempts. None were successful because I was destined to sit at Maharaj's feet and no one else's. The need from Maharaj's point of view was for a translator who could understand intuitively what he was trying to convey, and who also had a more than adequate knowledge of the English language and understood the Western mind. So it so happened that this body-mind mechanism called Ramesh satisfied all those three conditions.

Two months before Maharaj's death, he was very ill. He was lying down but he was still able to get to the room upstairs to give the talks. He wanted to go downstairs so, for the first time ever, he said to those present, "You can continue to ask your questions," and pointing at me said, "He's authorized to answer them."

He went downstairs, but there were no questions, so obviously there couldn't be any answers. Two people who were near me said, "Look, if you don't talk Maharaj will come in and get angry." I said, "But there are no questions. I was authorized to answer questions, not to talk on the subject." Maharaj came back and asked what was going on. I said, "Nothing. There were no questions, so there were no answers." He grumbled something.

Then, two days before his death, he must have remembered his earlier authorization but he also knew that I wasn't speaking. It was two days before his death and he was so ill that he could only whisper. In order to hear him, his personal attendant had to literally bend down and place his ear on Maharaj's lips. In that state of weakness, he suddenly got up on his elbow and shouted at me in his normal voice which hadn't been heard for two months, "Why don't you talk?!" Then he fell back. Frankly, I thought that was the end, but he still survived for two more days.

So that is why I talk. But, mind you, it is not my usual practice to go around the world talking to people. Mostly I just sit at home. If Totality sends some people to me, I talk to them. I talk because there is a need of it. Need, not from my point of view, but from the point of view of Totality.

◻◻◻

— KRISHNAMURTI —

When Krishnamurti says, "You are the world and the world is you," is that an intuitive understanding?

Yes. That you and the world are not separate. It means, simply, that all there is, is the functioning of Totality.

Each has his way of talking. Therefore Krishnamurti says, "You and the world are the same." I would be inclined to say, "All there is, is Consciousness functioning through this totality of manifestation."

Incidentally, I revere Krishnamurti. He was a great teacher. The trouble, however, is that Krishnamurti still spoke to the individual although he did remind you of the fact that all there is, is what-is in the present moment, in the here and now. He repeated that any number of times.

Nonetheless, his role in life was to talk to a large number of people and it had to be at a level which people could understand. And for that to be so, he had to speak to the individual. In many cases, the "individual" raised a block.

Once, a group of people from Krishnamurti's state came to Bombay to hear him give probably his last talk in Bombay. They telephoned me, "We've come here to hear these talks. When Krishnamurti's talks end, could we come there to see you?" I said, "Of course."

We talked for one or one and a half hours. When they were leaving, one member of the group hesitated and came back. He said, "I have one last question. What you have said has made things so clear, I wonder why I had to go to Krishnamurti for thirty years?"

I said, "Maharaj begins where Krishnamurti ends. Obviously your thirty years with Krishnamurti were a preparation. What made you come here at this moment? Those thirty years! And if you hadn't labored with this problem for thirty years, the talk we had could not be so illuminating."

He left with a great sense of relief.

🞏🞏🞏

11

METAPHYSICAL QUESTIONS

– THE MEANING OF LIFE –

So, the question comes to me of the meaning of life. I like to feel that life has a meaning, since I'm in the middle of it. And what you say seems to take that away.

Yes.

That's what I think I have some trouble with.

If you go to the seashore, you might see a child building a sand castle. When it is time to go home, he demolishes it. And if you ask him, "What is the meaning of your constructing the castle with a lot of time and love, and then demolishing it?" he will probably tell you he doesn't understand the question. All he can say is, "I *like* to build the castle, and then I *like* to demolish it!" It's just a game.

That's a tough answer.

You see, the meaning of life... who wants to know?

Well, this is where the buck stops.

I do understand. Definitely. But not to worry, it is all part of the game!

◘◘◘

– SAMADHI –

I've been taught that there is some sort of a transformation that can come about in a person's character by going into samadhi.

No, madam. After you come back from the *samadhi*, you'll still be the same person with the same characteristics with which you were conceived and created. There is the old chestnut of a story about a *yogi* who went into *samadhi* and when he came back he told his disciple, "I'm terribly hungry, bring me some food." But by the time the food was brought he had gone back into *samadhi*. So, when he finally comes back from *samadhi* again he asks, "Where's my food?"

After twenty days of *samadhi* or twenty years of *samadhi* he still came back to the same moment.

◘◘◘

If I understand you correctly, when there's some stimuli, you witness it. If there isn't any, you go into a non-witnessing state?

Yes.

Is that the same thing they call samadhi?

No, that is what I call the non-witnessing state, which Ramana Maharshi calls the natural state. *Samadhi* is an abnormal state.

For the average person, there is continual involvement. When that involvement and the "me" and the thinking mind disappear, what remains is the witnessing state. Whatever is happening is merely witnessed. When there is nothing to witness, no thought is arising, then the mind goes deeper into the non-witnessing state. In that non-witnessing state sounds are heard, smells are smelled, but in an extremely passive way. They have no meaning, but consciousness is still present, so it can again go into the witnessing state when necessary, smoothly and easily without any deliberate effort. Consciousness is still present, so if someone calls your name or there is a sound, then you go back into the witnessing state. Witnessing and non-witnessing are the states in which the *jnani* resides. The non-witnessing state is the normal state and the witnessing state happens if there is something to witness.

When you say that samadhi *is abnormal, do you mean that* samadhi *is not to be desired?*

No. It's just not normal. *Samadhi* is abnormal in the sense that it goes deeper than the natural state. That state of *samadhi* can happen.

Is there any value to a forced samadhi?

I don't know. Those who go into it do think so. You go into the sea, you come out, you dry yourself. If you go into the sea again, you come out and dry yourself. This keeps on happening.
What Maharaj used to say is, "If you go into *samadhi* for two hours, two days, two years, or two thousand years and come out, there you are back again in phenomenality!" What is the point?

You come back. Oh, I see. You can't say that you were transformed as long as you perceive, in phenomenality, as an individual?

Correct.

What is the difference between deep sleep and samadhi?

Deep sleep is basically a physical happening. *Samadhi* is a psychic happening. Your body is a psychosomatic apparatus. Deep sleep is more a somatic happening. *Samadhi* belongs more to the psychic part of the body.

How do I know the difference when I go into samadhi? *I know deep sleep.*

That is the physical, you see. But actually you do know. You have such moments every day. They may not be recognized, but you do have moments when there is a deep sense of peace. They may be fleeting moments, but nonetheless, those moments are there. And when you come out of them, you do realize that in those moments when you weren't aware of yourself, when the "me" was not aware of itself, there was a sense of well being. And then the mind promptly says, "I want more of those moments."

◘◘◘

– SAMSKARAS –

Ramana Maharshi often talked about samskaras *that have to be worked out. My understanding of what you call inherent characteristics is that* samskaras *may be something similar.*

Samskaras are the natural inherited characteristics plus the conditioning which takes place because of the surroundings in which you are born.

Would an example of a natural characteristic be that I am impatient?

Characteristics of temperament, yes.

And conditioning on top of that?

Yes.

Where are these samskaras *at the point of death?*

These *samskaras* are merely thoughts, they are not objects. The *samskaric* concepts go into the totality of memory and some of those will be conveyed into some new organism when it is conceived. Which of them will go where, we don't know.

❑❑❑

– REINCARNATION –

Time is a tricky thing. When we talk about reincarnation in the sense of impersonal tendencies or samskaras *having some continuity, we're talking about time in a linear way. It implies there were lifetimes prior to this one, the pieces of which came together and created our current phenomenal manifestation.*

From the other point of view, the manifestation occurs spontaneously and from that perspective, there is no linear time and thus no continuity.

That is correct. So when we are speaking of reincarnation this way, we're dealing just conceptually with the multitude of phenomena. But from the point of view of a *jnani* who is *not*, all of this is just swept aside. In other words, there was never any "me" earlier to project itself into a new "me" now.

So when we're discussing phenomena as identified individuals, we can borrow from phenomena and conceptualization and entertain reincarnation. Then from the other point of view, when there is no "me," all this dissolves?

Correct. It becomes irrelevant.

But until that point, we play in the field of phenomenality.

We play in the field of phenomenal conceptualizing.

Ah! Thank you.

❑❑❑

– ARE GOD AND CONSCIOUSNESS THE SAME THING? –

Are God and Consciousness the same thing? If not, what's the difference?

None. No difference. They are just names. The Absolute, *Nirvana*, God, the Eternal Subject, Awareness, whatever. All there is, is That. What name you give to That is immaterial.

❏❏❏

– MYSTICAL PROPERTIES OF THE GURU'S PRESENCE –

Since everything material is really an illusion, a conceptualization, is it possible to speak in terms of states of Consciousness, gradations of Consciousness?

As a concept, certainly.

I was thinking about the fact that certain masters and gurus and jnanis are able to give an experience of a higher state of consciousness to other people by not necessarily even touching them but just by being there.

Yes. You mean there is an altered state.

Yes, sort of. Yes.

You know, in 1987 I was taken to a place called Altered States somewhere in Los Angeles. There were various kinds of apparatus. There was one enclosed tank of heavily salted water where you float by yourself and after a while you're in an altered state. Then there was another mechanism for you to alter your body's electrical impulses and you apply that to yourself so that the brain is quieter. And another where there was a reclining chair with a roller which goes up and down your back and after a while you are in an altered state.

Well, what I was wondering is, what's going on with the guru and the disciple in a the situation where there aren't any of these mechanical things operating?

If these altered states can be produced by certain machines, why should such altered states not happen in the presence of some special body-mind organisms?

Well, that's it. I mean, there's an energy change.

You see, you can give it any label you want, but what you're talking about must necessarily be at a mechanical level, at the level of phenomenality.

In some books, it is written that the presence of a jnani *makes* samskaras *disappear from those people who are present. What do you say?*

It may or may not, depending upon the destiny of that organism. But one thing is certain. The *jnani* wouldn't say it was his presence which brought it about.

A true jnani *would not say that. A false one might.*

(laughing) You see, there is something false only because there is something genuine.

∎∎∎

– BIOLOGICAL CHANGES AFTER ENLIGHTENMENT –

Krishnamurti and others mention that when awareness or understanding takes place, there's a tremendous change in the brain cells, it becomes a whole new brain. Would you comment on that?

I don't know the biological processes. Frankly, I wouldn't be interested. Somebody asked me about *kundalini*. I don't know about *kundalini*. Some biological changes that take place may technically be called *kundalini* awakening. Frankly I know nothing about it. I've never been interested in these matters. The *yogi* here may teach you something about it, but I don't know anything about these matters.

◻◻◻

– EFFECTS OF SEEKING ON THE BODY-MIND –

Ramesh, on the way to becoming more aware I've noticed that my writing skills, for instance, were getting weaker...spelling, things like that. I seem to be in a state of absence-forgetting. Is that something that occurs on the way to...

No, I'm afraid not!

Before my seeking I never had these problems. Now sometimes my mind stops and I cannot do even a very easy action. A very little calculation takes me hours to do because my mind doesn't think. It never happened to me before. What is this?

I'm sorry, I can't explain it. But I would say it wouldn't be correct to attribute this result to the seeking. Now, it could be that a certain path, certain practices would produce dangerous consequences. That can happen. But if that has happened, even then it's not your fault. Your being elected to a particular path is not in your hands.

Something else. With Ramana Maharshi, my mind stopped completely. I could not talk to anyone.

Yes, but I really wouldn't associate it with the seeking. Phrases such as, "the stopping of the mind" can cause misconceptions. Last year, someone who used to attend these talks who was supposed to be looking after our needs, started an affair with a married woman. One evening, when we were eating together, he said, "This woman is so good for me, she makes my mind stop."

I said, "If you want to have an affair with her that is your business, by all means go ahead and do it. But don't associate any spiritual aspect with this affair!"

◻◻◻

Sometimes I have to do a project, but my mind stops and I go into spontaneous meditation and cannot complete the project. Does this have something to do with the seeking or with the progress?

No, it has nothing to do with your seeking. Seeking will take its own course. So it's no use blaming the seeking for interfering with your normal, working life. What interferes with the working mind is not the seeking. It is the thinking mind which interferes with the working mind. It is the "me" wanting something.

Also, could it not be that behind all this talk of the effects of the seeking, it is the "me" wanting to create an impression of being a special seeker?

ᗐᗐᗐ

– MIRACLES –

What is the significance of miracles?

Nothing.

Are they a diversion of some type? I mean you can't have a Course without the miracles.

No. Miracles are simply events which the human mind cannot explain with its existing knowledge.

Consciousness is creating these miracles for a purpose, is it not?

No. Except to enjoy.

To enjoy the play. And it distracts the different entities to believe in them.

Yes. So if you mean, are these things created so the pseudo-entities that think they are independent entities should get further involved? Yes, indeed.

Therefore the game, this *lila* goes on.

ᗐᗐᗐ

– SIDDHIS –

I was thinking about gravity and levitation. The body becomes light in altered states, right? So what happens to gravity? How does it happen that gravity does not work?

You see, again, your question involves the matter of mechanics. If it is mechanical, science will explain it someday, if it is not able to do so now. All these curiosities are merely at the level of mechanics.

A hundred years ago they did not know about radio waves, so radio was a miracle. Maybe a hundred years from now all these *siddhis* will be perfectly explainable in scientific terms. But what's the point?

ㅁㅁㅁ

What is the silent transmission?

A concept, nothing more.

How would somebody coming to you, who knew nothing about Advaita, learn about it unless they are verbally told?

What effect verbal instruction will have is neither in my hands nor in the hands of the man who listens. The only difference is, I am not concerned at all, whereas the poor devil is very concerned.

How would that person come to you and get that understanding?

A mysterious force sends him to me.

Is that an energy?

Yes, you can call it that. Consciousness in action is energy.

Other teachers I've seen, always have gold light around them. I sit around them and my mind gets quiet. There's a tangible presence. With you there's nothing. You're just here, nothing special.

I am glad. The point about this understanding is its ordinariness. There's one great advantage where I'm concerned: if there is an impact, you don't have to wonder if it is the magnificent physical presence that brought it about. If there's an impact, there's an impact.

The whole thing has been brought to a circus standpoint with a lot of these concepts.

In the circus, they keep going round and round and round!

◘◘◘

– MANIPULATING THE MANIFESTATION –

Some people believe that they create their reality. They sit and they imagine that they will have a big income and a big income comes. They say, "I visualized a big red Cadillac. Look, I have a red Cadillac."

The body-mind organism was using visualization as part of the functioning process.

These people believe that they are in charge of their own reality, instead of just acknowledging that it's the Totality that is functioning.

But the reality which they think they produce is *in* that basic illusion. If some other body-mind organism is concerned, then what happens? Does this person who creates reality control the lives of the other people who come into that reality?

If you follow the thought through, they would have to, and yet they can't.

Correct. So, they *think* that their mentation causes a certain appearance in Consciousness.

What you're saying then is, if income or a car or whatever their goal was to create, gets created, that was all part of the plan anyway?

Absolutely correct.

◘◘◘

– ASTRAL TRAVEL –

Can Consciousness perceive without the presence of a physical body?

Consciousness needs a psychosomatic apparatus in order to make an objective expression of itself.

How then does astral travel happen? If I'm sitting here and suddenly I see something which is thousands of miles away, it can't be that I see it with my body.

No, it's Consciousness which does the observing through an instrument. Please understand, you are nothing other than a mere instrument which is totally useless without Consciousness.

What I cannot understand is, if I'm sitting here and I close my eyes, my body would not be present a thousand miles away, so how can I perceive what is happening there?

Why not? What makes you think anything that happens in the universe needs to be understood by any individual instrument? Whether this instrument exists or not, whatever happens in the universe will continue to happen. See?

The theory of relativity had to be given to mankind, as I said before, and it was given at the appropriate time through an instrument which was evolved scientifically highly enough to receive it. Whatever happens in the universe is a functioning of Consciousness which does not need any conceptual support from any instrument.

Are you saying that it's the same kind of phenomenon, Einstein receiving the thoughts, as it is for me to perceive something one thousand miles away?

Yes, precisely. The whole problem arises because the "me" says that it has observed something. The most important, relevant fact is forgotten: that observing has happened through an instrument. No "me" has anything to do with it.

◘◘◘

Sometimes people die and then they see themselves lying down on the operating table as the doctor brings them back from death. Again, it looks like Consciousness can perceive without the physical body because they see the physical body there.

Yes, but that physical body was therefore not dead. What are supposed to be after death experiences are not, cannot be, *after* death. They can only be *near* death experiences. After death there is no consciousness in the body. No experience can happen, no image can arise in the mind, if the body is dead.

So you are saying that I will not experience my death?

You will experience only the approach of death. You can only experience the approach of the deep sleep state. You cannot experience the deep sleep state. See what I mean? The moment before you fall asleep...

The ego is gone.

Yes. But once you fall asleep, who is experiencing the deep sleep state? So you can experience the approach of death, but the moment that death happens to you there cannot be experience because there is no you. That is the point I am making.

◘◘◘

– HEALING –

Ramesh, what is healing?

Healing? It depends on how you use the word. The doctor would consider healing to be healing a wound. The psychotherapist would consider healing to be healing the split in the ego.

But what is the source of whatever all that is about?

The source is always Consciousness.

How can one become a useful instrument in that way?

If you want to be useful, you can do whatever you think you need to do to be useful, but whether what you do is going to be useful or not, and to whom it is going to be useful, is all something that will have to be construed by the persons affected.

This body-mind organism has been conceived and created with certain characteristics so that particular actions will take place through that body-mind organism. All actions through the body-mind organism are circumscribed by the natural characteristics with which this body-mind was conceived. And those characteristics were implanted at the moment of conception.

So the idea is just not to get in the way?

Nobody can get in the way.

So how does healing work?

The healing, whether it succeeds or not, is an act. It is part of the functioning of Totality. The healer does, conscientiously, what he thinks is best, to the best of his ability. But what effect that healing will produce at any particular moment in any particular case is not in his hands.

❐❐❐

– DIRECTING ONE'S ATTENTION AT THE MOMENT OF DEATH –

If you want to make sure that when you leave the body you're going into samadhi *and not becoming an amoeba, what do you do? (laughter)*

What do you mean by "you"?

Is it a matter of focus, then?

No, wait a minute. To whom are you referring? The ordinary person?

I am referring to myself.

In that case you are assuming that you will know the precise moment when you are going to die and at that moment you'll ask the question, "should I do this or should I do that?" What makes you think you will be given the special privilege of knowing the moment when you are going to die?

But I've read that at the moment of death it is critical to be focused, to have your compass targeted in the right direction. So, how do you do that?

I am not concerned with doing that. I am just not concerned with doing anything. You may think you are doing something. I *assure* you, you are not. There is no individual doer. Focusing, or whatever, will happen if it is to happen. No "you" can have anything to do with it.

🞎🞎🞎

– DEATH –

When I was a child, in our community there were people who died at eighty, ninety years old, and all of them knew when they were going to die, within a week. They prepared themselves. They washed the clothing they wished to be buried in and placed it next to their bed. They bought the coffin and many other things. They knew exactly, but these were very healthy persons. They were simple folk. They were not mentally sophisticated. In fact, I was the only one who finished high school.

So, you see, in that kind of basic living the intuition is at a high level.

They knew exactly.

More than the time of death, the attitude toward death will be most important, you see.

When you die, your body decomposes. When I wake up in the morning just one day older, the fear of that is there.

The "me" assumes that it will continue to remain in this body-mind after death. Some people have gone so far as to have the body frozen after death. Such is the extent to which this identification of the "me" with the body can go!

In the West, death has a really bad press. People in the East are more accepting of death. Here, we're not supposed to die.

No, it's the same in the East. If anything, more! It is not the culture, but the understanding of nonduality, seeing one's true nature and the true nature of all manifestation, which gets rid of the fear of death.

My own feeling is that the understanding of nonduality is definitely stronger in the West than in the East. In the East, most are still concerned with dying a Hindu or dying a Muslim and going to their own separate exclusive heaven. Organized religion is still so strong there.

I don't think that I'm afraid to die. I don't want to die, I'd prefer not to die, but I am afraid of dying in a plane crash or in an accident or something like that.

What you are saying is that deep down there is an understanding of what death is about, that basically there is no fear about the phenomenon of death, but there is a fear about the process of death, you see? There is fear about the process of death being painful or whatever. That's a totally different thing. Someone who is very sensitive to pain will be more concerned about the process of death. It is not unnatural to be afraid of the process of death.

🞏🞏🞏

– MAHARSHI'S ENLIGHTENED COW –

I read that Ramana Maharshi said that sometimes an animal can become fully realized. Is this true?

I know, it's the story of Ramana Maharshi's cow. I don't know what Ramana Maharshi had in mind.

All right, it's out of context.

In Tiburon, when I was talking, there was a cat in the place. The cat's name was BC. So each day when the talk started it would come and jump in my lap and it would remain there for quite some time. So the joke used to be that "If anyone was going to be enlightened in this place, it had to be BC, the cat."

🞏🞏🞏

– RAISING SPIRITUAL CHILDREN –

I have a general question about raising children. What kind of environment is a good one in which children can develop spiritually?

I would very earnestly suggest that no effort be made to raise children spiritually. It can create a tremendous sense of confusion. In fact, it is the desire to raise children spiritually that often causes them to grow up with a tremendous sense of guilt, and causes them enormous misery.

If you let God develop them spiritually as He sees fit and not consider it your responsibility, both you and the children will be happier. The sense of right and wrong, a combination of discipline and freedom has to be worked out, of course. Beyond that though, to tell them about right and wrong or to tell them what they should do and shouldn't do, to an extent that makes them feel bound, can be, in my opinion, a tremendous burden. Let your own behavior be the example.

The basis of spirituality is not guilt or burden. The basis of spirituality is relaxed freedom. This is not generally understood, so it is thought that spirituality is something that one must seek with tremendous effort and concentration. It isn't. I assure you it isn't.

Don't make it, as you say, a federal case. Let the seeking take its own course!

❑❑❑

– THE DILUTION OF TRUTH IN ORGANIZED RELIGION –

When the Supreme court building was being built in Washington, somebody got the idea that it would be a nice thing to hang portraits of the founders of the great religions. The portraits were commissioned and put up on the walls. When the Moslems found that there was a picture of Mohammed, they raised hell and the picture was taken down and put in the basement and it's still there...

Didn't they object that the Prophet should have been put in the basement?!

Maybe, but what occurred to me was, when Mohammed originally asked that pictures not be made of him, what he had in mind was that he wanted his people to concentrate on a bodiless Self rather than the embodied self, concentrate on the atman *rather than the* jiva. *If he were around today, he may not have thought it was all a very big deal.*

Yes, it's always really a matter of perspective. When you narrow the perspective you're always going to get into difficulty.

In the broader perspective this transcendental philosophy, this Advaitic philosophy is the base of all organized religions. What happens is, the subsequent interpreters, the mediators, come in and narrow the perspective. The subsequent interpretations in every religion have caused a tremendous void between the original philosophy and its interpretations.

❏❏❏

12

REGARDING EMOTIONS

– GENERAL DISCUSSIONS –

Whenever I get angry or have any intense emotion, I say to myself that the reason I have that emotion is because I still consider myself as a separate entity. Now, would you say that that was the reason that a person experiences any strong emotion? Or could there be other reasons as well?

That is the only reason.

Well then, if the fact that the person thinks of himself as an entity is the only cause of that person experiencing strong emotions or anger, again I have to go back to the fact that you said that Maharaj got angry!

But that was just a way of speaking. Along with that, I also said that if one happened to ask, "Maharaj, why are you getting angry?" he would probably spontaneously and genuinely have asked, "Who is getting angry?"

You say, "I get angry, I want to purify myself." Maharaj would know that it was not Maharaj who was getting angry. It is a subtle but enormous difference.

Didn't we just agree that the only cause of anger is that this thing considers itself as a separate entity?

Yes, but Maharaj was not an entity getting angry. There was no entity identifying itself with an emotion which arose spontaneously in that body-mind mechanism. That is why Maharaj would say, "There is anger, I am not angry. There is great pain but I am not in pain."

So when I get angry...

You say, "I am angry, I should not be angry. Anger drains me of energy and creates a lot of enemies." All of that is involvement horizontally, in duration.

So, the next time I get angry, then the best course would be...

No! There would be no course! (laughter) I'm not playing on words. Your problem is so common and so important. Next time you get angry, the thing to understand is that there is nothing you can do about it. That is the basic understanding.

It's just the function of Consciousness.

Yes! Let the understanding have a chance.

I'm getting the fact that you're on automatic pilot and whatever happens to you happens and you just let it.

Exactly!

That's it?!

Exactly! That's it. That is precisely it! And the deep intuitive conviction of it will produce a tremendous sense of freedom. An intellectual effort to comprehend it will bring nothing but frustration.

That's what I was looking for. Thank you.

◘◘◘

Sometimes I feel such gratitude, I feel forced to create a God to be grateful to. It doesn't make sense to me. I don't know what to do with this upwelling.

The mind says, "I must do something. I must create something to which this gratitude can be dedicated." But why? Let it well up and overflow. Let it come up in the form of tears or whatever. That's all right. You didn't create that sense of gratitude, it happened. Let it happen. That is the natural outcome of this understanding. The intellectual understanding doesn't produce that welling up of gratitude.

◘◘◘

What is the function of emotion?

Emotion, like a thought or a desire, arises in the mind. The arising of any thought or emotion or desire is always spontaneous. You cannot *will* a particular emotion to arise nor can you keep it from arising.

Once it arises, you can either get involved in it as the ordinary person does, or if there has been some understanding then witnessing takes place and the involvement in that emotion or thought or desire gets cut off.

Are emotional patterns according to the nature of that particular individual?

Yes. Once the emotion arises, further involvement, according to a certain pattern, will depend on the characteristics of that particular organism. Quite so.

◘◘◘

– LOVE AND COMPASSION –

*Is there something which loves something else or is it all imper-
sonal?*

There is no subject which loves any object. There *is* love,
there *is* compassion, there *is* humility, charity, whatever you
call it. The distinction between the manifest and the unmanifest is only notional.

It's not an emotion, then?

Oh no! Far from it. Exactly the opposite of emotion.

*Would you say it was the love of the noumenal for the phenome-
nal, because they really are the same?*

Yes. Why not?

◻◻◻

*What about universal love that many people speak of? Is that
just another concept?*

Yes, but universal love is another name for the understanding of polarity, understanding that all objects, all human beings are objective expressions of that same universal
Being.

When you tell someone to "Love thy neighbor" he may
say, "Why should I love my neighbor, he's a nasty specimen.
He kicks my dog, chases my cat up the tree. Why should I
love him?" But when this understanding begins that all
objective expressions are of the same Being, then love or
compassion arises.

Then it is not just "Love thy neighbor" but "Love everything."

Yes. That is what the understanding produces. Everything in this manifestation is your neighbor, indeed is your
Self.

Your Self in an impersonal sense.

Yes, indeed, yes. There's a beautiful Sufi story in which one of the Sufis cried out in public, "I am God!" and he was stoned to death by the pious crowd.

That night, one of the persons who had stoned him had a dream. In that dream he saw God welcoming the dead Sufi with open arms. So the stone-thrower asks God, "You sent the Pharaoh into hell because he said, 'I am God.' The Sufi said the same thing but you're welcoming him to heaven."

God replied, "When the Pharaoh said, 'I am God,' he was thinking of himself. When this Sufi said, 'I am God,' he was thinking of Me."

❑❑❑

GLOSSARY

advaita	Non-duality (*a*= negative particle + *dvaita*= duality) The most important branch of Vedanta philosphy
ahankara	Ego
ananda	Bliss; joy (one of the three elements of the ultimate Principle: *Sat-Chit-Ananda*)
avatar	Incarnation; descent of a diety
aum	The word and the sound denoting *Brahman*, the ultimate Principle; the symbol of the Supreme Self, the most sacred *mantra*
Avyakta	The unmanifest (*a*= negative + *vyakta*= manifest)
bhakti	Devotion; adoration as a way of salvation
bhakta	Devotee
bhoga (bhogi)	Experience (er) of sensual reactions
Brahma	One of the gods of the Hindu Trinity; *Brahman*, the creator; *Vishnu*, the preserver; *Shiva,* the destroyer
Brahman	The Absolute, the Ultimate Reality
Chetana	Consciousness
Chit	Universal Consciousness
darshan	Seeing; meeting
dharma	Inherent property; natural characteristic (also, a firm code of conduct and duty)
dhyana	Meditation
Guru Puruima	The full moon day in July/August on which the disciples renew their dedication to the *Guru*
Ishwara	The supreme lord and master of the universe in Hinduism
japa	Literally "muttering," the repetition of the name of God

jiva	The individual identified consciousness (as opposed to *Shiva*, the impersonal, Universal Consciousness)
jnana	Knowledge; especially of one's true nature
jnani	One who Knows
karma	Action: the principle of causality
Kundalini Yoga	The system of *yoga* which concentrates on the psychic centers *(chakras)* in the body in order to generate a spiritual power called *shakti*
lila	The play of God; the Cosmos looked upon as a divine play
Mahavakya	Literally, "great saying"; more specifically, it refers to four *Upanishadic* quotations which affirm the reality of the Self: 1) That Thou Art; 2) I am *Brahman*; 3) This Self is *Brahman*; 4) *Prajuana* (Conciousness) is *Brahman*
manana	Meditation; discriminative understanding through reflection
maya	Delusion; the veiling power which conceals the real and projects the unreal
moksha	Liberation
nama rupa	The phenomenal world of name and form
nididhyasana	Remain settled after profound meditation
Nisarga	Natural State
paravritti	Literally highest *(para)* course of conduct *(vritti)*; transformed action
prajna	Pure awareness; unselfconcious knowledge; intuitive understading
samadhi	Superconscious state
vairagya	Indifference to wordly matters
Vedanta	Literally, the end of the *Vedas*; one of the six schools of Hindu philosophy
Vedas	Four collections of Hindu scriptures from 2000 BC to 500 BC; "Revealed Knowledge," the most sacred, the ultimate authority for Hindus
Yama	The Hindu god of Death

Also By Ramesh S. Balsekar

A Duet of One
Here Ramesh uses the *Ashtavakra Gita* as a vehicle for an illuminating look at
the nature of duality and dualism
Softcover — 224 Pages $16.00

Experiencing The Teaching
In this book many facets of Advaita (non-duality) are examined and illuminated
through a series of 24 dialogues. Ramesh's ability to cut through to the simple
heart of complex ideas is a joy to experience.
Softcover — 142 Pages $11.95

The Final Truth
A comprehensive and powerful look at Advaita from the arising of I AM to the
final dissolution into identification as Pure Consciousness.
 Softcover — 240 Pages $16.00

Your Head In The Tiger's Mouth
A superb overview of the Teaching. Transcribed portions of talks Ramesh gave
in his home in Bombay during 1996 and 1997.
Softcover — 472 Pages $24.00

A Net Of Jewels
A handsome gift volume of jewels of Advaita, selections from Ramesh's writings
presented in the format of twice daily meditations.
Hardcover — 384 Pages $25.00

From Consciousness To Consciousness
This wonderful collection of letters between Ramesh and several of his disciples
explores the very heart of the *guru*/disciple relationship.
Softcover — 80 Pages $11.00

Ripples
A brief and concise introduction to Ramesh's Teaching. Perfect to give to friends.
Softcover — 44 Pages $6.00

If unavailable at your bookstore, these titles may be ordered directly from Advaita Press.

Send check or money order or Visa/Mastercard number (include expiration date) for the
indicated amount plus shipping as noted below to:

Advaita Press
P.O. Box 3479 CS3
Redondo Beach, CA 90277
USA

Shipping & Handling:
In **U.S.** — — — *Surface mail*: First book $3.00. Add 50¢ for each additional book.
Airmail: First book $5.50. Add 50¢ for each additional book.
Outside U.S. — *Airmail*: $10.00 per book. *Surface mail*: $3 per book Payment in U.S.
dollars via check or money order payable on a U.S. bank. No Eurochecks please.

More Books About Advaita

NO WAY -
for the Spiritually Advanced
by Ram Tzu
Blending paradox, wit, satire and profound insight Ram Tzu creates a view of spirituality that is truly unique.
"Ram Tzu is accessible from several levels of misunderstanding." ~ Ram Tzu
Softcover — 112 Pages $13.00

Consciousness and the Absolute
edited by Jean Dunn
The final translated talks of Sri Nisargadatta Maharaj, recorded just before his death in 1981. Includes four b/w photos.
Softcover — 118 Pages $12.00

I Am That - Conversations with Sri Nisargadatta Maharaj
A compilation by Maurice Frydman of Maharaj's conversations with seekers who came to him from around the world. This is the latest high quality American edition.
Softcover — 576 Pages $24.95

Seeds of Consciousness
edited by Jean Dunn
More translations of conversations with Nisargadatta Maharaj. This is a NEW EDITION of a once out of print title.
Softcover " 216 Pages $14.00

Prior To Consciousness
edited by Jean Dunn
Further insights into the teachings of Sri Nisargadatta Maharaj via translated accounts of his talks. NEW EDITION includes 5 new photographs.
Softcover —159 Pages $14.00

If unavailable at your bookstore, these titles may be ordered directly from Advaita Press.
— See previous page for ordering information —

Audio and Video Tapes Are Also Available

— Write Us For a Free Catalogue—